AGE DISCRIMINATION
AND DIVERSITY

This volume of essays is concerned with the discrimination against older people that results from a failure to recognise their diversity. By considering the unique combinations of discrimination that arise from the interrelationship of age and gender, pensions, ethnicity, sexual orientation, socio-economic class and disability, the contributors demonstrate that the discrimination suffered is multiple in nature. It is the combination of these characteristics that leads to the need for more complex ways of tackling age discrimination.

MALCOLM SARGEANT is Professor of Labour Law at Middlesex University Business School.

AGE DISCRIMINATION AND DIVERSITY

Multiple Discrimination from an Age Perspective

Edited by

MALCOLM SARGEANT

CAMBRIDGE
UNIVERSITY PRESS

CAMBRIDGE UNIVERSITY PRESS
Cambridge, New York, Melbourne, Madrid, Cape Town,
Singapore, São Paulo, Delhi, Tokyo, Mexico City

Cambridge University Press
The Edinburgh Building, Cambridge CB2 8RU, UK

Published in the United States of America by Cambridge University Press, New York

www.cambridge.org
Information on this title: www.cambridge.org/9781107003774

First published 2011

Printed in the United Kingdom at the University Press, Cambridge

A catalogue record for this publication is available from the British Library

Library of Congress Cataloguing in Publication data
Age discrimination and diversity : multiple discrimination from an age
perspective / [edited by] Malcolm Sargeant.
p.   cm.
ISBN 978-1-107-00377-4 (hardback)
1. Age discrimination.   2. Older people.   3. Ageism.   I. Sargeant, Malcolm.
HQ1061.A415   2011
305.2608–dc22
2011001814

ISBN 978-1-107-00377-4 Hardback

CONTENTS

FIGURES

vi

TABLES

CONTRIBUTORS

Editor

MALCOLM SARGEANT is Professor of Labour Law at Middlesex University Business School, UK. He is author of *Age Discrimination in Employment* (Gower, 2007) and *Age Discrimination* (Gower, 2010), and editor of *The Law on Age Discrimination in the EU* (Kluwer Law, 2008) as well as having written numerous articles including, recently, 'The default retirement age', *Industrial Law Journal* (2010) and 'Age discrimination and the national minimum wage', *Policy Studies* (2010).

Authors

SARA ALLIN is an assistant professor at the University of Toronto, School of Public Policy and Governance; a Senior Researcher at the Canadian Institute for Health Information and a visiting Fellow at LSE Health. Her research focuses on health systems and comparative health policy, in particular equity in access to health care. In January 2009 she completed her PhD in Social Policy from the London School of Economics.

DR JOSE-LUIS FERNANDEZ is Deputy Director and Principal Research Fellow at PSSRU, the London School of Economics and Political Science. An economist, he specialises in ageing policies, the analysis of funding systems, service productivities, the interaction between health and social care, and the economic evaluation of health and social care services. Amongst others, he has advised bodies such as the English Department of Health, the UK Treasury, the UK parliament's Health Select Committee, the European Union, the WHO and the World Bank.

DIANE GRANT is Reader in Community and Social Studies, Liverpool John Moores University. She gained her PhD in 1996, entitled 'Poverty in Britain in the 1990's: Rowntree re-visited', conducted at Liverpool John Moores University. She has researched and published in her research area interests which include poverty, social exclusion, age and gender discrimination. She was Research Director on two major bids funded by the European Social Fund into gender discrimination and ageist perceptions 2003–7.

KAREN M. KOBAYASHI is an Associate Professor in the Department of Sociology and a Research Affiliate at the Centre on Aging at the University of Victoria. She is a co-leader for the National Initiative on the Care for the Elderly's (NICE) Ethnicity and Aging team. Her research interests include the economic and health dimensions of ethnic inequality in Canada, intergenerational relationships and social support in mid and later life families, and the sociocultural dimensions of dementia and personhood.

SHARON KOEHN is a medical anthropologist who works with transdisciplinary teams in applied settings to explore the social and cultural dimensions of ageing, health and access to health care. She is a Research Associate at the Centre for Healthy Aging at Providence Health Care and a Clinical Assistant Professor in the Department of Family Practice at the University of British Columbia.

ALEXANDRA LOPES holds a PhD in social policy from the London School of Economics for a thesis on living arrangements and the well-being of older people in familialist social policy settings. Until early 2010 she was Director of the Department of Sociology of the University of Porto, where she works as a senior lecturer. Her research interests and experience include the analysis of inequality in old age, with a particular focus on theoretical and methodological instruments to address poverty in old age.

GABRIELLE MASTIN is a doctoral student in the School of Sociology and Social Policy at the University of Leeds. Her research examines systems of state consultation with elderly and disabled people.

MARK PRIESTLEY is Professor of Disability Policy at the Centre for Disability Studies at the University of Leeds, and Scientific Director of the European Commission's Academic Network of European Disability experts (ANED). He previously held an Economic and Social Research Council research fellowship on 'Disability, Social Policy and the Life

Course' and has published numerous works on the intersection of disability and generational issues.

LYNN ROSEBERRY, Associate Professor of Commercial Law, Department of Law, Copenhagen Business School, received her JD degree from Arizona State University College of law, her LLM degree from Harvard Law School, and her PhD from Copenhagen Business School. Before joining Copenhagen Business School, she was a practising trial attorney in Phoenix, Arizona. Her main research interests are employment law, discrimination law and legal theory, especially feminist and critical race theory.

ATHINA VLACHANTONI is a Lecturer in Gerontology at the Centre for Research on Ageing and the ESRC Centre for Population Change in the University of Southampton, UK. Her research interests combine the areas of ageing, gender and social policy. Her most recent publications include 'The demographic characteristics and economic activity patterns of older carers: evidence from the English Longitudinal Study of Ageing', *Population Trends* (2010); and (with J. Falkingham and M. Evandrou) 'Gender, poverty and pensions in the UK', in S. Chant (ed.), *International Handbook on Gender and Poverty* (Edward Elgar, 2010).

Ageism and age discrimination

MALCOLM SARGEANT

Introduction

This book is about the diversity of older people and the discrimination that results. Older people are often stereotyped according to their age. Age stereotyping is concerned with associating certain characteristics, or the lack of them, with certain ages. It in effect homogenises the particular age group as being all the same, rather than recognising any diversity within that age group (Robinson, Gustafson and Popovich 2008). There is an impression that older people share certain attributes, patterns of behaviour, appearances and beliefs (Ward *et al.* 2008). This stereotyping according to age is not restricted to older people of course and can apply to all ages and age groups. Here is a useful quote that illustrates how the issue of age pervades many aspects of the life course:

> Our lives are defined by ageing: the ages at which we can learn to drive, vote, have sex, buy a house, or retire, get a pension, travel by bus for free. More subtle are the implicit boundaries that curtail our lives: the 'safe' age to have children, the 'experience' needed to fill the boss's role, the physical strength needed for some jobs. Society is continually making judgments about when you are too old for something – and when you are too old.
>
> (Age Concern 2005)

This book is concerned with the effect on older people of age discrimination and ageism and how age relates to other diverse characteristics to create the potential for multiple discrimination.

Ageism

Age discrimination is a manifestation of ageism. This latter term, said to have been first used by Robert Butler MD in 1969, concerns the adoption of negative stereotypes of older people and the ageing process. Butler's short article was about the strongly negative reaction of white affluent middle-class residents to a proposal for a public housing project for the 'elderly poor' in their district. He described ageism as 'prejudice by one age group against other age groups'. Although he highlighted the issue of ageism, the events that he described were a mixture of prejudice based upon race and class as well as age. Interestingly, he described the age prejudice that was revealed as 'a deep seated uneasiness on the part of the young and middle aged – a personal revulsion to and distaste for growing old, disease, disability; and fear of powerlessness, "uselessness" and death'. There is, however, little evidence generally that societal prejudice against the old is a result of such animosity. Butler was writing at a time, in the USA, when the Age Discrimination in Employment Act 1967 had recently been adopted. In fact a report to Congress entitled *The Older American Worker–Age Discrimination in Employment* in June 1965 stated that 'We find no significant evidence of . . . the kind of dislike or intolerance that sometimes exists in the case of race, color, religion, or national origin, and which is based on considerations entirely unrelated to ability to perform a job.' Professor MacNicol (2006) has further described ageism as the 'application of assumed age-based group characteristics to an individual, regardless of the individual's actual characteristics'. The application of stereotypical images is something that is prevalent in society. Stereotyping refers 'to a set of assumptions held about an individual or situation based on previous experience or cultural norms. Once a stereotype is applied to an individual, it is assumed that they will behave in a certain way, in line with a fixed general idea or set of associated images' (Rake and Lewis 2009). There have been ample studies which illustrate the stereotypical images of older people such as those by Taylor and Walker (1994) and McGregor (2002). These studies illustrate how employers, for example, can hold views about older and younger workers which can influence career decisions affecting those workers. So younger workers are perhaps more IT friendly, more dynamic and enthusiastic, whilst older workers might be seen as more reliable but also more conservative. Many of the stereotypes of older people are negative ones and studies have shown how the media perpetuates these images. One study identified eight negative stereotypes used in the media (Schmidt and Boland 1986). These were those who were (1) eccentrics; (2) curmudgeons (grouchy, angry, uncooperative, nosey/peeping toms); (3) objects of ridicule or the brunt of the joke; (4) unattractive; (5) overly affectionate or sentimental; (6) out of touch with current/modern society; (7) overly conservative; and (8) afflicted (physically or mentally deficient). A later study (Sargeant 2008) of the national press in the UK found mostly negative stories about older people, which were about elderly criminals, elderly victims, elderly incompetence, eccentric behaviour, older people with animals, older people as record breakers and couples with a significant age difference.

It is not difficult to see how these perceptions lead to negative or less favourable treatment. Stereotypes are, by their nature, untrue. This is because they apply an image or allocate an attribute to a whole class of people but on an individual basis. Thus a statement that says that older people have problems with IT, for example, is actually saying that each individual older person has problems with IT. This is self-evidently not true. It is therefore the purpose of this book to identify the diversity of the older population and perhaps to present an argument that the current approach to age discrimination and ageism is inadequate.

Age discrimination

Age discrimination is widespread within the European Union. This is illustrated in a Eurobarometer survey of opinion in the twenty-seven EU Member States and three candidate countries.[1] One of the questions asked was:

> In our country, when a company wants to hire someone and has the choice between two candidates with equal skills and qualifications, which of the following criteria may, in your opinion, put one candidate at a disadvantage?

The responses included the following:

The candidate's age 48%
The candidate's skin colour or ethnic origin 48%
A disability 37%
The expression of religious belief (e.g. wearing a visible religious symbol) 22%
The candidate's gender 19%
The candidate's sexual orientation 18%

The same survey stated that 58% of respondents perceived age discrimination to be widespread (16% very widespread, 42% fairly widespread)

---

[1] Discrimination in the EU: a special Eurobarometer report 317 (2009), European Commission, http://ec.europa.eu/public_opinion/archives/ebs/ebs_317_en.pdf.

compared to 37% who believed it to be rare (10% very rare, 27% fairly rare). The majority view in all but six countries (Turkey, Ireland, Luxembourg, Denmark, Malta and Germany) was that it was widespread. Hungary had the most respondents agreeing, with 79% saying that age discrimination was widespread in their country. This was followed by the Czech Republic (74%), France (68%), Latvia (67%) and the Netherlands (66%).

In the USA also, after more than forty years since legislation on age was adopted (Age Discrimination in Employment Act 1967), the Equal Employment Opportunity Commission received almost 23,000 complaints about age discrimination in employment in 2009.[2] Other studies have shown that such age discrimination is still widely perceived as taking place (Neumark 2008).[3]

Of the 20 million people aged 50 or over in Great Britain, almost 9 million are aged between 50 and the State Pension Age (SPA).[4] The proportion of older workers in work has been increasing for some years. For example, in the second quarter of 1999, some 66.5% of the workforce between the ages of 50 and SPA and some 7.9% of those at SPA or above were in employment; by the second quarter of 2010 these figures had increased to 71.2% and 12.2%.

A UK Government consultation on age discrimination in employment (*Towards Equality and Diversity* 2003) confirmed how widespread was discrimination based upon age. Some 50% of respondents either had suffered age discrimination at work or had witnessed others suffering such discrimination. This discrimination took a variety of forms, such as being forced to retire at a certain age (22%), not being given a job they applied for (18%), being prevented from attending training courses (17%), being told age was a barrier to general advancement (17%), assumptions being made about abilities due to age (15%) and being selected for redundancy because of age (13%). Older workers were less likely to be in paid work than younger groups and when they did work they were more likely to be working as self-employed or part-time.

It also stated that there was a greater risk of becoming economically inactive beyond the ages of 50 and 55 years; and that the chances of men

---

[2] See www.eeoc.gov.

[3] Neumark (2002) cites a survey in which two thirds of respondents felt that age discrimination in the workplace did exist.

[4] This, in 2010, was 60 years for women and 65 for men; the two retirement ages are to be equalised over the ten years up to 2020.

Table 1.1 *Percentage of unemployed out of work for twelve months or more*

Age	18–24	25–49	50 and over
2008	19.9	28.8	37.6
2009	19.9	23.9	30.3
2010	25.5	36.8	43.3

leaving inactivity for paid work were sharply reduced after the age of 50 and 'were close to zero for those over 60'. For women the chances of moving out of inactivity were much reduced after the age of 40 and were 'particularly uncommon for those in their late 50s' (*Characteristics of Older Workers* 1998). Table 1.1 shows figures for long-term unemployment available from the UK Office for National Statistics.[5]

Younger age groups suffered during the years 2008–10 but the rate for older workers has been consistently high.

Older workers are more likely to be working part-time or in some form of flexible working. The likelihood of part-time working increases with age, so that, for example, whilst 13.4% of the 45–54-year-old population in the UK work part-time, some 22% of those 55 or over work part-time. The older a worker becomes, the more likely he or she is to be self-employed and to work part-time. He or she is less likely to be in a permanent job and will, on average, earn a lower gross hourly wage than younger age groups. The relationship with age is even more pronounced when one breaks down the figures for those aged 50+ into five-year age groups; for example, 20.2% of men aged between 50 and 54 are self-employed. This increases to 22.7% for those aged 55–60; 27.9% for those aged between 60 and 64; and 40.8% between 65 and 69.

Ageing populations

This issue is important because it can affect an increasing proportion of the population. The United Nations Report on *World Population Ageing* (2009) commented that population ageing is unprecedented, pervasive, profound and enduring. It is unprecedented because the increase in the

---

[5] www.statistics.gov.uk; Labour Market Statistics, August 2010. The figures presented are for the period April to June in each year.

Table 1.2 *Percentage of population aged 60 and over, 65 and over, 80 and over, by region and sex (UN Report on World Population Ageing, 2009).*

Region	60+			65+			80+		
	Total	M	F	Total	M	F	Total	M	F
World	10.8	9.7	11.9	7.5	6.6	8.4	1.5	1.1	1.9
Africa	5.3	4.9	5.8	3.4	3.1	3.7	0.4	0.3	0.5
Asia	9.7	9.0	10.5	6.6	5.9	7.2	1.1	0.9	1.3
Europe	21.6	18.5	24.5	16.2	13.2	18.9	4.1	2.7	5.4
Latin America and Caribbean	9.8	8.9	10.6	6.8	6.0	7.5	1.4	1.1	1.7
Northern America	18.0	16.2	19.7	12.9	11.2	14.5	3.8	2.8	4.8
Oceania	15.1	14.1	16.0	10.6	9.7	11.6	2.8	2.2	3.5

population over the age of 60 accompanied by reductions in the proportion of those under 15 is 'without parallel in the history of humanity'. By 2045 the number of older persons in the world is expected to exceed the number of children for the first time. It is pervasive because it affects nearly every country in the world. It is profound because it will have major consequences for all aspects of human life. Lastly it is enduring because it is a process that has been continuing since the nineteenth century in the developed world. As fertility levels are unlikely to rise again to the high levels seen in the past, the report forecasts that population ageing is irreversible. The pace of change is greatest in the developed countries, but the change is happening everywhere. It is illustrated by the increase in the median age of the world's population. According to the UN report the median age[6] for the world's population is 28 years. The country with the youngest median age is Niger at 15 years; the oldest is Japan with a median age of 44 years. By 2050 the world's median age is expected to increase by ten years. It will only remain below 25 in nine countries, most of which are African; the oldest population will be in Japan, which is projected to have a median age of over 55 years (see Table 1.2).

It is noticeable how much 'older' Europe and Northern America are, when compared to other parts of the world. Oceania follows closely, but this is because Australia and New Zealand have a much older population

---

[6] Defined as the age when half the population is below it and half above.

than the rest of the region, so the figures appear much higher than they would be without these countries.

The reasons for the change are, of course, a combination of a declining fertility rate and a lengthening of people's life spans. In the EU, for example, the total fertility rate (i.e. the average number of children per woman) has declined from 2.64 in 1960/64 to 1.50 in 2005 (Europe's Demographic Future 2007). In numerical terms this means, for example, that there were 5.1 million children born in the twenty-seven Member States of the EU in 2005 compared to 7.6 million forty years earlier in 1965 (*Demography Report 2008* 2009). In terms of living longer, the figures are equally clear. In the USA, for example, a person reaching the age of 65 had an average life expectancy of an additional 18.6 years[7] (19.8 years for women and 17.1 years for men). A child born in 2007 could expect therefore to live for about thirty years longer than a child born in 1900 (*A Profile of Older Americans* 2009).

Such a structural change in the demographic makeup of the world's population has consequences. There are many more older people in work, or who wish to work. Retirement ages devised to meet the needs of a different demography become less relevant. There are additional strains on the resources necessary to fund pensions, health care and social care, some of which are illustrated in this book. Mostly, however, there needs to be a new attitude towards age and the older population. Older people need to be given equal treatment with those of other ages. This means the tackling of age discrimination. Below, we consider further what this means in practice.

Framework for diversity

Age is a characteristic that, if we are fortunate, will come to each of us. The result of this ageing process is not a uniform greying population who share the same identity and appearance. The older population is as diverse as any other age group within the population. It will consist of people from different ethnic backgrounds, different genders, and so on. Age is an extra dimension to the scope of discrimination that people may suffer. It is often the combination of age with another apparent disadvantage that may multiply the discrimination suffered. One study (Tackey *et al.* 2006), for example, highlighted the exceptional difficulties suffered by older Pakistani and Bangladeshi men:

---

[7] Figure is for 2007.

Looking first at personal characteristics, it was evident that age represented a significant barrier to work, especially for men in their 40s and
50s. It is striking that at the age where most people of working age in
Britain are at the height of their productive capability, a large number of
Pakistani and Bangladeshi men had stopped working altogether. Age was
linked directly with people's health, and Pakistani and Bangladeshi men
were likely to suffer multiple health problems, which also prevented them
from working. Age also excluded older men from new forms of skilled
employment, particularly because the only skills they possessed were
limited, outdated and no longer relevant to the changed industrial economy of Britain.

The Law Commission of Ontario has produced a study called 'Theoretical
and economic approaches to understanding ageism' (Spencer 2009). It
states that most discussion of ageism has come from the sociological,
psychological and gerontological fields. This diversity is reflected in this
book. It is perhaps difficult, if not impossible, therefore to devise a theoretical approach that satisfies all these disciplines. The study suggests that
there are a number of ways of looking at ageism. It might be an issue
specifically related to old age or it might be looked at as having its roots in
earlier life when society's perceptions add 'layers creating disadvantage or
special burdens'.

The Ontario study examined a number of different theoretical
approaches, including feminist legal theory and a disability related
theory. The feminist approach might state that a woman's subordination
in law results from an assumption that the male adult is the norm and
women represent a deviation from that norm. Using a similar approach,
one might speculate that the younger adult is the norm and that the
lesser regard for the elderly results from their being a deviation from that
norm. If, for example, one were to postulate that, in age terms, the ideal
employee/customer was an adult aged between 30 and 35, then one can
equally postulate that the further an individual strays from this age
norm, in either direction, the more likely it is that the individual will
suffer detriment. In this approach it is the oldest and the youngest who
will suffer most disadvantage, as, for example, in the employment field.

One might then build on this 'ideal age' model by also considering
issues related to disability. According to the Law Commission of
Ontario's analysis, 'people in the disability community have actively
resisted efforts by gerontologists or other to suggest that there may be
certain shared interests'. If this is correct, then it is an error. There is a
very close link between disability and age which suggests that the
approach taken in tackling disability discrimination may be of use

Table 1.3 *Percentage of disabled people for age groups (UK)*

Age group	Percentage of population disabled	Numbers (000s)
16–24	9.7	668
25–34	12.4	850
35–49	34.2	2,353
50–59/64	43.7	3,001
All	100.00	6,871

when considering age discrimination. In all, some 10.8% of the population of Great Britain, for example, have a disability or limiting long-standing illness.[8] Over 60% of these are aged 55+ and over 40% are aged 65+. This is of particular interest when one discusses issues related to mandatory retirement ages, as it is likely that many older workers will suffer both age and disability discrimination.

Almost 80% of disabled people of working age in the United Kingdom are over the age of 35, including some 43.7% of all disabled people of working age[9] who are over 50 years of age. The chances of becoming a disabled worker therefore increase with age (Table 1.3).

Part of the explanation for this is that health problems associated with ageing itself account for a higher proportion of disabled at older ages. It is likely to be independent of social and economic circumstances to a greater extent than the main causes of disability at younger ages. At younger ages, although many fewer people become disabled overall, nearly one quarter are the result of accidents (Burchardt 2003).

In the USA, over 51 million people are reported to have some level of disability (some 18% of the population) and over 32 million are reported to have a severe disability (12% of the population). The link with age is clear, as the same statistics reveal that some 72% of those over the age of 80 have a disability.[10]

The closeness of age and disability as issues is perhaps further illustrated when considering the medical and social models of disability. The

---

[8] These and subsequent figures, unless otherwise stated, are taken from *Disability Briefing May 2007*, published by the Disability Rights Commission, now absorbed into the Equality and Human Rights Commission.

[9] Up to 60 years of age for many women and 65 for men.

[10] See Disability History in America, http://disabilityhistoryinamerica.wetpaint.com/page/Disability+Statistics+In+America.

medical model focuses on the individual and postulates that an individual's inability to work or participate in society is a result of the disability. The individual has an impairment which needs to be paid attention to. In a sense, the problem is the disability and the person who has the disability. It is for the individual to adapt to society's norms. The social model, on the other hand, treats disability as a loss of opportunity to participate in society and work. The problem is not the individual but society. Barriers exist in society which stop people with a disability from fully participating. These barriers can relate to the inaccessibility of the physical environment such as buildings or to the stereotypical attitudes of society about disabled people.

It is possible to apply these models to old age and perhaps build a model which focuses on the limitations of older people (resulting, as with disability, from stereotypical attitudes) in contrast to one which focuses on the barriers that society puts in the way of older people which are similar to those in the disability social model. In such a scenario, a compulsory retirement age becomes a barrier to participation in the workforce imposed by society. One can take this analogy further and argue, because of the close link between age and disability, that there should be an element of positive discrimination such as that of providing a duty of reasonable accommodation to older workers, in the same way as such a duty is owed to the disabled (Sargeant 2005). One of the reasons why one might do this is because of the fear of employers that older recruits will become disabled.

Regulation

When considering the regulation of age discrimination, it is clear that age is often treated differently, and more negatively, than the other grounds of unlawful discrimination, such as sex, race and disability. Advocate General Mazák stated in the Age Concern case at the European Court of Justice,[11] that 'the possibilities of justifying differences of treatment based on age are more extensive'. Essentially more exceptions to the principle of equal treatment are allowed in respect of age. The requirements of the labour market, for example, may take precedence over the rights of older workers. An illustration of this is Advocate General Geelhoed's statement in *Sonia Chacon Navas*[12] that

---

[11] Case C-388/07, *The Incorporated Trustees of the National Council on Ageing (Age Concern England) v. Secretary of State for Business, Enterprise and Regulatory Reform*.
[12] Case C-13/05, *Sonia Chacon Navas v. Eurest Colectividades SA*.

the implementation of the prohibitions of discrimination of relevance here [disability and age] always requires that the legislature make painful, if not tragic, choices when weighing up the interests in question, such as the rights of disabled or older workers versus the flexible operation of the labour market or an increase in the participation level of older workers.

Both the UK and the USA have legislated measures aimed at stopping discrimination on the basis of chronological age. The UK did not do this until 2006 when, in response to an EC Directive,[13] it adopted the Employment Equality (Age) Regulations, which have now been largely superseded by the Equality Act 2010.[14] The USA has a much longer history of age legislation, having adopted the Age Discrimination in Employment Act (ADEA) in 1967. Both measures are limited to stopping discrimination in employment only. The UK is proposing to extend this coverage to include other areas, such as facilities, goods and services, as a result of the adoption of the Equality Act 2010.

The Equality Act 2010 provides some protection for all age groups who are in or seeking work.[15] This includes protection from direct and indirect discrimination, although it is possible objectively to justify discrimination if it can be shown to be 'a proportionate means of achieving a legitimate aim'. It is also possible to provide benefits related to length of service or seniority, and such benefits if related to periods of more than five years can be justified by an employer if this 'fulfils a business need of his undertaking (for example, by encouraging the loyalty or motivation, or rewarding the experience, of some or all of his workers)'. Apart from these and other exceptions, the original Regulations introduced a default retirement age of, usually, 65 years. It is somewhat bizarre that the introduction of regulations designed to tackle age discrimination were seen as the opportunity to introduce a major piece of age discrimination such as this. Fortunately the Government elected in 2010 promised to phase out this mandatory retirement age from 2011.

The ADEA is limited to providing protection for those who are 40 or older.[16] It includes protection from disparate treatment and, since the Supreme Court decision in *Smith v. City of Jackson, Mississipi*,[17] for disparate impact. It also has exclusions such as that for small

---

[13] Directive 2000/78/EC establishing a general framework for equal treatment in employment and occupation, OJ L303/16 2.12.2000.

[14] SI 2006/1031; for a full analysis see Sargeant (2006).

[15] Generally, see Sargeant (2007).   [16] Section 12(a).   [17] 544 U.S. (2005).

employers,[18] a bona fide occupational qualification[19] and seniority.[20] Most importantly, when compared to the UK, the mandatory retirement age has been removed.[21] Although legislation concerning discrimination on the grounds of age was contained in a different statute than that which applied to race and sex, there had been a common assumption that a similar approach would be taken in each when a complainant wanted to show that discrimination had taken place. This has been limited by the decisions of the Supreme Court. In *Gross v. FBL Financial Services*[22] the Supreme Court appears to have denied that there was a shared approach and made it much more difficult for plaintiffs to show age discrimination in 'mixed-motive' cases. In this case Mr Jack Gross claimed that he had been demoted because of his age and he claimed a violation of his rights under ADEA. At the District Court the jury was instructed by the court to enter a verdict for him if he proved that he was demoted and that his age was a motivating factor in the decision to demote him. In the event, the jury found for Mr Gross. On appeal this decision was reversed and the court held that the jury had been incorrectly instructed as to when an employee alleges that he or she has suffered adverse treatment because of a mixed-motive case (i.e. when there are a mixture of permissible and impermissible reasons). The Supreme Court subsequently held that a plaintiff bringing such a claim must prove that age was the 'but-for' cause of the action. The burden of proof does not switch to the employer to show that it would have taken the action regardless of age, even if there is evidence that age was a factor.[23] The ADEA was to be treated differently from the other grounds of discrimination such as race and sex because the plaintiff now had to show that age was the reason the employer decided to act. It appears subsequently that some lower courts have interpreted this to mean that age must be the sole cause of the discriminatory action. Thus it becomes almost impossible to bring an age-related mixed-motive claim, considerably weakening the scope of the ADEA.

It is not always easy to show that age is the only, or dominant, cause of discrimination, as now seems to be required within the USA. In Australia the Age Discrimination Act 2004 originally contained a dominant reason test and this may be why it has not been effective. It provided that, where an act is done for two or more reasons, that act will only be

---

[18] Those with fewer than twenty employees; Section 11(b).   [19] Section 4(f).
[20] Section 4(f).   [21] By amendments to the legislation in 1978 and 1986.
[22] 129 S. Ct. 2343 (2009).   [23] See www.law.cornell.edu/supct/html/08–441.ZS.html.

discriminatory if the person's age was the dominant reason for the doing of the act. This test was eventually withdrawn by legislation in 2009. In the UK, the Equality Act 2010 provides, in a limited way, protection from direct discrimination on multiple grounds. Combined discrimination occurs when a person is discriminated against on the grounds of more than one protected characteristic. The Act limits this to two characteristics. Thus Section 14(1) states that 'a person (A) discriminates against another (B) if, because of a combination of two relevant characteristics, A treats B less favourably than A treats or would treat another person who does not share either of those characteristics'.

A complainant would need to show that there was less favourable treatment in relation to the combination of the two characteristics. The relevant characteristics which can be combined in this way are age, disability, gender reassignment, race, religion or belief, sex and sexual orientation (Section 14(2)).

The issue of multiple discrimination is considered in depth in chapter 2 and referred to by many of the other authors in this book. Whether one adopts an additive, intersectional or other approach (Hannett 2003), there needs to be an acceptance that discrimination on the grounds of age is often linked to other types of discrimination. We have discussed the close relationship of age and disability (see above and chapters 8 and 9), but a similar story can be told about age and gender (see chapters 3 and 4), age and ethnicity (see chapter 7), age and sexual orientation (see chapter 6), etc. Indeed, one might consider the particular issues of older migrant women (chapter 7), for example, to show how the different grounds for discrimination can come together and require specific action.

The purpose of this book is to highlight this diversity and some of the research that has taken place in aspects of the field. It is a contribution to a debate about the need to consider specific issues related to the diverse population of older people.

Bibliography

A Profile of Older Americans 2009. Administration on Aging, US Department of Health and Human Services

Age Concern 2005. *How Ageist Is Britain?* London: Age Concern

Burchardt, T. 2003. *Being and Becoming: Social Exclusion and the Onset of Disability*, ESRC Centre for Analysis of Social Exclusion, Report prepared for the Joseph Rowntree Foundation, CASE report 21

Butler, R. N. 1969. 'Age-ism: another form of bigotry', *Gerontologist* 9: 243–6

Characteristics of Older Workers 1998. DFEE Research Report RR45

Demography Report 2008 2009. European Commission, Luxembourg

Europe's Demographic Future 2007. European Commission, Luxembourg

Hannett, Sarah 2003. 'Equality at the intersections: the legislative and judicial failure to tackle multiple discrimination', *Oxford Journal of Legal Studies* 23(1): 65–86

Law Commission of Ontario 2009. 'Theoretical approaches to understanding ageism'

MacNichol, J. 2006. *Age Discrimination: An Historical and Contemporary Analysis*. Cambridge University Press

McGregor, J. 2002. 'Stereotypes and older workers', *Journal of Social Policy* (New Zealand) 18: 163–77

Neumark, David 2002. 'Staying ahead of the curve: the AARP Work and Career Study', A National Survey Conducted for AARP by Roper, A.S.W., September 2002

   2008. 'Reassessing the Age Discrimination in Employment Act', AARP Public Policy Institute, Washington, DC

The Older American Worker – Age Discrimination in Employment 1965. Report of the Secretary of Labor to the Congress under section 715 of the Civil Rights Act of 1964. Washington, DC

Rake, C. and Lewis, R. 2009. *Just Below the Surface: Gender Stereotyping, the Silent Barrier to Equality in the Modern Workplace?* Fawcett Society, www. fawcettsociety.org.uk/documents/Just%20Below%20the%20Surface.pdf

Robinson, Tony, Gustafson, Bob and Popovich, Mark 2008. 'Perceptions of negative stereotypes of older people in magazine advertisements: comparing the perceptions of older adults and college students', *Ageing and Society* 28: 233–51

Sargeant, M. 2005. 'Disability and age – multiple potential for discrimination', *International Journal of the Sociology of Law* 33: 17–33

   2006 'The Employment Equality (Age) Regulation 2006: a legitimisation of age discrimination in employment', *Industrial Law Journal* 35(3): 209–28

   2007 '*Age Discrimination in Employment*. London: Gower

   2008 'Age stereptypes and the media', *Communication Law* 13(4): 119–24

Schmidt, D. F. and Boland, S. M. 1986. 'Structure of perceptions of older adults: evidence for multiple stereotypes', *Psychology and Ageing* 1(3): 255–60

Spencer, Charmaine 2009. 'Theoretical and economic approaches to understanding ageism', in *Older Adults*, LCO Funded Paper, Law Commission of Ontario

Tackey, N. D., Casebourne, J., Aston, J., Ritchie, H., Sinclair, A., Tyers, C., Hurstfield, J., Willison, R. and Page, R. 2006. *Barriers to Employment for Pakistanis and Bangladeshis in Britain*, Research Report DWPRR 360, Department for Work and Pensions

Taylor, P. and Walker, A. 1994. 'The ageing workforce: employers' attitudes towards older people', *Work, Employment and Society* 8(4): 569–91

Towards Equality and Diversity: Report of Responses on Age 2003. London: Department for Trade and Industry

Ward, Richard, Jones, Rebecca, Hughes, Jonathan, Humberstone, Nicola and Pearson, Rosalind 2008. 'Intersections of ageing and sexuality', in Richard Ward and Bill Bytheway (eds.), *Researching Age and Multiple Discrimination*. London: Centre for Policy on Ageing, www.cpa.org.uk

World Population Ageing 2009 2009. New York: Department of Economic and Social Affairs, United Nations www.un.org/esa/population/publications/WPA2009/WPA2009_WorkingPaper.pdf

2

Multiple discrimination

LYNN ROSEBERRY

Introduction

The term 'multiple discrimination' has begun appearing regularly in EU policy documents since the adoption of the anti-discrimination directives in 2000[1] that expanded the number of prohibited discrimination grounds in EU law from two (sex and nationality) to seven (race, ethnic origin, age, sexual orientation, and religion or belief). The 2000 Directives themselves do not contain any provisions defining or prohibiting multiple discrimination, but their preambles include statements asserting that especially women are often the victims of multiple discrimination.[2] The 2000 Council Decision establishing a Community action programme to combat discrimination states that equality of women and men requires action on multiple discrimination, and that new practices and policies to combat discrimination should include multiple discrimination.[3] In 2008 the European Commission announced the use of 'new governance mechanisms to address the issue of multiple discrimination', inter alia, 'through ... providing funding for smaller networks of NGOs representing intersectional groups'.[4] In the decision establishing the 'European Year of Equal

---

[1] Council Directive 2000/43/EC of 29 June 2000 implementing the principle of equal treatment between persons irrespective of racial or ethnic origin, OJ L 180, 19/07/2000, pp. 22–6 and Council Directive 2000/78/EC of 27 November 2000 establishing a general framework for equal treatment in employment and occupation, OJ L 303, 02/12/2000, pp. 16–22.

[2] See Recital 14 in Directive 2000/43 and Recital 4 in Directive 2000/78. Interestingly, the recitals of the gender equality directives, even those adopted after the 2000 directives, Directive 2004/113 and Directive 2006/54, do not mention multiple discrimination.

[3] 2000/750/EC Council Decision of 27 November 2000, OJ L 303, 2.12.2000, pp. 0023–0028, Recitals 4 and 5.

[4] Communication from the Commission to the European Parliament, the Council, the European Economic and Social Committee and the Committee of the Regions, 'Non-discrimination and equal opportunities: a renewed commitment', COM(2008)420 final, p. 9.

Opportunities for All (2007) – Towards a Just Society', the Preamble's Recital 14 states that the European Year 'will also seek to address issues of multiple discrimination, that is discrimination on two or more of the grounds listed in article 13 EC'.[5]

The term 'multiple discrimination' has not yet been used in any binding EU legislation. However, on 2 April 2009 the European Parliament added provisions on multiple discrimination to the Commission's recent proposal[6] for a Council directive on implementing the principle of equal treatment between persons irrespective of religion and belief, disability, age or sexual orientation other than in the field of employment and occupation. The European Parliament proposed adding to the directive's text a provision explaining that the directive's framework for combating discrimination includes multiple discrimination within its scope.[7] It defines multiple discrimination as follows:

Multiple discrimination occurs when discrimination is based:

(a) on any combination of the grounds of religion or belief, disability, age, or sexual orientation, or

(b) on any one or more of the grounds set out in paragraph 1, and also on the ground of any one or more of
  (i) sex (in so far as the matter complained of is within the material scope of Directive 2004/113/EC as well as of this Directive),
  (ii) racial or ethnic origin (in so far as the matter complained of is within the material scope of Directive 2000/43/EC as well as of this Directive), or
  (iii) nationality (in so far as the matter complained of is within the scope of Article 12 of the EC Treaty).

This definition of multiple discrimination makes explicit that, at least within the scope of the proposed directive, discrimination claims may be based on any combination of the seven grounds of discrimination currently covered by EU anti-discrimination law, although the material scope of the protection against multiple discrimination is limited to discrimination outside employment.

The inclusion of an express obligation for Member States to ensure that cases of multiple discrimination can be addressed within the scope of the proposed directive raises a number of questions of interpretation

---

[5] Decision 771/2006/EC establishing the European Year of Equal Opportunities for All (2007) – Towards a Just Society [2006] OJ L 1462/1.

[6] Council Directive COM(2008)426. The original proposal only repeated the recitals mentioning multiple discrimination that appear in the preambles of the 2000 directives.

[7] *Ibid.*, Article 1(1).

(European Network of Legal Experts 2009: 10–11). However, this chapter will leave such questions of interpretation aside and focus instead on the more general question of what a prohibition against 'multiple discrimination', defined simply as discrimination based on any combination of two or more prohibited grounds of discrimination, contributes to European anti-discrimination law.

The object of this chapter is to identify the problems the concept of 'multiple discrimination' is intended to address and to evaluate the extent to which including 'multiple discrimination' within the scope of prohibitions against discrimination resolves these problems.

In the first part of the chapter, I trace the development of the concept of 'multiple discrimination' to the concept of 'intersectionality' and the anti-essentialist feminist critiques on which it was based. Although age has rarely figured in anti-essentialist feminist critiques or in intersectionality scholarship, I will show how these critiques are equally applicable to discrimination based on age together with other grounds. I will argue that neither anti-essentialist feminist critiques nor 'intersectionality' have been particularly helpful in providing analytical tools for dealing with discrimination on multiple grounds within the current framework of European and American anti-discrimination law, and that the concept of 'multiple discrimination' by itself contributes nothing new to resolve this problem.

In the second part of this chapter I argue that the usefulness of the concept of multiple discrimination is shaped and limited by assumptions about identity that are inherent in the legal orders of western liberal democracies. In order to exploit the potential of the concept of multiple discrimination to make a real difference in addressing experiences of discrimination on multiple grounds, I suggest that we reconsider these assumptions in light of post-structuralist and modern psychological theories and research on identity formation. These theories suggest that identity categories are socially constructed concepts that are essential to the construction of social hierarchy and that discrimination occurs when people occupying dominant positions in the hierarchy use their power to construct a social framework that maintains their privileged position and keeps subordinate identity categories in their subordinated positions.

I conclude the chapter with suggestions on how to develop a modified post-structuralist approach to the concept of discrimination, and demonstrate how it may be applied to multiple discrimination based on age and other protected characteristics.

The development of the concept of multiple discrimination

The organising focus of the civil rights and women's movements that led to the development of American anti-discrimination law was the Aristotelian concept of equality – likes should be treated alike, and unlikes should be treated differently (Roseberry 1999: 355–7). These movements argued that race and sex are illegitimate grounds for disadvantageous treatment with regard to a range of social and economic rights. The civil rights movement, which was led by black men, e.g. Martin Luther King and Jesse Jackson, was primarily a struggle against public and private practices of racial segregation and denial of social and economic opportunities to black Americans. The feminist movement, which was led by middle-class white women, was primarily a struggle for access to the employment and educational opportunities of the most privileged class – white men.[8] In the civil rights movement, the implicit comparator was white people, without regard to the differences between men and women. In the feminist movement, the implicit comparator in most cases was white men. Both movements focused on single grounds of discrimination, and the phrase "Blacks and women" was commonly used as a collective label for the categories of people regarded as being the main targets of discrimination in American society (Spelman 1988: 114–15). White feminists as well as black civil rights activists commonly argued that the problems black women faced were caused by racism and not sexism, thus the 'women' in the phrase 'Blacks and women' were understood to be white (hooks 1981: 1–13).

In 1981, bell hooks offered the first systematic examination and critique of the view that race and sex discrimination are two separate but comparable phenomena in her book *Ain't I a Woman*.[9] Pointing out

[8] This was 'the problem that has no name' that Betty Friedan identified in her book *The Feminine Mystique* (1963). Friedan claimed that women as a group were dissatisfied with their lives because they are urged, if not forced, to forsake their educations and any thoughts of careers in order to devote themselves to the roles of housewife and mother.

[9] The idea that race and gender were not unitary categories and were unhelpful to understanding the subordination of black women began appearing in political and historical literature published by American black feminists at the end of the 1970s and in the early 1980s. In 1977 the Combahee River Collective, a black lesbian feminist organisation based in Boston, spoke of being 'actively committed to struggling against racial, sexual, heterosexual and class oppression', and advocated 'the development of integrated analysis and practice based upon the fact that the major systems of oppression are interlocking' (Combahee River Collective 1977). Historical work in the 1980s by American black feminists include Davis (1981) and Giddings (1984). However, it seems that bell hooks was the first to articulate the idea that gender and race are inseparable identity characteristics that set black women apart from black men and white women.

that white feminists often drew analogies between 'women' and 'blacks', hooks asserted that the use of these analogies exemplified white feminists' 'support of the exclusion of black women from the women's movement' and that 'what they were really comparing was the social status of white women with that of black people' (hooks 1981: 8). Hooks rejected this comparison because it represented a failure on the part of white women to recognise the privileges associated with being white and their complicity in racial oppression of black men and women. Hooks insisted on the inseparability of racism and sexism in the lives of black women.

> My life experience had shown me that the two issues were inseparable, that at the moment of my birth, two factors determined my destiny, my having been born black and my having been born female ... [T]he struggle to end racism and the struggle to end sexism were naturally intertwined ... to make them separate was to deny a basic truth of our existence, that race and sex are both immutable facets of human identity.
>
> (hooks 1981: 12)

By the late 1980s and early 1990s feminists' 'tendency to posit an essential "womanness" that all women have and share in common despite ... racial, class, religious, ethnic, and cultural differences' (Spelman 1988: ix) had been given a name, 'essentialism', which became the target of sustained theoretical criticism by feminists in various disciplines (Spelman 1988; Fuss 1989; Harris 1990).[10] American anti-essentialist feminists focused their attention on explaining why and how feminist theory should broaden its representational base in order both to accurately describe differences among women's experiences of oppression and to lay the foundation for more effective strategies for combating those different forms of oppression.[11]

In her book *Inessential Woman*, Elizabeth Spelman presented a comprehensive philosophical analysis of the problems essentialist feminist theories leave unexamined. Spelman argues that feminist theories have generally proceeded on the assumption or belief that the differences among women are less significant than what they have in common

---

[10] Spelman is a philosophy professor, Fuss is an English professor, and Harris is a law professor.

[11] A parallel debate about the interrelationships of gender, ethnicity, race and class and the notion of 'triple oppression' of 'racial' and ethnic minority women was occurring in Europe, primarily among British feminists (Anthias and Yuval-Davis 1983; Yuval-Davis 2006). However, this debate remained primarily in Britain and had apparently little impact on policy-makers or legal scholars (Yuval-Davis 2006: 194).

largely because most well-known feminist theorists were white, middle-class women who represented their own experiences as the condition of all women:

> It is not as if, in the history of feminist theory, just any group of women has been taken to stand for all women – for example, no one has ever tried to say that the situation of Hispanas in the southwestern United States is applicable to all women as women; no one has conflated their case with the case of women in general. And the 'problem of difference' within feminist theory is not the problem of, say, Black women in the United States trying to make their theories take into account the ways in which white women in the United States are different from them.
>   . . . A measure of the depth of white middle-class privilege is that the apparently straightforward and logical points and axioms at the heart of much of feminist theory guarantee the direction of its attention to the concerns of white middle-class women.
>
> (Spelman 1988: 3–4)

The primary problem Spelman identifies in connection with the conflation of the condition of one group of women with the condition of all is not just that the concerns of other groups of women remain unaddressed. Rather, essentialist feminist theories served to preserve the privileged status of some women over others (1988: 16). She explains:

> If feminism is essentially about gender, and gender is taken to be neatly separable from race and class, then race and class don't need to be talked about except in some peripheral way. And if race and class are peripheral to women's identities as women, then racism and classism can't be of central concern to feminism. Hence the racism and classism some women face and other women help perpetuate can't find a place in feminist theory.
>
> (1988: 112–13)

Thus, when straight, white, middle-class female feminist theorists do not reflect on how they may occupy a privileged position, even when discriminated against, in relation to other women – for example racial or ethnic minorities, or gay poor women – their theories do not take sufficiently into account how, being based in their own experience, they may perpetuate the oppression of other women, and even some men. Spelman argues that it is especially because 'white middle-class women have something at stake in not having their racial and class identity made and kept visible that we must question accepted feminist positions on gender identity' (1988: 112).

One year after the publication of Spelman's *Inessential Woman*, American legal scholar Kimberlé Crenshaw introduced the concept of intersectionality as a way of accounting for the experiences of women with different backgrounds and experiences in feminist theory and anti-racist politics (Crenshaw 1989). Crenshaw argues that black women often experience 'double-discrimination' – the combined effects of practices which discriminate on the basis of race and sex simultaneously, and that these experiences should be understood as occurring at the intersection of race and sex discrimination (1989: 149). According to Crenshaw, the reason feminist theory, anti-racist politics and legal doctrine have been unable to account for black women's experience of discrimination is the conviction that black women's experience of discrimination can only be explained as occurring along a single axis of discriminatory treatment that can be traced to their race or sex.

Crenshaw clearly draws on the anti-essentialist critique in choosing her starting point in the differences among women, but her concept of intersectionality goes further. Anti-essentialist critiques have tended to focus on identifying the multiple aspects of identity and how they interact in order to remedy feminist and anti-racist theorists' focus on gender and race in isolation from each other and additional aspects of identity such as class. Crenshaw focuses her critique on the way we define discrimination, which includes more than identification of identity categories. She makes the experiences of black women the starting point of her critique, explaining that by doing so:

> it becomes more apparent how dominant conceptions of discrimination condition us to think about subordination as disadvantage occurring along a single categorical axis. I want to suggest further that this single-axis framework erases Black women in the conceptualization, identification and remediation of race and sex discrimination by limiting inquiry to the experiences of otherwise-privileged members of the group.
>
> (1989: 139–40)

The single-axis framework to which Crenshaw refers is the legal framework that proceeds from a definition of wrongful discrimination that requires the identification of a specific class or category.[12] Another

---

[12] Both American and EU law require that claimants identify the class or category with regards to which they claim protection from discrimination. For example, Title VII, the US federal employment discrimination act, 42 U.S.C. §703(a) provides:

It shall be an unlawful employment practice for an employer –

element in this framework is the requirement either that the discriminator intentionally targets a category for discrimination, or that the discriminator adopts a process or practice that somehow unintentionally disadvantages all members of a particular category (1989: 150).[13] Further, a discriminator is assumed to treat all people within any given protected category (race, sex, age, religion, etc.) similarly, and any significant variations within a category are taken to indicate that the group is not being discriminated against (1989: 150). For example, when black women are not hired but white women are, it is taken to indicate there is no sex discrimination.[14] Consequently, combining two or more categories into one discrimination claim is generally not allowed.

As Crenshaw points out, 'Underlying this conception of discrimination is a view that the wrong which antidiscrimination law addresses is the use of race or gender factors to interfere with decisions that would otherwise be fair or neutral' (1989: 151). The approach is 'process-based' rather than outcome-based, which leads the courts to ignore the material conditions of those 'who are victimized by the interplay of a number of factors' (1989: 151). Instead they focus their attention on determining whether race or sex or some other protected category has 'interfere[ed] with the process of determining outcomes' (1989: 151). Moreover, Crenshaw points out that the 'but-for' analysis prescribed by the single-axis framework of discrimination law limits our understanding of sex and race discrimination to the experiences of those 'who are privileged but for their racial or sexual characteristics' (1989: 151). Crenshaw asserts that the only people who are privileged but for their race are whites, and the only people who are privileged but for their sex are men. Thus, Crenshaw observes, 'If Black women cannot conclusively say that "but for" their race or "but for" their gender they would be treated differently', their experiences of discrimination remain unrecognised

(1) To fail or refuse to hire or to discharge any individual, or otherwise to discriminate against any individual with respect to his compensation, terms, conditions, or privileges of employment, because of such individual's race, color, religion, sex, or national origin; or

(2) To limit, segregate, or classify his employees or applicants for employment in any way which would deprive or tend to deprive any individual or employment opportunities or otherwise adversely affect his status as an employee because of such individual's race, color, religion, sex, or national origin.

[13] In EU law these kinds of discrimination would be recognised as 'direct' and 'indirect' discrimination respectively.

[14] See, e.g., *DeGraffenreid v. General Motors*, 413 F. Supp. 142 (Eastern District of Missouri 1976).

and unremedied (1989: 152). If, as Crenshaw asserts, only white women can say they are privileged but for their sex, and only male racial minorities can say they are privileged but for their race, anti-discrimination law does not begin to address the full extent of discrimination in society but focuses only on the most privileged 'victims' of discrimination.

As the foregoing discussion has shown, anti-essentialist feminist critiques and intersectionality theory developed from the insights of (younger or middle-aged) American black feminists who were concerned primarily with the intersection of gender and race. Perhaps rather unsurprisingly, age has not been subjected to the same scrutiny as an additional intersectional category. There have been very few law journal articles discussing multiple or intersectional discrimination from an age discrimination perspective, and it remains under-theorised. A few authors have examined the ways in which age and gender (Crocette 1998; Ryan 1999; Porter 2003) and age and disability (Barnes 2001/2002) interact in cases of discrimination, although they do not always identify these cases as examples of intersectional or even multiple discrimination.

For example, it has been noted by a number of legal and other commentators that because physical appearance is a chief measure of a woman's worth, and because youth is generally associated with beauty, older women find themselves the targets of more negative treatment than older men, especially in occupations where appearance is believed to be important. In such occupations, women with grey hair and wrinkles are generally regarded as being too old and unattractive, whereas men with grey hair and a few wrinkles are regarded as distinguished authorities (Porter 2003: 94–7). Older women also experience increased pay inequality. In the United States, women's median earnings peak at age 44, whereas men's peak at age 55 (Porter 2003: 97–9). The older women get, the wider the pay gap grows. Despite these statistics, the discrimination claims of older women have had mixed success. Courts have rarely recognised 'older women' as experiencing discrimination because they refuse to treat 'older women' as a special class, in much the same way as they refused to recognise 'black women' as a special class. They generally choose to compare all women with all men regardless of age difference (Crocette 1998; Porter 2003). These comparisons usually erase the evidence of discrimination experienced by older women.

With regard to age and disability Alison Barnes (2001/2002: 274–7) has noted that American attorneys specialising in serving the elder population rarely use the provisions of the Americans with Disabilities Act (ADA) to pursue a client's claim of employment discrimination, even though many impairments commonly associated with ageing may be sufficient to qualify an individual as disabled, as compared with 'the average person', the standard used by the Americans with Disabilities Act. At the very least, elderly disabled people suffering from chronic diseases and their symptoms might qualify as 'persons with disabilities' under the ADA (Barnes 2001/2002: 277). Barnes (2001/2002: 274) believes that the infrequent use of the ADA in age discrimination cases is an 'oddity' that is best explained by the fact that the ADA was a political response to 'the claims of disabled individuals of working age who could not get jobs because of fear, or mistake, or prejudice that undervalues their real capabilities'. In contrast, older people with health problems and chronic conditions have been thought to be interested in retirement rather than employment. Further, Barnes (2001/2002: 274) considers that most older people would not identify themselves as having disabilities. However, Barnes does not attempt to analyse these cases as intersectional claims, but rather engages in a fairly technical examination of how older people might be able to make use of both the Age Discrimination in Employment Act and the ADA (Barnes 2001/2002: 276–7).

Nevertheless, the concept of intersectional discrimination seems particularly applicable to age-related discrimination, because ageing in modern western cultures is often understood as being synonymous with disability, at least in the context of employment. Stereotypes about disability combine with stereotypes about age to construct a view of the elderly that is different from discrimination against disabled young people. Numerous studies have shown that age-related declines in intellectual ability are minimal and are related more often to disease than to age, and that there is little evidence to support the view that older workers cannot learn new tasks (Eglit 1997: 677). Nevertheless, older workers are often perceived as being or becoming less productive, less motivated, unreceptive to change and/or untrainable because of age-related declines in intellectual ability, or they may be perceived as potential financial burdens on the organisation owing to health problems and higher salaries. These images of older people incorporate views on both ageing and physical ability/disability, which are difficult to separate.

The interest in examining discrimination occurring along more than one axis, as evidenced by the (limited) literature on ageing and gender and ageing and disability, indicates that the main insight of Crenshaw's concept of intersectionality – that analysis of discrimination as occurring along the axis of a single identity trait does not adequately account for disadvantages suffered by persons with more than one identity trait that is commonly targeted for discrimination – seems to be generally accepted (Goldberg

2009: 124). However, use of various terms to describe this phenomenon in the academic literature suggests that some reservations about the meaning and usefulness of the concept of intersectionality remain.[15] Legal scholarship on the subject has focused a great deal of attention on whether discrimination on multiple grounds should be understood as being 'additive', 'compound' or 'intersectional' discrimination (European Network of Legal Experts 2009: 9–12). Each of these terms indicates a particular perspective on the nature of the problem to be addressed.

'Additive' discrimination is understood as signifying the view that discrimination against particular targeted groups – such as ethnic minority women – is primarily an additive phenomenon that can be broken down into components corresponding to individual prohibited grounds of discrimination (Abrams 1994: 2482–92; Roseberry 1999: 336–7). Thus, for example, discrimination against ethnic minority women is understood as consisting of discrimination on grounds of sex plus ethnicity. According to this concept, a person may be discriminated against on several grounds in a single instance, but the role of the different grounds can still be distinguished (European Network of Legal Experts 2009: 3). However, this view of discrimination is precisely the one that anti-essentialist feminists criticised and which led to Crenshaw's development of the concept of intersectional discrimination. According to these theorists, it is not possible to disentangle the different grounds of discrimination. For example, Spelman asserts: 'It is highly misleading to say, without further explanation, that Black women experience "sexism and racism." It suggests that Black women experience one form of oppression as Blacks (the same thing Black men experience) and that they experience another form of oppression as women (the same thing white women experience)' (Spelman 1988: 122).

'Compound' discrimination may be understood as describing a situation in which someone is discriminated against on several different grounds at different times (Makkonen 2002: 10).[16] It is intended to

---

[15] These terms include, inter alia, 'additive discrimination', 'compound discrimination', 'intersectional discrimination', 'intersectional inequalities' and 'intersectional disadvantage' (Makkonen 2002; European Network of Legal Experts 2009: 3–5).

[16] Makkonen (2002: 10) refers to this kind of discrimination as 'multiple discrimination', but I call it 'compound discrimination' here because it seems she is suggesting that the effect of the different kinds of discrimination – differentiated on the basis of which ground seems to be targeted – is compounded over time. In my view, the term 'multiple discrimination' as used in international legal and policy documents, including the amended proposal for the new EU anti-discrimination directive, does not correspond to Makkonen's definition.

convey the idea that some persons are burdened by an accumulation of distinct discrimination experiences. For example, a disabled woman in her fifties may be discriminated against on the basis of her age in access to education or job training, while she was discriminated against on the basis of her sex with regards to promotions when she was younger, and on the basis of her disability in a situation in which a public office building is not accessible to persons with wheelchairs. However, anti-essentialists and intersectional theorists have argued that 'it is not as if one form of oppression is merely piled upon another' (Spelman 1988: 122). Intersectional discrimination signifies the view that discrimination based on several grounds produces very specific types of discrimination, in which the several grounds operate and interact with each other so that it is not possible to determine which ground of discrimination is determinative in a given case. Nor can the kinds of discrimination experienced by persons having multiple targeted identities be reduced to cumulative experiences of discrimination on different grounds.

The concept of intersectionality has itself run into difficulty as the challenge of accounting for differences within identity categories has led to ever more complex identity combinations (Conaghan 2009: 30–1; Goldberg 2009: 124). Joanne Conaghan observes, 'This seems a project of limitless scope and limited promise . . . [I]t ensures that the focus of intellectual, political and legal energy is directed towards the infinite elaboration of inequality subgroups, engendering a slow but steady march towards conceptual fragmentation and, ultimately, dissolution. In the meantime, other ways of thinking about and theorising the problem are lost from view' (Conaghan 2009: 30–1). Nancy Ehrenreich has called this problem 'the infinite regress problem' and traces it to intersectionality theory's emphasis on the need to avoid ignoring differences within identity categories in order to avoid hiding practices of exclusion and unfair treatment behind traditional single-axis approaches to discrimination (Ehrenreich 2002: 267). As we recognise ever more complex identities groupings, existing recognised identity groups tend 'to split into ever-smaller subgroups, until there seems to be no hope of any coherent category other than the individual' (2002: 267). The individual seems to be the only possible unit of analysis, which precludes analysis of group-based oppression.

Ehrenreich identifies three additional problems which arise from intersectionality theory's preoccupation with identifying complex identity categories: the 'zero sum problem', the 'relativism problem' and the 'battle of the oppressions' (2002: 266–7).

The 'zero sum problem' refers to the tendency to conclude that conflicts among the interests of different subgroups make it impossible to further the interests of all (2002: 267). This conclusion seems to follow from some intersectionality theorists' suggestion that dominant individuals belonging to a category generally regarded as a target for discrimination, e.g. 'women', are unable to recognise and address the subordinated situation of less powerful members of the group, e.g. 'black women', not because of ignorance but because of their 'investment in their own privilege' (2002: 268).

The impression that it is not possible to promote all groups' or subgroups' interests at the same time may suggest that discrimination can only be combated by prioritising among the various identity groups' interests. Accordingly, different identity groups engage in 'the battle of oppressions', in which they compete for the role of 'most oppressed' (2002: 269). However, because there is no agreement on the measure to be used in comparing oppressions, and intersectionality theory has also pointed out that even oppressed individuals may be dominant in some situations, it seems nearly impossible to claim that any given group is always oppressed (2002: 269).

Intersectionality theory's recognition that even oppressed groups include dominant and subordinate members, and that everyone 'has both oppressor and oppressed statuses (depending on the context)', leads to 'the relativism problem' (2002: 267). While the insight that members of oppressed groups may also be oppressors 'reveals a commitment to avoiding the repeated error that identity groups have made in universalizing their own views', it is devastating for anti-discrimination law and politics, for it comes very close to suggesting that everyone is oppressed (2002: 271). From there it is a short cognitive distance to the conclusion that no one is more oppressed than anyone else and therefore there is no discrimination. As Ehrenreich points out, 'The very notion of oppression, which implies inequality and differential treatment, is rendered meaningless if all people suffer from it in equivalent ways' (2002: 271).

Both Ehrenreich and Conaghan suggest that while intersectionality theory has made a substantial contribution to understanding the limits of single-axis analyses of discrimination, it does not by itself solve any of these problems because it has focused on identity analysis rather than on the relations and processes that create inequality (Ehrenreich 2002: 254–5; Conaghan 2009: 29). Thus, intersectionality serves 'as little more than an *exhortation* to take account of complexity' in theorizing about discrimination (Conaghan 2009: 28–9).

Given that there is considerable disagreement about how to opera-
tionalise the insights of intersectionality theory within anti-
discrimination law, the definition of 'multiple discrimination' in the
amended proposal for a new EU directive appears to indicate an intention to avoid taking sides in the debate about how to conceptualise
discrimination based on more than one protected characteristic
(European Network of Legal Experts 2009: 3–6). The definition merely
makes explicit that discrimination on more than one prohibited ground
may occur and that the directive is intended to cover this kind of
discrimination. It does not indicate whether 'multiple discrimination'
should be understood as representing 'additive', 'intersectional' or
'cumulative' discrimination. Even if it had, the foregoing discussion of
the problems with conceptualizing discrimination on multiple grounds
indicates that these problems cannot be solved simply by choosing one
or the other variation of the concept.

In the next part, I consider how to shift the focus from accurately
representing complex identity categories to the relations and processes
that create inequality and the extent to which doing so moves the
discourse of multiple discrimination beyond being a mere exhortation
to offering a practical and effective alternative to the single-axis framework that has shaped anti-discrimination legal doctrine.

Moving from identity to process[17]

To get beyond intersectionality's concern with accurately representing
complex identity categories, it is useful to consider the theory of identity
upon which the legal systems of the liberal democracies in western
industrialised countries are based. These build upon liberalism's commitment to individual autonomy, which assumes that an individual's
identity is the result of the individual's own process of becoming 'a
self . . . marked by strong boundaries that are theoretically possible to
maintain against the claims and incursions of others' (Abrams 1999:
810–12). According to such theories, social influence may be important
in defining this self during childhood and adolescence, but once an
individual reaches maturity, social influences are assumed to have only
minimal influence on the individual. Social influences are kept at a
distance from the internal motivational structure of the actor in order

---

[17] The following discussion draws on soon to be published work I have done on dress codes
and Muslim women (Roseberry, in press).

to maintain the position that personal autonomy, and thus also personal responsibility for one's choices and actions, exists as more than merely an ideal (Abrams 1999: 810–12).

In the last decades of the twentieth century, a collection of theoretical projects that belong to the post-structuralist movement in philosophy 'denounced liberal individualism for its ... notions of the individual as an autonomous agent free to shape his or her destiny' (Carle 2005: 319–20). Post-structural theories of identity hold that all human knowledge and action are social constructs. Accordingly, there is no 'self' outside a social context. No self exists separate from or prior to social context. Thus, post-structuralist theories of identity tend to reject the possibility of complete, and in some cases even partial, individual autonomy. As a consequence, post-structuralist theories have difficulty accounting for any possibility of bringing about social change through acts of will (Carle 2005: 339). Feminist and other progressive theorists engaged in framing legal and political strategies for combating identity-based oppression have been dissatisfied with post-structuralist theories of the constructed self for this very reason.

Intersectionality theory's focus on describing identity categories seems to build on the liberal view of identity as it tends to focus on the experiences of the individuals experiencing discrimination rather than on what social processes converge to create those experiences which are part of constructing the identity categories. It is only important to be sure one has fully understood which identity category one belongs to if one subscribes to the liberal view that identity is stable and marked by strong boundaries. However, this understanding of identity is difficult to reconcile with the social processes that create inequality. If one accepts the post-structuralist assertion that identity is socially constructed, the social processes that create inequality may be understood as the social construction of identities that include assignment of unequal value. Furthermore, if identity categories are not the stable essences suggested by liberal theories, it becomes less important to determine what category a given individual belongs to, and more important to find out what social meanings are being assigned to that individual in a given situation. Such an approach seems to hold out considerable promise in understanding and dealing with 'multiple' discrimination. One may ask, however, whether the promise of this approach is fatally limited if it includes extreme scepticism about the efficacy of individual acts of will.

Kathryn Abrams has attempted to resolve this problem by developing a theory that allows for the possibility of self-definition and self-direction – which she calls agency, to distinguish it from liberal autonomy – while at the same time recognising that the process of self-definition is powerfully shaped by the forces of social construction in a context of unequal power relations (Abrams 1999). Abrams describes self-definition as 'determining how one conceives of oneself in terms of the goals one wants to achieve and the kind of person, with particular values and attributes, one considers oneself to be', but asserts that the possibility of self-definition arises first when the individual becomes aware of the extent to which one's conception of self is socially constituted (1999: 824). She observes:

> A woman may become aware, for example, that images or attitudes she has regarding her body, her competence to perform certain tasks, or her strength or vulnerability in relation to others, are shaped by norms that describe these matters at least partly as a function of gender. Developing this awareness does not permit her to transcend these socially conditioned visions of self, but it allows her greater room in which to affirm, reinterpret, resist, or partially replace them . . . Though she does not have recourse to some complete, pre-social self that can be uncovered, she may draw on moments of insight that arise from her reflection on her experience, or attitudes she holds that are shaped by other social influences. This process of reflection and comparison, which is facilitated by her awareness of certain self-conceptions as socially shaped, may allow her to identify more strongly with certain images and strive for greater distance from others.
>
> (1999: 825–6)

Abrams further asserts, as many feminists do, that the social or cultural norms that embody negative judgments about women's competence and bodies 'do not simply make it more difficult for women to develop independent self-conceptions' (1999: 826). These negative norms often prevent women from ever developing self-conceptions that contradict these negative judgments and which are a necessary condition for even imagining the possibility of choosing a path that does not conform to limiting gender stereotypes. However, Abrams manages to find room for agency in the fact that everyone has a range of attributes that are assigned various positive or negative meanings in a particular culture, 'so that our ability to define ourselves in positive and authorizing ways may be assisted by some of these meanings, and undermined by others' (1999: 826–7). Abrams asserts that it is through social dialogue that a woman may become aware that 'her self-conception does not simply reflect her own shortcomings, but is a function of views and expectations that are instilled socially' (1999: 828). Here lies the possibility of charting a life path different from the paths laid out by gender stereotypes.

Psychological theories of identity lend scientific support to Abrams' modified post-structuralist theory of identity. Erik Erikson, the psychoanalytic theorist who coined the term 'identity crisis', is generally credited with introducing the idea that social relationships are crucial to the construction of individual identity. Abrams' description of the process of reflection and comparison that is part of what she calls 'self-definition' is remarkably similar to Erikson's description of the process of identity formation:

> In psychological terms, identity formation employs a process of simultaneous reflection and observation ... by which the individual judges himself in the light of what he perceives to be the way in which others judge him in comparison to themselves and to a typology significant to them; while he judges their way of judging him in the light of how he perceives himself in comparison to them and to types that have become relevant to him. This process is, luckily, and necessarily, for the most part unconscious except where inner conditions and outer circumstances combine to aggravate a painful, or elated, 'identity-consciousness'.
>
> (Erikson 1968: 22)

Erikson's account of the process of identity formation has also provided the basis for psychological explanations of the subjective experience of identity-based social oppression. American psychology professor Beverly Tatum characterises the experience of racism in relation to Erikson's reference to 'outer circumstances' that create a 'painful identity-consciousness' (Tatum 2002: 21). Tatum explains that this painful identity-consciousness shows itself in the fact that when we reflect on who we are, we identify those aspects of our identity that belong to a socially disadvantaged category as having more importance than others. To illustrate this point, Tatum recounts how she regularly gave her students a classroom exercise which consisted of completing the sentence 'I am ... ', using as many descriptors as they can think of in sixty seconds. Tatum noticed that students of colour usually mention their racial or ethnic group, women usually mention being female, Jewish students often say they are Jews, and students who are comfortable about revealing it may mention being gay, lesbian or bisexual (2002: 21). On the other hand, white people did not mention being white, men did not mention their gender, nor did heterosexuals mention their sexual orientation. Tatum explains these omissions in the following way:

That element of their identity . . . is taken for granted by them because it is taken for granted by the dominant culture . . . [T]heir inner experience and outer circumstance are in harmony with one another, and the image reflected by others is similar to the image within. In the absence of dissonance, this dimension of identity escapes conscious attention . . . The aspect of our identity that is the target of others' attention, and subsequently of our own, is often that which sets us apart . . . as "other" in their eyes.

(2002: 21)

In the United States, otherness is commonly defined on the basis of race or ethnicity, gender, religion, sexual orientation, socio-economic status, age, and physical or mental ability, and, as Tatum points out, each of these categories has a form of oppression associated with it: racism, sexism, religious oppression, heterosexism, classism, ageism, and able-ism, respectively (2002: 22). Each form of oppression involves a group considered dominant, which is systematically advantaged by their membership in the dominant group, and a group considered subordinate, which is systematically disadvantaged. Like Abrams, Tatum also points out that most of us possess both dominant and targeted traits, so that in some situations we may be targeted for domination while in other situations we may target others (2002: 22).

These observations suggest that whether one is dominant or targeted for discrimination in any given situation depends on the particular configuration of dominant and targeted traits present in the situation and which dominant traits come to the fore through the exercise of power. The determination of whether a given policy or practice amounts to the kind of oppression that should be covered by prohibitions against discrimination is not so much a question of identifying whether the claimant can be assigned to a protected identity category as making an assessment of the relationships of dominance and subordination, which tend to trace targeted identity categories, that are present in the case. Discrimination is thus not just any action based on a collection of irrational feelings and stereotypes about certain identity categories in society. Rather it is best understood as the use of power by persons who can claim membership in a dominant identity group to bring about, maintain and enforce a social and economic hierarchy in which targeted identity groups are excluded from social and economic opportunities from which members of the dominant identity group derive some material benefit. Tatum explains it this way (2002: 23): 'Dominant groups, by definition, set the parameters within which the subordinates operate ... [T]hey hold the power and authority relative to the subordinates.'

In order for this understanding of discrimination to translate into legal practice, courts must be led to recognise the existence of dominant and subordinate identity categories and be able to recognise how these identity categories are constructed. Instead of trying to determine whether the alleged discriminator was considering an identity category as a factor in his or her decision-making, courts must instead focus on which identity categories may be present in a given situation and what positions they occupy in relation to each other in the social hierarchy, recognising that the prohibited grounds of discrimination – race or ethnicity, gender, religion, sexual orientation, age, and physical or mental ability – indicate which identity categories lend themselves to oppression.

Psychological and sociological research on racism and discrimination indicate a way of mapping systems of identity-based oppression in individual cases.

First, Dovidio and Gaertner have shown that in the United States overt forms of prejudice have declined in frequency while a more subtle, often unintentional form of prejudice among white Americans has appeared (Gaertner and Dovidio 1986: 62). They call this 'aversive racism' and note that white 'aversive racists' generally have strong egalitarian values and deny any personal prejudice but still harbour negative feelings or beliefs about minority groups that lead them to discriminate, often unintentionally, when their discriminatory behaviour can be justified on the basis of some factor other than race (Gaertner and Dovidio 1986: 66). This observation matches the point Tatum has made with her class exercise: members of dominant groups can avoid awareness of their dominance, and explain the existence of inequality on the basis of norms that work to preserve their privileged status without referring to the prohibited grounds of discrimination. It seems reasonable to assume that this description of 'aversive racism' may also apply to other grounds of discrimination so that it is possible to speak of 'aversive sexism', 'aversive homophobia', etc. In each case, people who engage in or support behaviour that results in denial of social and economic goods to subordinated identity groups often seek to justify such behaviour by referring to personal characteristics and behaviours, which are presented as individual characteristics without any particular connection with a targeted identity category, and without referring to any particular ground of discrimination.

For example, in *Rogers v. American Airlines*,[18] Renee Rogers sued American Airlines after being fired from her job, which involved extensive customer contact, because she refused to comply with American Airlines' grooming policy prohibiting employees in certain employment categories from wearing an all-braided hairstyle. Rogers asserted that the 'corn row' hairstyle which she wore has a special significance for black women and became popular after a famous black actress appeared on a national broadcast of the Academy Awards presentation several years before.[19] The court held that the grooming policy was not racially discriminatory because it applied equally to members of all races, and because the all-braided hair style is not worn exclusively by black woman. Moreover, the defendants had pointed out that Renee Rogers first appeared at work in the all-braided hairstyle soon after 'the style had been popularized [among white women] by a white actress in the film "10"'.[20] Finally, the court emphasised that the hairstyle was an 'easily changed characteristic, even if it is socioculturally associated with a particular race or nationality'.[21]

Second, sociologist Lawrence Bobo's group position theory supports the psychological explanation of dominance outlined above (Bobo 1999). According to this theory, racial prejudice is 'best understood as a general attitude or orientation involving normative ideas about where one's own group should stand in the social order vis-à-vis an out-group' (1999: 449–54). High-status group members are concerned about their group's relative status-group ranking as compared with perceived subordinate groups, and will articulate their own values in such a way that the group maintains cohesion and excludes unwanted others. In order to maintain the group's status, members of the dominant group 'must make an affectively important distinction between themselves and [perceived] subordinate group members . . . linked to ideas about the traits, capabilities and likely behaviours of subordinate group members' (1999: 454).

While the research described above focused on racial prejudice, I believe similar observations can be made about any kind of identity-based oppression. It supports the general point that even people who sincerely profess support for egalitarian values remain acutely aware of group status issues and may seek to defend the privileges they derive from being in a position of dominance in a given situation by targeting persons *they associate* with out-group identity for discriminatory

---

[18] 527 F. Supp. 229 (1981).   [19] *Ibid.*, 231–32.   [20] *Ibid.*, 232.   [21] *Ibid.*

treatment. I emphasise the words 'they associate' to stress that the key element in the practice of discrimination is that the discriminators participate in the construction of the identity of the out-group targeted for disadvantageous treatment. The individual members of various out-groups do not all possess one and the same identity. Everyone is a mixture of multiple, socially constructed identities. However, the fact that individuals who are identified as members of various out-groups have complex identities that do not fit within one identity category is not important for purposes of the maintenance of systems of dominance and subordination. What *is* important to those protecting their dominant positions is to make sure the out-groups remain subordinated. They do so by justifying disadvantageous treatment of persons they believe to be members of one or more out-groups in relation to themselves by describing the basis of the discriminatory treatment as consisting of particular traits or behaviours, which can be linked to dominant identity categories or characterised as matters of personal choice, thus transferring responsibility for the disadvantageous treatment to the target of discrimination.

Powerful incentives operate to ensure that the urge to keep subordinated groups in their place remains hidden, as identity-based oppression has become increasingly and widely understood to be not just illegal discrimination but also morally reprehensible conduct. This makes it difficult for those who experience discrimination to pinpoint the basis for the disadvantageous treatment they suffer. However, Abrams' modified post-structural approach towards identity formation and the social psychological research on racism point towards a way of resolving the puzzle of combating discrimination based on multiple grounds.

Conclusion: towards a modified post-structuralist approach to (multiple) discrimination

The modified post-structuralist understanding of identity formation and racism outlined above indicates that anti-discrimination law should avoid requiring victims of discrimination to single out one particular ground of discrimination as the basis for their claims. Rather it should focus on determining whether the claimant possesses one or more characteristics that serve as markers of membership in one or more identity categories that correspond to the prohibited grounds of discrimination and whether the discriminatory treatment disadvantages persons possessing those characteristics. For example, in regard to the black female employees in the *DeGraffenreid*[22] case in the United States, this determination could be made on the basis of evidence that women as a group (regardless of other factors) and blacks as a group (regardless of other factors) are over-represented on the lower rungs of social and economic privilege, e.g. lower average incomes, under-representation among the highly educated. This evidence should then be regarded as indicating that white people are likely to adopt attitudes and practices that protect their racial privilege and that men of all races likewise adopt attitudes and practices that protect their gender privilege. By doing so, they participate in the construction of an identity category 'black women' that is invested with the traits and characteristics necessary for persons possessing the dominant racial and gender identity characteristics to justify their participation in processes that subordinate 'black women'. Thus, whereas the court in *DeGraffenreid* refused to recognise the category 'black women' because of its adherence to the single-axis framework criticised by Crenshaw, the post-structuralist approach demonstrates how 'black women' can become an identity category that is subjected to specific forms of discrimination that disadvantage them in ways that the categories 'white women' and 'black men' are not.

In cases of employment discrimination against older women, the analysis must begin with the recognition that they possess the characteristics of two identity categories that are protected by anti-discrimination legislation: old age and gender. Thus, it is likely that their experience of discrimination involves both categories and is constructed by social processes that ensure that youth and maleness maintain their positions in the social hierarchy. This can only be accomplished by subordinating older women. Neither age nor gender can be removed from the analysis without losing an essential aspect of the discriminatory practice.

The infinite regress problem described by Ehrenreich becomes less of a problem – if not resolved – with the recognition that the basic grounds of discrimination may be combined in myriad ways in any given individual and serve to mark the main structures of social oppression. They tend to operate to protect the privileges that attach to the racial, ethnic, religious, gender, sexual orientation, physical ability and age characteristics around which society is organised. The subordination of anyone on the basis of any combination of these grounds serves to maintain and enforce the social structures of oppression. Combinations of multiple discrimination grounds should therefore not be brushed aside as exotic,

---

[22] *DeGraffenreid v. General Motors*, 413 F. Supp. 142 (E.D. Missouri 1976).

unlucky, irremediable coincidences of several subordinated characteristics in one person.

Finally, the modified post-structuralist approach outlined here
requires that judges take into account their own positions in the social
hierarchy in relation to the parties in discrimination cases because this
approach locates the process of oppression not just in the defendant's
treatment of the claimant but in the social construction of dominant and
subordinate identities in which everyone participates. This approach
makes it clear that those who benefit from norms necessary to the
maintenance of structures of oppression find it hard to reject those
norms as unjustly discriminatory. Accordingly, judges are compelled
to recognise that they may be just as prone to avoid awareness of their
dominance as anyone else who has enjoyed racial, gender and other
identity-based privilege, and that they are also just as prone to explain
the existence of inequality in a given case on the basis of norms that work
to preserve the identity-based privileges they have enjoyed.

Regardless of whether the complaint is based on one or several
discrimination grounds, this alternative approach would require the
court to recognise that, in order to provide effective protection against
discrimination, it must take into account all the prohibited grounds of
discrimination that may be implicated in order to determine whether the
defendant's justifications can be accepted. All grounds of discrimination
that can be identified with the claimant must be considered in order to
account for relationships of dominance between the claimant and the
defendant and between the claimant and the court. The explicit and
implicit norms that apply to construct dominant and subordinate categories – for example, age, ethnic origin, religion and gender may converge in cases concerning school dress codes that have the effect of
excluding Muslim headscarves – must be considered and a determination made as to whether these norms are operating in a given case to
maintain the lines between dominant and subordinate categories.

The main obstacle to changing legal approaches to these cases is
teaching judges and litigators to see the multiple identity categories
represented in themselves and in the parties before them, and the
relationships of dominance and subordination that lie at the root of
discrimination. It undoubtedly also requires new legislation to redefine
discrimination, so that it clearly includes considerations of relationships
of dominance and subordination based on the prohibited grounds of
discrimination, and to clarify the legal basis for considering all grounds
of discrimination that may be implicated in a case.

Bibliography

Abrams, K. 1994. 'Title VII and the complex female subject', *Michigan Law Review* 92: 2479–540

1999. 'From autonomy to agency: feminist perspectives on self-direction', *William and Mary Law Review* 40: 805–46

Anthias, F. and Yuval-Davis, N. 1983. 'Contextualizing feminism: gender, ethnic and class divisions', *Feminist Review* 15: 62–75

Barnes, A. 2001/2002. 'Envisioning a future for age and disability discrimination claims', *University of Michigan Journal of Law Reform* 35: 263–303

Bobo, L. 1999. 'Prejudice as group position: microfoundations of a sociological approach to racism and race relations', *Journal of Social Issues* 55: 445–72

Carle, S. 2005. 'Theorizing agency', *American University Law Review* 55: 307–93

Combahee River Collective 1977. 'A black feminist statement' available at www. feministezine.com/feminist/modern/Black-Feminist-Statement.html

Conaghan, J. 2009. 'Intersectionality and the feminist project in law', in Grabham *et al.* (eds.), 21–48

Crenshaw, K. 1989. 'Demarginalizing the intersection of race and sex: a black feminist critique of antidiscrimination doctrine, feminist theory and anti-racial politics', *University of Chicago Legal Forum*, 139–67

Crocette, S. 1998. 'Considering hybrid sex and age discrimination claims by women: examining approaches to pleading and analysis – a pragmatic model', *Golden Gate University Law Review* 28: 115–74

Davis, A. Y. 1981. *Women, Race & Class*. New York: Random House

Eglit, H. 1997. 'The Age Discrimination in Employment Act at thirty: where it's been, where it is today, where it's going', *University of Richmond Law Review* 31: 579–748

Ehrenreich, N. 2002. 'Subordination and symbiosis: mechanisms of mutual support between subordinating systems', *University of Missouri-Kansas City Law Review* 71: 251–324

Erikson, E. 1968. *Identity: Youth and Crisis*. New York: Norton

European Network of Legal Experts in the Field of Gender Equality 2009. *Multiple Discrimination in EU Law: Opportunities for Legal Responses to Intersectional Gender Discrimination?* Brussels: European Commission, Directorate-General for Employment, Social Affairs and Equal Opportunities

Friedan, B. 1963. *The Feminine Mystique*. New York: Dell Publishing Co.

Fuss, D. 1989. *Essentially Speaking: Feminism, Nature and Difference*. New York: Routledge

Gaertner, S. and Dovidio, J. 1986. 'The aversive form of racism', in S. Gaertner and J. Dovidio (eds.), *Prejudice, Discrimination and Racism*. Orlando, FL: Academic Press, 61–89

Giddings, P. 1984. *When and Where I Enter*. New York: W. Morrow

Goldberg, S. 2009. 'Intersectionality in practice', in Grabham *et al.* (eds.), 124–58

Grabham, E., Cooper, D., Krishnadas, J. and Herman, D. (eds.), 2009. *Intersectionality and Beyond: Law, Power, and the Politics of Location*. Abingdon and New York: Routledge-Cavendish

Harris, A. 1990. 'Race and essentialism in feminist theory', *Stanford Law Review* 42: 581–616

hooks, b. 1981. *Ain't I a Woman*. Boston: South End Press

Makkonen, T. M. 2002. *Compound and Intersectional Discrimination: Bringing the Experiences of the Most Marginalized to the Fore*. Åbo Akademi University

Porter, N. 2003. 'Sex plus age discrimination: protecting older women workers', *Denver University Law Review* 81: 79–111

Roseberry, L. 1999. *The Limits of Employment Discrimination Law in the United States and European Community*. Copenhagen: Dansk Jurist og Økonomforbundets Forlag

  In press. 'The assimilationist anti-discrimination paradigm and the immigrant Muslim woman: suggestions on how to re-conceptualise discrimination claims', in D. Schiek and A. Lawson (eds.), *EU Non-Discrimination Law and Intersectional Discrimination*. Farnham: Ashgate

Ryan, K. 1999. 'Compound discrimination: closing the loop in age and sex claims', *Colorado Lawyer* 28: 5–18

Spelman, E. 1988. *Inessential Woman: Problems of Exclusion in Feminist Thought*. Boston: Beach Press

Tatum, B. 2002. *Why Are All the Black Kids Sitting Together in the Cafeteria?* New York: Basic Books

Yuval-Davis, N. 2006. 'Intersectionality and feminist politics', *European Journal of Women's Studies* 13: 193–209

3

Older women, work and the impact of discrimination

DIANE GRANT

Introduction

The aim of this chapter is to shed some light on the impact discrimination has on older women (50 +) and to investigate how their under-representation in the workforce may be partly attributed to a combination of past and present age (and gender) discrimination. It is suggested that a tension exists for older women in attempting to access employment as being at odds with their experiences of gendered ageism, the gendered assumptions of both the family and wider society and their sufferance of gendered disadvantage and discrimination. Each of these aspects has created barriers to women's participation.

Despite being at the forefront of the fight for equal opportunities with women of all ages, older women are now looking back at a lifetime of endeavours to achieve equality with men, while facing further prejudicial treatment as older women in the form of ageism. For women, the consequences of growing older in a society that values youth and beauty, and the disadvantaging attitudes of employers and society in general, have served to limit the desires and expectations of older women to receive equal treatment in the workplace, thus resulting in a reduction in presence and constraints on prospects to redress the imbalance. All of this creates a disillusionment with the efficacy of legislation to combat discrimination.

Their experiences highlight that unfair treatment in the labour markets, and in training, access and education, results in internalisation of negative and unfair treatment. A large contingent of women, striving to attain an acceptable work–life balance, chose to work part-time, often under pressure from society, family and their own commitment to the provision of childcare within the home. The interpretation of part-time

work as being low-status, low-skill work, accompanied by few employment rights, further diminished the value of women's contribution to the
economy and society.

Past experiences and missed opportunities within work and the education system created a mistrust of fair treatment at work (perceived to
be based upon ageist assumptions by employers) and a lack of belief in
their own ability to achieve educationally, thus potentially damaging any
policy interventions aimed at improving work or educational opportunities for older people. The thought of re-entering education or work or
training later in life, after prolonged detachment, is fraught with feelings
of anxiety (Grant *et al.* 2006).

The chapter is divided into two sections. The first section explores the
context of women and work; policy responses to the disengagement of
older people with work; and key research into age (and other forms of)
discrimination. The second section concentrates on the voices of women
over 50,[1] who were interviewed just prior to the implementation of the
Employment Equality (Age) Regulations. Here they talk about their
recollections of work, education and experiences of discrimination as
both younger and older women.

Background

Attention from policy-makers in the UK regarding the under-representation
of older people in the labour force resulted in various measures designed to
remedy age discrimination. A consultation paper issued by the UK
Government in 1998 requested the views of employers, trades unions, and
organisations representing older people and individuals, on ways which
could be used to address age discrimination in employment. The responses
culminated in the voluntary code of practice, setting out a framework of
measures to encourage and promote employment of older workers (DfEE
1999). As a voluntary code, this achieved limited success. The evidence in
both the media and academia was mounting, with discrimination against
older workers seemingly continuing unabated. The Employment Equality
(Age) Regulations were enacted in October 2006. Four years later, in

---

[1] Prior to the implementation of the Employment Equality (Age) Regulations 2006,
   Liverpool John Moores University embarked on a three-year research project funded
   by ESF Objective 3. Data were gathered from 1,035 men and women over 50 and 178
   employer representatives, on issues concerning age and gender stereotypes. The interviews with women over 50 form the basis of the second section.

October 2010 (at the time of writing this chapter), the Equality Bill is set to supersede the previous legislation on discrimination, to provide a framework of discrimination law which protects individuals from unfair treatment and promotes a fair and more equal society.[2]

Despite the legislation aimed at providing fairer treatment for older people, evidence suggests there has been a decline in the numbers of over 55s in the workforce, whilst the proportion of older people (45 to 59) will increase by a quarter up till 2021 (Sargeant and Lewis 2008: 229). Many are experiencing difficulty gaining entry to the jobs market. According to Bytheway (1995) and Bytheway and Johnson (1990: 32), we are all of a particular age and are in the process of ageing, and as such 'any unwarranted response to any age' can be construed as ageism. Defining at which age one is classed as 'older' brings about different responses from various authors. Do we mean over 40, 50 or 60, or those that have retired from paid employment, or, as some studies found for women in their mid-forties, simply being judged as older? (MacNicol 2006). Ageism is believed to be experienced differently by men and women, with some authors finding that older women are facing the dual oppressions of age and gender discrimination. The glass ceiling is now being replaced with the silver ceiling and the emergence of 'lookism' (Itzin and Phillipson, 1993; Granleese and Sayer 2006).

Women now in their fifties and sixties witnessed and experienced the inequalities of access to equal opportunities prior to the legislation in the 1970s, and many of them now find they are less likely than their younger counterparts to be able to compete in the jobs market for a variety of reasons. The 1970s Sex Discrimination Act (SDA) and Equal Opportunities Act (EOA) legislation heralded an end to discriminatory practices which had pervaded most areas of women's working lives. In the intervening years women's position within employment increased. However, evidence has since emerged to illustrate that discriminatory practices were part of their everyday experiences.

Women and work

Women once left work upon marriage (for example in the teaching profession). However, today most women leave work upon the birth of a child and generally can return to work after basic maternity leave

---

[2] Government Equalities Office, see www.equalities.gov.uk/equality_act_2010.aspx.

(Maguire 1995). Hence, there are older women in society today who had a combination of different experiences regarding employment following childbirth. Many of today's older women would have been influenced by their own experiences as daughters (and mothers) in post-war Britain. Literature published by the Government in 1947 emphasised the work of women as being "temporary, helping in a crisis. . . and doing women's work in factories" (Cmd 7046 (1947)). Women themselves viewed work in the same way and took on the double burden of home and employment, accepting it as specifically a female practice. Women's participation in employment increased slowly: by 1951, 31% of women were employed, reaching 45% in 1987 in part owing to discrimination legislation, contraception being more readily available, the need to supplement the family income and the aspiration to raise family living standards (Summerfield 1994). The female contribution to the family purse through engagement in part-time employment had long been denigrated as pin money, yet it was a crucial lifeline for the working-class woman, often supplementing the low income of her husband or partner by taking on part-time or low-paid employment to keep the family out of poverty. Thus the part-time earnings of women were regarded as an important and growing component of family income (Harkness Machin and Waldfogel 1997).

Older women in the sample had faced mixed experiences following childbirth. As already stated, some women left work upon marriage, while others typically left upon the birth of a child. Upon re-entry, some had to look for new employment while some employers accepted others back into previous employment. Women would then work (intermittently and mostly part-time) between the births of subsequent children. Whilst this pattern is certainly different for single and divorced women, the identification of a cause of age disadvantage for older women is made by Groves, that in today's society and with the aid of the Sex Discrimination Act 1975, 'the younger the woman, the more paid work she is likely to have done and the better qualified in formal terms she is likely to be', as compared to her older female colleague (Groves 1993: 43). Thus the challenges women formerly faced in accessing and progressing in employment can partly be attributed to the gaps they took out of employment, at a time when it was expected that women would set aside career aspirations to raise their children, compared to the experiences of working women of today who are (mostly) legally protected in employment after childbirth.

Despite older women's marginal attachment to the labour force, they have faced gender discrimination and challenges in gaining an equal footing in the workforce. Throughout the struggle for fair treatment, they contended with the insidious undermining of their contribution to work, both paid and unpaid, through both discriminatory practices and, stereotyped attitudes of a 'woman's place' being in the home. Many older women experienced age discrimination throughout their younger employed life; employers freely questioned their plans for starting a family or getting married, or implied a loss of mental acuity as women aged, to be used in the process of selection or de-selection. Whilst unlawful under the SDA, it was nonetheless widespread. According to Groves, 'discrimination, when it did occur, was more implicit than explicit, expressed through double standards and judgments made on account of women's real or perceived age' (Groves 1993: 43).

The ageing population has now led governments to prioritise extending the working lives of people in the UK, beyond the current retirement age. This requires attitudinal change by employers to ensure older people are able and willing to participate. Thus the prevailing myths attributed to older workers need challenging. For older women, the combination of ageist and sexist treatment places them at a disadvantage and undermines their efforts to access work and to progress within the workplace, threatening to impede government objectives to increase the labour market participation of older people.

Age UK,[3] in an analysis of employment statistics,[4] found that two in five people aged 50+ were long-term unemployed (LTU),[5] with rates of LTU older women rising by a third in 2009 (TUC 2009), the highest percentage increase among all age groups. Whether leaving work before State Pension Age is due to an economic downturn or through choice depends upon the sector women find themselves in. In the private sector, women who generally undertook low-skilled work, often part-time and specifically gender-related, would not have recourse to an occupational pension scheme as management in the private sector was under no obligation to provide this, whereas women in some areas of the public sector would in general be able to access an occupational pension following early exit. Thus disadvantage throughout the working life can be a precursor to poverty in later years, with many experiencing female pensioner poverty. Previous studies have shown that early exit from labour markets can lead to poverty, lower-skilled male workers

---

[3] Age Concern and Help the Aged merged in 2010 to become AgeUK.
[4] www.ageuk.org.uk/latest-press/50-plus-workers-trapped-in-long-term-unemployment/.
[5] Unemployed for more than twelve months.

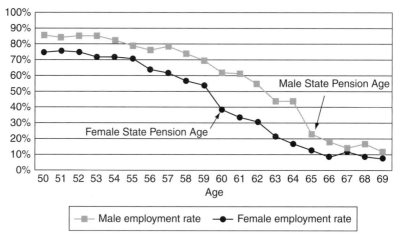

Figure 3.1   Male and female employment rates by age, autumn 2004. Source: Labour Force Survey 2004; www.dwp.gov.uk/docs/volume2.pdf.

being likely to be living on low incomes at 60. However, women were much more likely than men to be poor when aged 60+. The reason for this was the shorter working life of women, unstable attachment to work, and the predominance of part-time working. As older women were much more likely to be living without a partner, this 'substantially increased the risk of low income, even for women that had worked for much of their life' (Bardasi and Jenkins 2002).

Whilst recent trends show increased employment in the over 50s today, they also reveal a decline associated with age, around the age of 50 and beyond. Figure 3.1 illustrates that the age at which female employment declines is around 50, and that it declines more rapidly than male employment.

Women working outside the large public sector organisations tend to be found in occupations where workplaces are smaller, for example in retail, care and personal services or hospitality, with more households being dependent solely or primarily on the woman's wage as the major part of the family income. In past recessions, men bore the brunt of becoming laid off or made redundant, but trade unions now believe this is changing, with women facing increasing rates of redundancy, rising to almost double the rate of increase in male redundancies, because of care home closures and the loss of small retail chains (for example, Adams, Rosebys and Ethel Austin). With around 44% of part-time workers being older women without dependent children, many were found to be over-represented in private sector low-paid employment.[6]

The current recession is expected to affect future employment in the public sector. Public sector work has provided many women with the kind of flexibility they require, in those traditional occupations women have tended to undertake. Compared with the more rigid work patterns associated with the private sector, women can often negotiate flexibility within a public organisation. In a review and response to the first budget of the incoming UK Coalition Government in May 2010, Yvette Cooper,[7] formerly Secretary of State for work and Pensions in the outgoing (Labour) Government, produced a report on the forecast of projected cuts in public expenditure, in which she expressed her concern for women in this sector being disproportionately affected as jobs in the sector start to diminish.

Detachment from the labour market

The reasons for premature detachment from the labour market have evolved from an 'early retirement culture' which has been associated with a variety of push and pull factors. Push factors include ill health, redundancy, discrimination and the difficulties in combining work with caring roles. Pull factors are predominantly associated with having more economically advantaged circumstances whereby individuals can choose to leave work before their retirement age. The combinations of these two factors identified in early detachment have been described as the 'two nations' of early retirement (Arthur 2003; Lissenburgh and Smeaton 2003). Push factors are often located within lower social classes who have experienced redundancies or are long-term unemployed, with inadequate skills or reduced health (Banks and Tetlow 2008). For those who can choose when to leave employment, unconstrained by financial insecurity and often taken care of through income from an occupational pension, the future can mean taking on other interests whilst in good health.

For these two groups, the implications of social policies designed to increase participation in the workforce for the over 50s are quite distinct. Losing one's employment after the age of 50 is more likely to lead to long-term unemployment or inactivity compared with job loss at

---

[6] www.tuc.org.uk/extras/womenandrecession.pdf.
[7] Yvette Cooper, *Guardian on Sunday*, 4 July 2010.

younger ages. In the UK, older workers are over-represented among the long-term unemployed. However, this underestimates the problem of unemployment in this age group, as many older people, although wanting to work, move directly to early retirement, becoming part of the 'hidden unemployed'. It is known that a variety of structural and individual barriers exist in attracting such people back into work and for employers to retain older workers. These include discrimination and discriminatory perceptions of older people, a lack of current skills, or being unable to access suitable training or educational opportunities (Green 2003).

On a psychological level, being defined as old can result in a person becoming susceptible to identity degradation (Berger 2006), perpetuating detachment from labour markets. Furthermore, women also disappear from the workforce to provide intergenerational care (Mooney and Statham 2002). The Equal Opportunities Commission found in 2004 that many women, when faced with the burden of providing care and undertaking work, either reduced their commitment to work or left employment completely.

The impact of ageism, sexism and lookism

Ageism has generally only been referred to in a gender-neutral framework. However, age discrimination is not gender neutral. Granleese and Sayer (2006) identified female appearance as being important in the judgment of colleagues in academia. However, stereotyping and labelling associated with age, gender or appearance are precursors to disadvantaged treatment resulting in discrimination. Gender inequalities are compounded over time and internalised by women; as women grow older, the 'social pathology' of ageing affects women more than men, in terms of how they age and the perception that looking older may have on their opportunities (Itzen and Phillipson 1993; Duncan and Lorretto (2004). Women appear as more vulnerable to such pressures than men. Indeed, internalisation of previous discriminatory experiences is made complex by the realisation that in today's society an older women no longer conforms to the modern standards of youth and beauty, leaving some more prone to low self-esteem, depression and anxiety (Saucier 2004). In a society that embraces 'youth, beauty and the commercialised images of happiness and well being' (Sontag 1972: 29–38), such preoccupation with 'looks' has led women to take action to hold back signs of ageing through the use of beauty treatments (Clarke and Griffin 2008).

The fear of losing one's job through ageist perceptions, often identified by the visible signs of ageing, is quite legitimate. A study of the BBC (an organisation with a very high public commitment to equal opportunities) found that its older workers over the age of 50 (over a fifteen-year period) were increasingly whittled away from its workforce (Platman and Tinker 1998). Academic studies support the assumption that ageism for women is also bound up in sexism, and have found that women are thus 'subject to a "double standard" of ageing' (Sontag 1972) and to gendered ageism (Rosenthal 1990), by virtue of their simultaneous membership of the categories 'old' and 'female', and now facing the additional burden of 'lookism'.

Lookism is an appearance-related form of discrimination experienced differently by women in various scenarios. Granleese and Sayer (2006) found that non-academics viewed academics as being 'career driven by their lack of attractiveness and/or poor appearance'. Being a young female academic meant playing down one's 'looks', as this was perceived as disadvantageous to their careers. Relating factious appearance-based judgments to women's work trivialises women's contribution, reduces the value of their skills, disregards their important attributes and stifles motivation, thus imposing an additional barrier for older woman to break down in the workplace.

Factors affecting access to opportunities

A number of issues related to the experiences of older women and labour market attachment have been raised, yet, as research has identified, it is not only access to labour markets that is important, but also access to learning for qualifications to improve the chances of gaining better-paid employment and opportunities for progression within work. For some, the years during which they were bringing up their children was also an era of increasing technological advances. Being detached from the labour market also meant detachment from on-the-job training, creating a further disadvantage when applying for employment. Academic studies have pointed to a particular kind of disadvantage for the older woman of a certain age. Gender pay gaps have been attributed to the fact that most women did not have the same opportunities as men to build up a career or to earn the equivalent of males because of their childrearing and caring responsibilities (Women's Equality Unit (site now archived)).[8]

---

[8] http://webarchive.nationalarchives.gov.uk/20080905235643/equalities.gov.uk/.

The dominant ideology within organisations emerging from recessions in the 1990s was towards ensuring a younger workforce as a buffer against an ageing population, equated with low growth and economic stagnation. Despite the forecasts of a changing demography in the coming decades, Metcalf and Thomson (1990) found recruiters in the 1990s, whilst aware of the changing demography set for the future, had adhered to recruitment practices which were built upon age-related assumptions and generalisations. The negative stereotypes of the older employee included 'inflexibility, resistance to change, unwillingness to learn, poor health and lack of drive, energy and ambition', subsuming the more positive associated characteristics of reliability, maturity, loyalty and commitment. Arguably, many of those individuals who believed they had been discriminated against because of their age would assert that whilst legislation may be in place today, it is not the legislation that needs policing, but those who hide behind the well-intentioned policies whilst harbouring ageist and sexist assumptions.

In an attempt to identify whether there were employment inequalities between men and women, an analysis of data by the Department of Work and Pensions over a thirty-year period from 1973 to 2003 found that the Female Employment Disadvantage had been reduced dramatically (including the employment disadvantage associated with motherhood in particular), meaning that it was more likely that younger women would now have more chances of obtaining work compared to women over 50. However, a new employment disadvantage associated with being a woman aged over 50 began to emerge during this period (Berthoud and Blekesaune 2007).

Older women's rationale for undertaking paid work and their experiences of work have undergone transformation over time. For many women, the burden of gendered assumptions that provision of care within the family and society should be provided by women may indicate why part-time work predominates. Census data revealed that 10% of women were carers and that care-giving increased with age, reaching a peak between the ages of 45 and 59. This in part explains why many older workers can only work, or choose to work, part-time hours, or drop out of work altogether because of caring commitments.

The Equal Pay Act 1970 and the Sex Discrimination Act 1975 had gone some way to ensuring that women and men would be treated equally in the workplace, yet, despite this, data[9] continue to indicate

---

[9] Low Pay Estimates (ONS April 2008), see www.statistics.gov.uk/pdfdir/1pay1108.pdf.

that women were more likely to be found in part-time work and be more concentrated in three occupational groups, clerical, personal services and retail, with only 10% of women in professional occupations and 11.5% in managerial positions. In comparison to other countries in Europe, in 2009 the employment rates for the over 55s in the UK were 57.5%, the same as Denmark, but lower than Sweden at 80% and Norway at 68.7%.[10]

Perceptions of past discrimination

This second section will focus on the key themes of discrimination as identified by the women in the study, which supports and adds to current literature on how experiences of the past, in work, in education and in periods of economic inactivity have been bound up with age.

Age discrimination was found to operate when people were just starting out in their employment. Occasionally, some rationalised this as being negative treatment rather than discrimination. This was more apparent for those who entered manual labour occupations after their initial schooling. It was a period they could look back on and perhaps identify as a learning process or a kind of initiation into adulthood. Some interviewees felt that they had experienced discrimination in terms of the pay they received, whereby organisations based the pay scales on age rather than experience. When age discrimination occurred in later years, the women viewed this more seriously as this placed limitations on their opportunities and was to impact quite markedly on individual life chances. Hence accepted ageist practices were traced back to being initially played out largely in the labour market, being identified with the pay and rewards that went with 'age'.

Too young or too old?

A common example of discrimination many women identified was that of age barring, preventing women from applying for a job because of age limits in job advertisements. The study found that women both had experienced discrimination in the past owing to their age, and were continuing to come up against discrimination in later life. Although age limits in job adverts are mostly illegal, current evidence has been

---

[10] See http://epp.eurostat.ec.europa.eu/cache/ITY_PUBLIC/3-04082010-BP/EN/3-04082010-BP-EN.PDF.

found (post the 2006 legislation) of ageist language within the wording of job advertisements.[11]

In the not too distant past, ageist adverts were much more blatant, creating myriad emotions related to the inequality of opportunity that such practices had in holding women back in accessing employment or progressing. Women spoke of being hurt, angry, upset and frustrated at being unable to show potential employers what they as 'older' women could offer. 'I remember coming home and saying to Mum, "I'm thirty-six and I'm written off already – I can't believe it" – and I didn't feel old, but it made me feel worthless' (female, 55, working).

There were also examples of the negative effect that the double jeopardy of gender and age discrimination could have upon the individual. Such experiences and the internalisation of negative messages provoked feelings of frustration, thus lowering expectations for advancement in a situation in which they had little control. Alternatively, women decided to subordinate any work aspirations to concentrate on other aspects of their lives, over which they could exert some control.

> I think at the time it just made me work harder. I feel I had to work twice as hard, but I think it made me a little bit introverted as well because you were frightened to discuss how you felt with other people and you (women) were in a minority ... I suppose at the time because I was younger and it was a career I'd always wanted, it made me stronger, but I also think that when my family came along, I had someone else to consider, so it was a disadvantage. I used to take things to heart and that is why I thought in the end, 'oh, I give up'. I think if I hadn't had any one else to consider I'd have dug my heels in.
>
> (Female, 50, job seeker)

Applying for an internal management post, this interviewee found later that her failure to get the job was clearly due to her age. Acceptance of obviously unjust contentious decisions could, for some, result in internalisation of the negative perception society would seem to place on them and their potential value in the workforce.

> I felt very disappointed and very hurt because I was told I hadn't got the job. When I went (left employment) it came out, that the people said, no, they wouldn't give it to me because I was too old at fifty-three, because they expected somebody younger ... they wanted it to run for x number

---

[11] 'Applicants should be graduates, ideally with not more than 2–3 years' experience in a commercial environment.' The supermarket was ordered to pay €5,000 and advised to amend future advertisements.

of years, so I didn't get it . . . I was disappointed, but afterwards I thought well, that is life.

(Female, 62, unpaid volunteer)

To remain in particular spheres of work required training, or to re-enter work might also necessitate a strong commitment to re-enter education in order to gain new qualifications. The following extract addresses the perceptions of self and others in relation to the issue of training and education as a person becomes older. 'I had an example of ageism today, Mary said to me. "Have you had your test yet?" she said. "Well", she said, "you've got to remember that as you get older it gets harder to take things in" and I didn't say anything, because I'm too polite, but I felt like screaming, No! No! it doesn't, it's just your perception of it' (Professional female, 57).

The 'problem' of being a woman

Many of the women interviewed had confronted classic gendered discourse about motherhood, the care of the family and their role within it. It was felt in their younger days (1960s, 1970s), that employers at that time thought women were only interested in work until they got married or had children.

Just after I was married I went for a job . . . it was an internal promotion and it was between me and two men . . . the men were the same age as me . . . less qualified than me . . . had a worse sickness record than me – because I was always careful or conscientious about my days off – so on paper it looked like me . . . but at the interview, this man said to me – this is the god's honest truth – he said to me, 'you've recently been married?' I said 'yes'. 'So you'll be having children in a few years time?' I said 'no, I don't intend to have any children for a long while yet'. 'But you will be having children?' It was an assumption he made without me saying anything. I didn't get the job, one of the men got the job, but I was so angry because I knew why they hadn't given it to me.

(Female, 55, working full-time)

Ageism in work

Ageist attitudes were perceived to be operating within the workplace. As one interviewee understood it, age discrimination had always been a part of the workplace culture, operating amongst work colleagues as well as management, and as such it was accepted as an inevitable part of growing older in employment.

> I remember when we went for a night out, the younger people that we had trained were coming up, I was now part time, and they were now full time. We were in a restaurant and I sort of came in slightly later, and I remember [x], who I had known for some time [say] 'oh, you are over there with the oldies' and then she was like, 'oh, I am sorry, I am sorry' . . . I was [saying] 'yeah you are right' . . . I remember being her age and doing it [myself]. That was interesting . . . you see there was no age discrimination then . . . it was just the way it was, there wasn't a label or a word for it, that's the difference.
>
> (Female, 55)

Age discrimination in recruitment was also cited as the reason why very few people thought that they would find suitable work or why they applied for 'inferior' jobs or jobs that they were over-qualified for. One interviewee explained how discrimination can undermine a person's confidence, causing them to be self-limiting or self-deselecting or to put themselves down.

> I think I got a couple of interviews but just didn't get anywhere with it, but by that time my confidence was really knocked. I wasn't performing very well because usually I can get interviews no problem and if I do get an interview I'm not saying I'd get the job, but coming back again now [pause] it took me a long time and it knocked my confidence a lot . . . I went for an interview, the person there fed back to me . . . she said that . . . I'd sort of given negative answers. I seemed to be identifying problems rather than solutions, so I must have had a negative turn of mind then . . . I'll undersell myself and I'll go for jobs that are less than £30,000 and I shouldn't.
>
> (Female, 50+, student)

There was an overwhelming feeling that older people have a lot to offer an employer but were not being given the opportunity to prove their worth or showcase their talents. Those women out of work in our study were keen and eager to work. Many had dependent children to support, or were single or divorced. It was felt that employer prejudice prevented the majority of them from regaining a place in the labour market or ushered them into work that was unsuitable, temporary or inferior. The waste of talent of people in their fifties and sixties was a common theme in the data.

> I feel a lot of older people have got an awful lot to offer and what happens is I think their experience of life is overlooked and the fact that maybe

they *can* pick things up quickly. I find, and I say it to myself all the time, 'well if only I could get in a place and they showed me exactly what to do, then I'd pick it up no problem'. But it's actually [going in with that bit of paper, which obviously a younger person will do because they're taught computers at school.

(Female, 50, job seeker)

Situations arose in work in which access to training opportunities was based upon age. Assumptions were made about perceived learning capabilities and mental acuity. The reinforcement of negative messages brought about self-doubt and lack of confidence, as relayed by this interviewee. 'I think for somebody of my age, you sometimes get a lot of ageism. I used to work in the enquiries department [public sector] and I had to go for . . . training. All I kept getting told was that 'we won't expect you to be able to do this, because you are an older person' and although they had this policy of non-ageism, no prejudice, it kept on getting dropped in the conversation.'

Although she enjoyed the job and the colleagues she was working with, she was always aware of her age, as being the oldest and not being as valued. She had not felt that way before she went to work in that organisation, but she found that the expectations they had of her, not being up to the training because of her age, made her 'feel' old. 'The training put years on me . . . I even put a complaint in about [it] – I mean she was a lovely girl, but she kept bringing up this thing, about, well, because you are older and fair enough I maybe wasn't as fast, I had never been great at geography but I mean I had only been there three months and I got the employee of the month, so I wasn't that bad!' (Female, 58, paid staff, voluntary sector).

Sexism in work

On reflection, the experiences women faced in conjunction with age were equally associated with sexism or lookism, as well as gender stereotyping. An older female manager in a male-dominated environment had been confronted with prejudicial behaviours.

I have also been referred to, even in my later years, as 'eye candy', or, 'we have got to have bit of glamour at this meeting', '[participant's name] will you come along?' . . . which is all very nice in one way, but you know if I wasn't . . . presented in that way, what would I be, the office croney? It is just not a very valuable way of assessing people's abilities I think.

(Female, 50, paid staff, voluntary sector)

Not only were past experiences of age and gender discrimination related to us, but current practice in the workplace was being witnessed. 'Only a few weeks ago we were going to do an exhibition down in Birmingham and they got two girls from telesales, and they were told to wear short skirts. I couldn't believe it. So they were picked to go down and told to wear short skirts' (Female, 50, paid staff, voluntary sector).

In response to a question as to the existence of sexism in the workplace this interviewee responded:

> Yes, yes . . . I think basically there's still a lot of sexism around, I think so, I'm pretty sure . . . We were laughing – although we make a joke out of it at work – you know, you get some of the bosses come in and they go, 'Can you make a cup of tea?' and they'll turn to a woman! They won't turn to the bloke, they'll turn to the nearest female, so it's there, in their heads.

Subjective decisions on who to put forward for training, based upon a person's age, is often couched in terms of the economic benefit or pay-back period the trainee may have within the company and, as such, older workers are misjudged. The literature has shown that workers who have considerable length of service are more likely to repay their firm with loyalty, unlike younger workers who move on with the acquired training certificates in their CVs.

As with age discrimination, the tendency to have experienced perceived gender discrimination was stronger amongst the younger end of the cohort, particularly those in the 50–54 age group. One possible explanation for this was that profound changes regarding women's employment and equal opportunity legislation, during the last thirty years, had impacted greatly on this group, simply by virtue of the fact that these women were more likely to have grown up and grown older under these changes. They witnessed the challenges, then and now, of gender inequalities being brought before the tribunals and courts, providing a drip-feed of evidence, reinforcing the experiences of those who had faced the hurdles associated with maternity, promotion and equal pay. When a new recruit told her employer that she was pregnant, her contract was terminated.

> They [employer] said, '. . . I must have known [that I was pregnant] and that I was taking the [training] place . . . that I was just messing around, because it takes you a few weeks you know to get trained . . . so they just said, 'you must have known you were pregnant' and I said, 'well I didn't' and they said, 'well we're terminating your contract'.
>
> (Female, 58, carer of family and home, not actively seeking work)

Others gave examples of negative gendered stereotypes that they had experienced during their working lives. One woman told how sexist 'jibes' and 'jokes' had become a part of her everyday existence. 'I was whistled at I think every day I came to work and not just by the students, there was a lot of sexist banter and comments, nothing specifically insulting, but just low-level boring crap ... and you can't be bothered to respond to it on a daily basis, so it just becomes part of your daily existence' (female, 50, paid staff, voluntary sector).

There were also examples of women in the sample who, in the 1970s, had taken advantage of the new legislation. They were the first to 'break though' and establish themselves in formerly male-dominated jobs, yet found themselves facing a new set of hurdles along the way. One woman recalled the trouble she had in being accepted in her post in a public institution which has had a long history of male domination.

> When I went into [x], it was 1976 so it was just after the Equal Opportunities, but you know some people had claimed ... for discrimination ... I mean if I'd claimed for some of the things that were said to me when I went [there], and the way we were treated, because we were women, not by all of them, some of them were brilliant. But some of the things that were said, you could have taken them to a tribunal. But at the time you didn't realise, you're only young and you felt that if you stepped out of line – that would be it – because they could do that at any time ... just say that you're not suitable, and they didn't have to give you an explanation.
>
> (Female, 50, job seeker)

The impact of work detachment

Time taken out of the labour market to have and raise children had a profound impact on the availability of opportunity and choice once women returned to work. Although many could return to their previous employer, they had fewer years of service (compared to men and to single women) in which to progress and move up the career ladder. For those women who entered the job market at that time, it was not only their gender and family status that conspired to discriminate but also their age preventing them from applying for a post.

> I was 36 years old and believe it or not, seventeen years ago they used to put on the notice board in the job centre [pause] they used to type it out [job advertisement] on a little postcard, so they would put something like, '18–30' and they would actually put that on ... (pauses) ... the numbers of jobs, jobs I could have done quite easily ... receptionist jobs,

answering the telephone . . . that would have got me back into the workplace and I could have coped with that.

(Female 55, working full-time)

Having the confidence to embark upon training after periods out of the
workforce created tensions and comparisons between themselves and
those who were more conversant with new technology.

> I've been on a computer course, but it's only the Learn Direct one, so I feel
> that the barriers are obviously my skills aren't up to date . . . a lack of
> confidence as well, because you realise that everybody else is up to speed on
> computers and things, and when you've been out of the full-time workforce
> for any length of time, you do lose your confidence and, you know, it's hard.
>
> (Female 50, job seeker/volunteer)

Part-time work: choice or necessity?

The demand for part-time employment may increase progressively with
age, and thus some people can choose to combine elements of work and
retirement. On the other hand, some are forced into part-time work
because of ill health or disability, redundancy, early retirement or the
unavailability of full-time work. Hence the growth in demand for part-
time work may include elements of both choice and necessity. However,
there was a clear demand for more flexible forms of working.

> I've been working since I was 15 and that's coming on thirty-five years,
> that's a lot of work, that's a long working life and now I'd rather do less
> work perhaps 3 or 4 days a week.
>
> (Female, 50–54, student)

> I mind my grandson a couple of afternoons a week and I've also got
> another granddaughter . . . I'm going to be here whenever I'm needed,
> because I enjoy doing that really as well. I would need to work . . . but to
> work twenty-five hours gives me the best of both worlds really.
>
> (Female, 50–54, working part-time)

An increasing number of middle-aged and older women had specific
care responsibilities for older family members (parents, spouse or partner) as well as younger (children, grandchildren). The Fawcett Society
ones found that over a third of grandparents help out with the care of
their grandchildren, either regularly or occasionally.

This interviewee enjoyed taking care of her grandchildren – it was a
role that she felt was deeply enriching.

A lot of my generation are starting to do unpaid work looking after the grandchildren because you feel responsible, you have to give them [off-spring] a helping hand, rightly or wrongly, and some children expect their parents to reduce their hours perhaps, if they're working full-time to make sure that their child is looked after.

(Female, 55, working full-time)

Another felt a sense of exploitation. 'I think the government plays on us ... at the end of the day they're stopping us from working because they know it's costing too much to put their babies into nursery' (Female, 54, job seeker).

Another aspect to part-time working is the issue of promotion within employment. This interviewee could not view this as an option. The perception she had was that, in order to progress a, person has to work full-time. 'I prefer working part-time but the problem with part-time work is that it can be difficult to move up. Basically, if I wanted a promotion I'd have to go full-time, which is ... I think, one of the problems for older women, for women in general – because I think a lot of women try.' Here a balance was struck between home and work life, and for that to succeed the compromises made were to accept the limited scope work could offer in terms of promotion. 'Even though my kids are older now, I mean my youngest is 14, I still want to be there sometimes when she gets home from school. I still want to be there if she wanted help with her homework. I still want to be there if she wants a shoulder to cry on' (Female, 50–54, working full-time).

The comments above suggest that for many women detachment from the labour market could be a rational choice, that women were making decisions that still reflected caring responsibilities, even though the detail of that responsibility might have changed over the years. So in some ways the greater flexibility gained from part-time work was a consequence of, and a precursor to, care provision. Regardless, however, of the reason for the take-up of part-time employment, we found that right across our sample the respondents were more likely to be working part-time now than previously.

To old to study?

The women were generally less confident about studying than the over-sixties. Younger age groups also had greater concerns about the demands of study and, interestingly, were more likely to believe that they were too old to study and appeared to have less confidence in their ability to learn. This interviewee recalls how lack of achievement at school was, in a way, expected of her, limiting the choices that were open to her.

> I was in the C stream so my expectations or the school's expectations of me was not [good] ... I wouldn't be suitable for going onto further education or anything like that. My only choices were to work in a factory or shop work you know that kind of work.
>
> (Female, 55, early retired)

Another said:

> I always felt that I had failed really because when I took the 11 plus I had an interview to go to the grammar school and I didn't pass. You can imagine the first couple of years of my schooling, I probably felt quite a sort of failure really.
>
> (Female, 54, returned to work in her forties)

There was a clear perception that Higher Education was not for the likes of them, with some institutions thought of as being exclusively aimed at younger people and not valuing the life experience gained by prospective older students. Whilst this suggests institutional failings in widening participation amongst older learners, the barriers were sometimes much more blunt.

> Then a course came up in [another college] so I thought I'll try there so I rang up and by then I think I was 49 or 50 and he [tutor] said. 'How old ... can I ask you how old you are?' I said, 'I'm 50'. He said, 'Won't you feel stupid in a class of 16–19 year olds?
>
> (Female 50+, unemployed)

Policies enacted to emancipate older women also served to reduce the importance of their contribution through their experience of persistent and often covert discrimination. The layering of ageism and ageist perceptions created insurmountable challenges and perpetuated discrimination against older women during their collective routes into (and out of) work.

Very few of the women had taken up study to increase their employability and even these were beginning to question whether study after middle age was going to be as profitable as initially thought. Comments suggested that they expected to face age discrimination when looking for work. Negative cultural perceptions about age and learning were at the back of their minds or had impacted on their study in some respect. Reasons for trying to improve qualifications fell into three categories: to re-train after redundancy, for increasing social contact and for personal development.

> I was the oldest person doing my final . . . this diploma . . . my tutor said to me 'why are you doing it?', because I was already qualified, but I just wanted to get in there, renew it all and find out what else is going on. She used to say to me 'you are so brave', and I used to think, 'is it because I am older', you know, what the bloody hell is she doing *this* for?
>
> (Female, 57, volunteer)

Conclusions

Intermittent work patterns in the past served to reduce the opportunities for women once they re-entered the workforce. Experiences of discrimination because of gender, race or disability were not unusual. Indeed the period was characterised by the sex-stereotyping of jobs, whereby the majority of women were channelled into female-dominated occupations like teaching and shop work. As one woman put it:

> There was a lower expectation of women actually progressing up the ladder. Women generally had to work twice as hard as men to achieve, particularly the higher positions within the system, and there was a cultural expectation that really it was the man who worked and provided and really women would work for a number of years until they got married and settled down.
>
> (Female, 50–54, working full-time)

Some women had to fight to enter jobs that were previously closed to them. One such woman applied for a job in her chosen career, only to be rejected and told that it was a 'male-only' position.

> To do the actual job I do now, I had to wait for the Equal Opportunities Bill and then re-apply, because they [employer] didn't take notice of me the first time. I applied for my first [x], and I was told that it was a male-only job, and then I applied again and they said 'no' they only employed men. I'm going back a long time ago – anyway they only employed men and then I reapplied when the Equal Opportunities Bill came in which must have been in the [pause] 70s. I wrote out a written application and attached a copy of the Bill.
>
> (Female, 50–54, working full-time)

It was enlightening to find how one interviewee had made a decision to try and gain promotion when she was 50. Supporting the evidence that some women are moving into managerial positions in the middle years, this interviewee explains how she decided to make the move.

> I just decided to change direction a year ago because I'd been with [x] for 18 years ... I saw this job advertised and I just read it, and I thought I could do that. It was just a spur of the moment thing, seeing that advert. I had thought about moving on – well I can't at my age ... When I say that, I thought, it's worth a try and I did ... I wouldn't say I'm ambitious ... I just got to the stage in [x] where you could do the job with your eyes closed. You go on automatic pilot. The chief executive said 'I thought you'd be here till you retired' and so did I, 'but if I don't do it now maybe it won't wait till I'm over 60, its going to be even harder' ... he was very pleased for me and very supportive. (Female, 58, change of career at age 50)

The women in this study provided evidence of disadvantage spanning thirty to forty years, and they confirm that discrimination is still functioning in the workplace and in the wider society in which it operates. Women's progression in the workforce has been slow to filter through, with many still encountering gendered assumptions, some breaking through the glass ceiling and many older employees now facing the silver ceiling of ageism. However, many older women have now dropped out of the competition for a full-time job, some preferring to undertake part-time or voluntary work, or combining this with caring for family members. Some failed to re-engage owing in part to internalised barriers, relating back to their lack of self-belief or confidence in their own efficacy, or because of previous rejection by employers. Thus, the overwhelming evidence of this study points to a legacy of negativity based on the dubiety of legislation, past personal experiences and current perceptions. Women believed that, whilst some progress had been made, it was too slow, too little and too late for them. There was a feeling of uncertainty or questionability regarding whether legislation could tackle ageism, or had the power of enforcement to make real changes in the attitudes required from society. Lack of rigorous action now, to reduce ageist perceptions, will in the future deny many older women the opportunity to show what they can really do. Without concerted efforts on the part of government, employers, the legal profession and society in general, we risk failing those very women who took up the challenge to confront inequality and provide a more equal society for the younger generation of today.

Bibliography

Arthur, S. 2003. *Money, Choice and Control: The Financial Circumstances of Early Retirement*. Bristol: The Polity Press/JRF

Banks, J. and Tetlow, G. 2008. 'Extending working lives', in J., Banks E., Breeze C. Lessof and J. Naztoo (eds.), *Living in the 21st century: Older People in England*. London: Institute for Fiscal Studies, 19–56.

Bardasi, E. and Jenkins, S. P. 2002. *Income in Later Life: Work History Matters*. York: JRF

Berger, E. D. 2006. 'Aging identities: degradation and negotiation in the search for employment', *Journal of Aging Studies* 20(4): 303–16

Berthoud, R. and Blekesaune, M. 2007. *Persistent Employment Disadvantage*. Research Report 416. Leeds: Department of Work and Pensions

Bytheway, B. 1995. *Ageism*. Buckingham: Open University Press

Bytheway, B. and Johnson, J. 1990. 'On defining ageism', *Critical Social Policy* 10 (29): 27–39

Clarke, L. H. and Griffin. M. 2008. 'Visible and invisible ageing: beauty work as a response to ageism', *Ageing and Society* 28: 653–74

DfEE 1999. *Labour Government's Code of Practice for Age Diversity in Employment*.

Duncan, C. and Loretto, W. 2004. 'Never the right age? Gender and age based discrimination in employment', *Gender, Work & Organisation* 11(1): 95–115

Ginn, J. and Arber, S. 1996. 'Gender, age and attitudes to retirement in mid-life', *Ageing and Society* 16: 27–55

Granleese, J. and Sayer, G. 2006. 'Gendered ageism and "lookism": a triple jeopardy for female academics', *Women in Management Review* 21(6): 500–17

Grant, D., Walker, H., Butler, N., Meadows, M., Hogan, M. and Li, D. 2006. *Gender Discrimination and Ageist Perceptions*: ESF Objective 3 Research report. Liverpool John Moores University

Green, A. 2003. 'Labour market trends, skill needs and the ageing of the workforce: a challenge for employability', *Local Economy* 18(4): 67–76

Groves, D. 1993. 'Work, poverty and older women', in M. Bernard and K. Meade (eds.), *Women Come of Age*. London: Edward Arnold, 43–63

Harkness, S., Machin, S. and Waldfogel, J. 1997. 'Evaluating the pin money hypothesis: the relationship between women's labour market activity, family income and poverty in Britain 1997', *Journal of Population Economics* 10(2): 137–58

Itzin, C. and Phillipson, C. 1993. *Age Barriers at Work: Maximising the Potential of Mature and Older Workers*. Solihull: Metropolitan Authorities Recruitment Agency

Lissenburgh, S. and Smeaton, D. 2003. *The Role of Flexible Employment in Maintaining Labour Market Participation and Promoting Job Quality.* York: JRF.

MacNicol, J. 2006. *Age Discrimination: An Historical Contemporary Analysis.* Cambridge University Press

Maguire, M. 1995. 'Women, age, and education in the United Kingdom', *Women's Studies International Forum* 18(5–6): 559–71

Metcalf, H. and Thompson, M. 1990. *Older Workers: Employers' Attitudes and Practices*, Brighton: Institute of Manpower Services

Mooney, A. and Statham, J. 2002. *The Pivot Generation: Informal Care and Work after Fifty.* Bristol: The Policy Press

Platman, K. and Tinker, A. 1998. 'Getting on in the BBC: a case study of older workers', *Ageing and Society* 18(5), 513–35

Rosenthal, E. R. 1990. *Women, Aging and Ageism.* London: Routledge

Saucier, M. G. 2004. 'Midlife and beyond: issues for aging women', *Journal of Counselling and Development* 82, 420–5.

Sargeant, M. and Lewis, D. 2008. *Employment Law*, 4th edn. Pearson Education

Sontag, S. 1972. 'The double standard of aging', *Saturday Review of Society* 23(1), 29–38

Summerfield, P. 1994. 'Women in Britain in 1945: companionate marriage and the double burden', in J. Obelkevich and P. Catterall (eds.), *Understanding Post War Britain*. London: Routledge, 58–72

TUC 2009 Women and the Recession, online www.tuc.org.uk/extras/womenandrecession.pdf

4

Still disadvantaged? Women in modern pension systems

ATHINA VLACHANTONI

Introduction

Ageism or age discrimination has gained greater policy significance since the 1980s, as a result of changing regulations in the area of work, retirement and pension entitlement, but also as a result of changing expectations of the structure of the life course and old age in particular. Such changes have, in turn, come about largely owing to demographic changes at the individual level, such as the steady increase in life expectancy for both men and women, and at the population level, such as the steady increase in the proportion of the population aged 65 and over. For example, between 1984 and 2009, the proportion of the British population aged 65 and over increased from 15 to 16%, an increase which was equivalent to 1.7 million more people. By 2034, the Office for National Statistics has projected that 23% of the population will be aged 65 and over (Office for National Statistics Online 2010).

Pension systems around the world have tried to address these challenges and their financial implications through a variety of measures and changes considered more or less radical, depending on the country context. For example, Holzmann *et al.* have distinguished between parametric and paradigmatic styles of pension reform, which change certain parameters or the overall set of financing principles in a pension system respectively (Holzmann, Mackellar and Rutkowski 2003). One of the key questions permeating pension reforms around the world is the extent to which they have taken differences in men's and women's life courses into account. Women's life courses have always been more diverse than those of men, particularly in relation to patterns of paid work and the provision of care within and outside the household. The implications for gender differences in pension accumulation over the life course and pension adequacy in later life are significant, particularly where pension reforms have not accommodated adequate diversity in the pathways towards pension entitlement.

This chapter explores key issues relating to women's position in modern pension systems, and the extent to which these systems have tried to accommodate for diversity in women's employment patterns and life courses. The rest of this chapter engages with these debates in the following steps. The next section explores the extent and nature of women's disadvantage in modern pension systems, drawing on examples from the European Union. The section after that discusses pension reforms which have taken place in Europe over the last thirty years or so, in response to demographic change and its financial implications, and the extent to which they have addressed diversity in terms of employment and caring experiences. The fourth section of the chapter discusses the most recent pension reforms in the British pension system from a gender perspective, illustrating policy changes which have aimed at pension adequacy for more women. Finally, the conclusion draws the main implications of this chapter for the future organisation of pension protection in modern welfare states, particularly for women.

The extent and nature of women's disadvantage in modern pension systems

Modern pension systems are faced with the triple challenge of population ageing, the resulting rise in expenditure on old age pensions and changes in the structure of their labour markets. These challenges have profound implications for women in particular, which are not immediately evident in the mainstream literature on pension reform in developed countries. For instance, population ageing affects women disproportionately because women tend to live longer than men on average. In addition, women constitute the majority of older people living in poverty, as a result of the way pension systems interact with women's typical employment patterns (European Commission 2006). Figure 4.1 shows that in all the selected countries in this figure, the proportion of women aged 65 and over facing a poverty risk was higher than the proportion of older men, and in countries like Bulgaria, Portugal, Finland and the UK, the gender gap was very significant. Cost-reducing policies which target rising pension expenditures are also more likely to disadvantage women than men, because women are more likely to have irregular ties with the labour market and therefore to

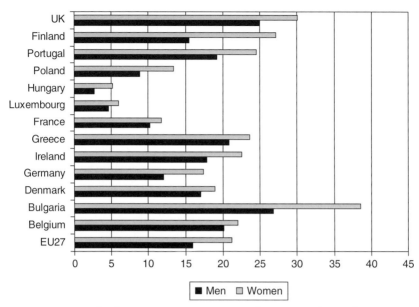

Figure 4.1   At-risk-of-poverty rate among men and women aged 65 and over, in selected EU countries, 2008. Source: Eurostat Online 2010a.

be more reliant on statutory pension provision (Luckhaus 1997; Rake 1999). Finally, the massive entry of women into the labour market has not always benefited women in terms of greater pension security, because women tend to constitute the majority of workers in part-time and less well-paid positions, where pension contributions may be irregular, interrupted or inadequate (Ginn and Arber 1998).

However, from a gender perspective, pension provision for women has always been a policy challenge, because systems of pension protection were not initially designed for women directly (Myles 1984). Rather, women were intended to be *indirect* beneficiaries of the pension system through the marital bond to their husbands, who, as full-time workers, were direct beneficiaries. This arrangement, although effectively contributing to the protection of women from the risk of poverty in old age, prevented women from accumulating individual pension savings and ultimately hindered their prospects for financial independence throughout their working life and especially in old age (Thane 1987). In welfare states with embedded patriarchal traditions, such as those found in southern Europe, women were still dependent on other male members of the family, such as their father or their brother, when the marital bond was absent. Undoubtedly, women's increasing ability to accumulate their own pension rights through employment has reduced their financial dependence on their spouse in old age, although their dependence on the state may still be the case if their pension income is relatively low. In spite of women's greater labour market participation, the design of pension systems has continued to be problematic because typical male working patterns are often the frame of reference for calculating pension entitlements. This practice has overlooked the gender differences in employment patterns and underestimated, or sometimes not valued at all, care provision within or outside the family (Jenson and Sineau 2001). As a result, typical male working patterns have tended to produce better pension outcomes than more diverse female working patterns in modern pension systems (see Sefton, Evandrou and Falkingham 2010). It is this continuous 'mirroring' of, and failure to address, the differences and inequalities in the division of paid/unpaid labour that creates an 'accumulated disadvantage' for women in terms of pension protection and can lead to women facing a greater poverty risk in old age than men (Rake 1999, Zaidi, Grech and Fuchs 2006).

Until the 1950s, when women's massive accession to the labour market began, first in the Nordic countries and followed by continental Europe, the assumptions of the 'male breadwinner model' were dominant. Within a marriage and a household, the man was the primary breadwinner and the woman was the primary care giver. According to this paradigm, a pension was provided directly to the man and this pension was sufficient to cater for the man's dependants. A woman's marital bond to a man entitled her to financial security during her life and during old age, even in the case of her husband's death. The policy assumptions in this arrangement about men and women, more implicit then than now, not only were prevalent in the field of pension provision, but rather permeated welfare provision in continental Europe more broadly (see for example Lewis 1992; Sainsbury 1999). By the mid-twentieth century, when more women began to receive a pension in their own right, as a result of increasing labour market participation, the pension problem for women had already begun to surface. Traditionally designed pension systems around Europe have since reflected the gender differences in employment patterns and in wages, in addition to the unequal division of unpaid and care labour in the private sphere. The degree to which a pension system reflects such gender inequalities is evident in the way it combines redistributive and non-redistributive elements in its pension entitlement structure (Leitner 2001). For example, the closer the link between earnings and the pension income, the more are women disadvantaged, because female employment records tend to be shorter, interrupted and in lower-paid jobs. Women are also more likely to be disadvantaged when occupational pension schemes place high thresholds of eligibility in terms of years of service, earnings or the level of contributions (Ginn, Daly and Street 2001). Pension systems can do a lot to compensate women for such inequalities, for example by providing flat-rate benefits and by calculating the pension income according to the 'best' income years of employment, rather than the last (Rake 1999).

The literature on women and pensions has outlined the challenge of pension protection for women, through both country-specific and comparative studies of pension systems. For example, one part of the literature discusses gender differences in terms of the pension incomes as a result of an unequal division of paid and unpaid labour (Rake 1999; Ginn, Street and Arber 2001; Ginn 2003). Another strand of research has focused on elements of pension systems which particularly affect the female population, such as the rules for pension sharing after a divorce (Price 2003), differences in the ages of retirement (Ginn and Arber 1995), the number of years over which pension contributions can be made (Leitner 2001) and the provision or not of care credits for the purpose of pension accumulation (Vlachantoni forthcoming). The literature on women and pension provision/reform rightly refrains from assuming homogeneity for the female population, as pension entitlement is different for women who work, are married and/or have children, or not. Finally, much of the literature on women and pension provision has developed in parallel with the debate on pension reform, trying to map the impact of broader trends of reform on women in particular. Such research has warned of the danger for women specifically of the general trend towards greater privatisation of pension provision (Luckhaus 1997; Ginn 2001; 2002; Street and Ginn 2001; Bardasi and Jenkins 2004).

A large part of the explanation for gender differences in pension entitlement lies with gender differentials in employment records, particularly during a time of change within European labour markets. The typical working patterns of men and women have always differed, even before the changes in the configuration of European labour markets from the late 1970s onwards (Kohli and Novak 2001; Orloff 2002). The demand for labour gradually shifted away from the manufacturing and

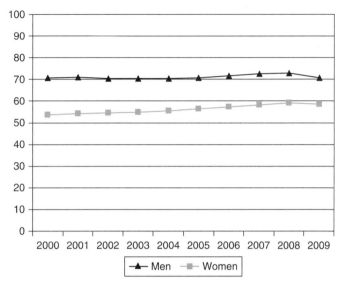

Figure 4.2 Men's and women's employment rates in the EU-27, 2000–8. Source: Eurostat Online 2010b.

agricultural sectors towards the service sector, and it was women who mostly filled this gap in the labour force, especially in the early part of the 1980s (OECD 2002). These trends certainly narrowed the gender gap in terms of labour market participation (see Figure 4.2), yet the gender differences in the type of employment, which also affect pension accumulation, have not been altered. Men tend to have continuous working records until retirement, while women tend to interrupt their working lives in order to care (Ginn, Street and Arber 2001). Indeed, because women have always tended to do more caring than men, the increase in female labour force participation rates during the last two decades or so largely reflects women *combining* paid work, usually part-time, with caring obligations (Davis 1998).

The over-representation of women among part-time workers in Europe, but also the particular characteristics of part-time work, directly affect women's accumulation of pension contributions. For a start, part-time work tends to be concentrated in comparatively low-paid occupational sectors, such as the health, education and service sectors. In addition, the minority of male part-time workers tend to work at the very beginning and/or at the very end of their working life, while their female counterparts may spend their whole life in part-time employment, impacting differently on their lifetime and retirement incomes (Laczko and Phillipson 1991; Ginn and Arber 1998). Large variations are also found in the *length* of part-time employment, which, depending on the country's pension legislation, will affect the amount of the accumulated pension differently. For example, in Sweden and Denmark, the majority of female part-time workers are in 'substantial' part-time jobs (between 20 and 34 hours per week), often approaching the full-time norm of working hours in other parts of Europe, whereas in Germany, 'marginal' part-time work (up to 19 hours per week) is more widespread. Part-time work may therefore reduce individual earnings on which the calculation of a basic pension is based, it may result in a reduced access to occupational pension schemes depending on a country's pension regulations, and, finally, it may prohibit an individual from contributing to a private pension scheme (Luckhaus 1997; Ginn and Arber 1998). The adverse effects of part-time employment on pension acquisition can be mitigated in several ways, such as allowing workers with atypical employment records to 'buy' pension contributions (France and Germany), or not penalising workers for transferring their pension rights from one sector to another (Germany and Denmark), as is common in this mode of employment.

Part-time work and a lower participation in the labour market altogether are not the only reasons why women are more likely than men to end up with an inadequate pension income in old age. When women do work, they also tend to be paid less, creating a gendered pay gap which has persisted despite efforts at the European level to abolish all kinds of gender discrimination in the employment sphere (Orloff 2002). The measurement of the pay gap will depend on such factors as the occupational sectors compared, the level of education and the length of work experience, as well as the particular type of wages compared (hourly, monthly, annual), yet such factors affect the *extent* of the pay gap rather than whether is exists or not. For instance, women's gross hourly earnings in 2007 were on average 17.6% less than those of men across the twenty-seven European countries (Eurostat Online 2010c), reflecting structural inequalities, such as the over-representation of women in poorly paid occupations, but also career breaks in order to care for dependants (Orloff 2002).

Gender has always been central to the organisation of labour markets, and governmental intervention, through the combination of family and employment policies, can influence individual behaviour in these spheres immensely. In the context of pension provision this is important, as it determines who will provide care within the family and, more importantly, whether a woman will be able to accumulate a pension income in her own right through employment, or whether she will rely on an entitlement derived from her marriage (Ginn and Arber 1996). Historically, most of the care has been provided by female family members, and this has not changed even as more women have entered the labour market (Bubeck 1995; Jenson 1997). On the contrary, there is evidence that labour market changes have led to a 'modernisation' of the division of paid and unpaid labour (Orloff 2002), whereby women still do the bulk of unpaid work, but also work in the labour market (Gershuny, Godwin and Jones 1994; OECD 2002), while men's work and care patterns have largely remained the same. However, the relationship between childbearing and childcare and labour force participation rates is particularly complex.

One particular element of European pension systems which has featured in policy debates is the difference between men and women in terms of the retirement age (European Commission 2006). The establishment of different retirement ages has historically reflected the state's assumptions about men and women. In theory, earlier retirement was granted to women so that, first, the couple would enjoy their retirement simultaneously because women were usually younger than their husbands, and second, widows would receive social protection earlier (Fredman 1996). At the same time, the state could claim to recognise women's contribution to the household as well as to the labour market. In reality, the policy intention behind this arrangement was not entirely benign, as the difference in retirement ages also compensated for women's relatively low wages in the labour market *in addition* to their unpaid labour in the household (Arber and Ginn 1995). The age of retirement is an area where equal treatment is not immediately applicable under Community Law; rather Member States are obliged to examine their legislation periodically and establish whether the derogation from the European Directive 79/7/EEC on the equality principle is still justified in each case. Pension legislation in Europe relating to survivor benefits and childcare credits increasingly uses gender-neutral language. However, several Member States still have different retirement ages for men and women (Poland, Italy, Slovenia, Austria until 2024), but are in the process of gradually abolishing them (Steinhilber 2005; European Commission 2006). Current differences between men's and women's official and effective (actual) retirement age are shown for a selection of European countries in Figures 4.3a and 4.3b. The figures

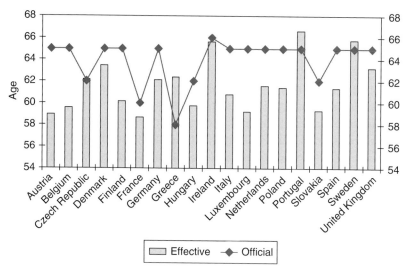

Figure 4.3a   Men's official and effective retirement age in selected EU countries, 2002–7. Source: OECD, Society at a Glance 2009.

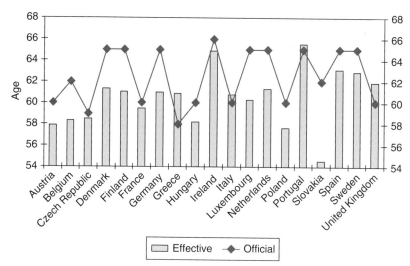

Figure 4.3b   Women's official and effective retirement ages in selected EU countries, 2002–7. Source: OECD, Society at a Glance 2009.

show that in most countries the official retirement age for men for the period 2002–7 was 65, whereas for women it was between 58 and 64. It is the gap between the official and the effective retirement age which constitutes the greatest challenge for European Member States in this area.

Unless labour markets are able to cater for care providers, and pension systems to compensate them with additional ways of building up pension entitlements, caring for children, or for elderly or long-term sick/disabled persons, indirectly contributes to gender inequalities in the accumulation of lifetime and retirement income (Luckhaus and Ward 1997; Ginn 2002). There are greater boundaries to pension policy in this respect than employment policy, partly because pension policy can only compensate for gender inequalities which first originate in the labour market. The principal compensatory measure in pension policy is the provision of care credits towards pension contributions for childcare that varies considerably between countries, while the provision of such credits for elder care is becoming increasingly important as the share of the elderly population rises (Vlachantoni forthcoming). The following section explores the ways in which modern pension systems have tried to address the combined challenges of population ageing, rising pension expenditures and changing labour markets, and the implications of such responses for women in particular.

Pension reforms and their gender implications

Although all pension systems have been under pressure to reform, the nature of the pressure, and by consequence the urgency for pension reform, is largely determined by the particular structure or 'model' of pension provision (Palme 1990). The tasks of preventing poverty in old age and replacing a worker's income following retirement have become more difficult for all pension systems, but within different systems this holds truth for varying reasons and to varying degrees which are context- and system-specific (Bonoli 2003). Modern pension systems have been categorised on the basis of different elements of their structures and distributional effects (Schokkaert and Van Parijs 2003). Within the pension reform literature, many analyses focus on the way pension provision is financed through different pillars (flat-rate via general taxation, earnings-related or savings) to broadly distinguish between *insurance-based* and *multi-pillar* pension systems, often referred to as

'Bismarckian' and 'Beveridgean' respectively (see for example Myles and Quadagno 1997; Hinrichs 2001; Myles and Pierson 2001; Bonoli 2003). Although modern pension systems are increasingly hybrids, which are composed of elements from different types of systems, this categorisation exposes the basic strengths and weaknesses of pension systems, particularly with regard to women and pension provision. In insurance-based systems, or social insurance systems, pensions are financed through earnings-related taxation, and, more often than not, such systems operate on a Pay-As-You-Go (PAYG) basis, whereby the current generation of workers pays for the pensions of the current generation of pensioners. Insurance-based systems typically provide a means-tested minimum pension for those who reach the age of retirement but have inadequate contributions, while private pension provision is typically under-developed in such systems. Multi-pillar pension systems, on the other hand, typically prioritise poverty prevention over income replacement in retirement by combining a flat-rate, basic pension with more developed pillars of occupational and private pension provision. Thus, the bulk of pension incomes in such systems is financed through individual contributions to pension funds, which may be state- or privately managed (Bonoli and Shinkawa 2005).

The structure of pension provision can also point to a number of inequalities from a gender perspective in terms of pension entitlement (Leitner 2001). Insurance-based systems may typically provide pension protection to more women through their working husbands (derived pension rights), compared with multi-pillar systems where the process of pension accumulation may be more individualised. Both types of systems, however, may hinder women's pension accumulation prospects by establishing minimum qualifying conditions (for example fifteen years of contributions at least), or by establishing formulae to calculate the pension income based on long periods of employment (for example the last or best ten years of employment). Women's employment records, whether short or interrupted, may deny them access to certain occupational schemes in multi-pillar pension systems, while in insurance-based systems such records may threaten women's qualifying conditions for the basic pension. Finally, the provision of additional credits which recognise care work within the family sphere are increasingly becoming important components of the structure of multi-pillar and insurance-based pension systems alike (see Vlachantoni forthcoming).

Beyond the impact of a system's structure on women's pension entitlements, the way pension provision is organised is one of the most important determinants of the nature of the pension reform (Disney and Johnson 2001). Population ageing, the resultant rise in pension expenditure and changes in the configuration of the labour force typically affect insurance-based and multi-pillar systems in different ways. In insurance-based systems, which are fundamentally based on earnings-related taxation, population ageing can combine with early retirement to shrink the contributory base which supports a continuously increasing number of claimants, thereby disturbing the contract between consecutive generations of workers. In political terms, the PAYG character which insurance-based systems usually have presents a further challenge for policy-makers. A switch to a multi-pillar system incurs the 'double payment problem', whereby younger workers are obliged to finance the pensions of current pensioners *as well as* their own pensions (Pierson 1997). In addition, older workers nearing retirement are likely to resist a reform which 'breaks' their contract with the state and forces them to contribute to private pensions towards the end of their working life. Consequently, pension reform in countries with insurance-based pension systems requires decision-making of both a financial and a political nature (Pierson and Weaver 1993; Pierson 1994).

The pension problem assumes a rather different form in multi-pillar pension systems, where the potential risk resulting from population ageing is largely born by employees and, to a lesser extent, their employers. The rise in the cost of the basic (flat-rate) pillar may be smaller owing to the typically smaller size of this pillar in such systems. However, population ageing can raise the cost of annuities purchased by individuals as the average life expectancy rises (Barr 2002). Since occupational pension provision is more developed in multi-pillar systems, the restructuring of the labour market is important in such systems. Ensuring the long-term sustainability of the pension system as a whole may therefore include a shift from typically more expensive, defined-benefit schemes (DB), where pensions are determined by the employee's salary and the years of work, to defined-contribution schemes (DC), where pensions are determined by contributions to individual employee accounts which potentially carry a higher risk and a lower return guarantee. Finally, the pension problem within multi-pillar systems may also relate to the lack of guarantees which generally characterises investment decision-making (Bonoli and Shinkawa 2005).

In trying to address diversity and gender inequalities, European pension systems have been guided by a broader pension policy agenda which developed rapidly after 2001 (SPC 2000; EPC 2001; CEU 2003). This agenda, focusing as much on the harmonisation of occupational pension provision in the light of increasing labour mobility as on the incorporation of gender equality in different aspects of European pension systems, has been promoted using the Open Method of Coordination (OMC) for Pensions as a tool (see European Commission 2001; Moerth 2004; Zeitlin 2005). Notwithstanding such coordination attempts, European Member States have approached the pension reform challenge in a variety of ways which reflect their pension systems, diverse social needs, fiscal resources and institutional capacities (Holzmann *et al.* 2003; OECD 2004; Whiteford 2004). Within this vast diversity, the literature has identified a broad tendency towards reducing the state's commitment to pension provision and shifting that responsibility to the individual and his or her employer (Bonoli and Shinkawa 2005). The gender implications of this shift are immense, since women tend to rely on statutory pension provision to a larger extent than men.

Pension reforms remain very context-specific, but it is possible to observe a broad trend which 'tightens' eligibility criteria for pension provision across the European Union and reduces the generosity of modern welfare states (Nye 2003). And although it may be difficult to ascertain clear shifts from one type of pension provision to another, the approaches to pension reform within Europe show at least some convergence. In the light of deteriorating dependency ratios, for instance, many welfare states have combined pension with employment policies to provide incentives for current workers to stay in the labour market at least until the retirement age, or longer. Such measures include the abolition of incentives for early retirement, the increase of the retirement age, the introduction of anti-ageing discrimination and the provision of continuous training for older workers. Again, within the realms of the labour market, several countries have devised incentives to push or pull people of working age into the labour market through the creation of new jobs and/or the creation of links between benefit receipt and paid employment. The establishment of incentives and a care infrastructure to allow more women to combine paid work with care is part of such policies, as are efforts to 'loosen' immigration regulations which can attract more economic migrants.

The magnitude of pension reform becomes more lucid in efforts within European systems to change the balance between the basic, occupational and private pillars of pension provision (Bonoli and Shinkawa 2005). Insurance-based systems have aimed to reduce the generosity of the basic pillar, and to introduce tax or other incentives in order to encourage greater participation in occupational and, to a lesser extent, private pension schemes (Davis 1998). Multi-pillar systems, on the other hand, have aimed to strengthen their occupational pension pillar, while maintaining a restricted basic pillar aimed at poverty alleviation. This can be observed through the shift from defined-benefit (DB) to defined-contribution (DC) schemes (Johnson, Conrad and Thompson 1989; Disney 1998) and the creation of opportunities to contribute to private funds, even in occupations which produce relatively low earnings (Bonoli 2003). Despite the differences in policy responses, the direction of pension reforms appears to point to a shift of the responsibility for pension provision away from the state, especially in insurance-based systems, towards the (employed) individual. The implications of this direction for women cannot be underestimated, both for women's position in the labour market and entitlements within the pension system, but also for women's undertaking of caring within the family sphere and the way they are viewed within modern welfare states more broadly (Ginn 2002).

The European Commission notes that 'pension systems may not be the appropriate place to compensate for the gender differences in earnings and career patterns, rather pension systems tend to mirror social circumstances, which highlights the importance of efforts to reduce gender gaps in employment, earnings and career patterns' (European Commission 2006: 90). Indeed, the ways and extent to which European pension systems have addressed the gender dimensions of the pension problem in their policy responses vary considerably. Some insurance-based systems, such as those in Belgium and Luxembourg, which have adhered to the principles of the male breadwinner model to a greater extent than multi-pillar models, have aimed to strengthen survivors' benefits, also in view of women's higher life expectancy on average (Leitner 2001). Other insurance-based systems, such as those in Austria and Germany, have reduced the value of survivors' pensions, but have instead tried to increase female employment rates and have provided better care credits (European Commission 2006). Pension sharing in the case of divorce was first pioneered in the German pension system and has been instrumental in keeping women out of poverty in old age, especially in insurance-based schemes where they are often assumed not to be in paid work. Within such systems, however, the principal way of recognising gender differences in working patterns remains the compensatory measure of recognising periods of care for dependants (Luckhaus and Ward 1997). Although such credits are only a partial compensation of time spent caring (Rake 1999), they are increasingly becoming a central part of pension policy towards women in both insurance-based (Germany, Greece) and multi-pillar (United Kingdom) pension systems. Still, fewer than half of all European countries, including Germany, the UK and Ireland, offer such credits for care *other* than childcare, at a time when elder care is rapidly assuming policy importance owing to population ageing (Vlachantoni forthcoming).

Multi-pillar pension schemes, which place greater emphasis on supplementary (occupational) and private pensions, tend to have fewer 'solidarity features' aimed both at restoring gender equality within pension provision and at securing an adequate income for women in old age (European Commission 2006). Under the assumption that the individual will be able to top up his/her pension income through other pillars of pension provision, women's prospects of pension accumulation in such systems are dire unless they can balance work and care. Some European countries with multi-pillar pension systems, like Poland, Sweden, Austria and Denmark, provide state- or employer-financed contributions into occupational schemes for periods of maternity or parental leave. Other countries, such as Ireland and the United Kingdom, have measures in place to encourage parents to contribute to supplementary pension schemes, whether they are employed at the time or not. Most of the European countries have also made it illegal for pension companies to use gendered life-tables in the calculation of pension entitlements, because it disadvantages women as they tend to live longer. Indeed, unisex tariffs in second- and third-pillar schemes are an important step towards greater equality, especially because women are generally less able to afford contributing to such schemes in the first place (Luckhaus and Ward 1997; Leitner 2001).

Women in the British pension system

This section explores some of the key issues relating to women in modern pension systems by focusing on a particular case study, that of the United Kingdom (UK). It discusses reforms to the British pension system introduced by the New Labour government over the last decade or so, and draws out the implications that these have for women in particular. The UK has a flat-rate pension scheme, which offers a basic pension based on a minimum contribution record, and additional private pension income depending on one's occupational and income status. After New Labour came into power in 1997, virtually all aspects of the British pension system underwent reform to a certain extent, with important implications for women's pension entitlement (see Falkingham, Evandrou and Vlachantoni 2010). This section summarises the most important reforms in the minimum safety net and the basic, earnings-related and private pension provision in the UK over the last decade or so. Until 1998, Income Support (IS) provided a minimum safety net for persons of all ages, who fell below a certain income threshold. In 1999 IS was replaced by the Minimum Income Guarantee (MIG), which targeted the poorest people aged 60 and over. Finally, in 2003, the MIG was replaced by the Pension Credit, which was composed of two elements. First, the Guarantee Credit, for those aged 60 in 2010, but gradually rising to 65 by 2020, and second, the Savings Credit, for those aged 65 and over who have made some provision towards their retirement income, for example in the form of savings. The combined weekly amount of the basic state pension and the Guarantee Credit in 2010 was £132.60 for a single person and £202.40 for a couple (Direct.Gov Online 2010). Although in theory the Pension Credit could potentially lift many pensioners out of poverty, its effectiveness is undermined by persistently low take-up rates. In 2008/9 it was estimated that between 27 and 38% of eligible pensioners did not claim the Pension Credit (DWP 2010a).

The reform of the Basic State Pension (BSP) was realised with the 2007 Pension Act. The Act promised to restore the link between the BSP and earnings, which had been broken in 1978, at some point between 2010 and 2015. The link between the BSP and prices during this period had meant that the value of the BSP had continuously dropped from 24% to approximately 16% of the national average earnings in 2008, according to the Pensions Policy Institute (PPI 2008). The 2007 Pension Act also changed pension entitlement rules for the BSP, which are expected to increase the proportion of women who can claim it. The minimum qualifying period for the BSP was thirty years for men and women, compared to thirty-nine years for women and forty-four years for men. Peter Hain, the Secretary of State for Work and Pensions in 2007, noted that, as a result of the Act, by 2010 around three-quarters of women retiring would be eligible for a full BSP, compared to only half of women if the reform had not been introduced. By 2025 the government estimated that more than 90% of women would be entitled to the full BSP (DWP 2007).

The 2007 Pensions Act also changed the eligibility criteria for the BSP for those providing care for at least twenty hours every week. Care credits were introduced in Britain in 1978 under the Home Responsibility

Protection (HRP) Act, which, rather than crediting carers' contributions, was designed to reduce the number of qualifying years for the entitlement to the BSP. Under this scheme, the number of qualifying years (thirty-nine for women, forty-four for men) for the BSP could be reduced. However, a carer still needed at least twenty years of National Insurance contributions in order to receive a full BSP. The HRP scheme had certain weaknesses which subsequent legislation sought to remedy. First, the reduction in the number of qualifying years was based on whole tax years (meaning that a carer needed to receive the Child Benefit or the Carer's Allowance for the whole tax year). Second, although HRP was available to carers of ill or severely disabled persons who received Income Support, the provision of care credits did not expand to cover care for elderly persons. Third, the HRP was initially designed to provide support to carers' entitlement to the BSP, thereby doing little to support or protect pension income from occupational and/or personal schemes. Since the early 2000s, some of these problems have been remedied through pension reform. For example, since April 2010, the HRP has been replaced by a system of weekly care credits available to those providing a minimum of twenty hours per week of care for children up to 12 years old or for severely disabled/ill persons. The 2007–8 pension reforms, coming into effect in 2010, aimed at 'providing an equality of opportunity to women and men to accumulate state pension entitlement in addition to pension entitlement to occupational and other private pension protection' (DWP 2006).

The earnings-related part of the British pension system has also undergone reform, with the State Earnings Related Pension Scheme (SERPS) being replaced with the State Second Pension (S2P) in 2002. The introduction of the S2P was partly aimed at supporting carers and those on low incomes in building pension entitlement beyond the basic state pension. In 2002, the HRP scheme was extended to support carers' entitlement to the S2P, which is planned to become flat-rate by around 2030. In contrast to the Pension Credit, which will soon be increasing in line with earnings, the flat-rate S2P is expected to increase in line with prices, thereby sustaining the risk of women with weak employment records facing poverty in old age. The enhancement of second-tier pensions, combined with the promised indexation of the BSP to earnings, addresses concerns raised by gendered analyses in the late 1990s (Falkingham and Rake 2001). According to the government's calculations, around 180,000 more people could gain entitlement to the S2P in 2010 through care credits, of whom 110,000 are women (DWP 2007).

Finally, reforms in occupational and other private pension provision is expected to benefit a smaller proportion of women compared to men, because fewer women contribute to private pension schemes, including occupational schemes (Falkingham *et al.* 2010). In 2001, the government introduced Stakeholder Pensions, aimed at boosting the income of middle-income earners as defined in 1998 (those earning between £9,000 and £18,500 per year). Subsequent research found that the introduction of Stakeholder Pensions had had no effect on overall pension coverage, and in fact coverage by any type of pension had decreased for the middle-income earners who had been the primary target of the measure (Disney, Emmerson and Wakefield 2010). By contrast, the introduction of Stakeholder Pensions appeared to have had a positive effect on pension coverage for women on low incomes, regardless of their marital status, who benefited from the increase in the joint contribution limits within households, also introduced by this reform (Disney *et al.* 2010). The 2007 Pensions Act also introduced Personal Accounts, which all employees aged 22 and over will be automatically enrolled on from 2012 onwards.

The change in government in 2010 has signalled the maintenance of the status quo in pension protection in the UK, and the restoration of the link between the BSP and earnings from April 2011 (DWP 2010b). At the same time, the debate on extending the retirement age for both men and women to 66 or beyond is also continuing. Considering that women tend to rely on state pension income to a greater extent than men, the commitment of the previous and current governments to raising the value of the BSP, in combination with the change in pension entitlement rules, will go a long way to ensuring an adequate income in later life for many more women. However, in terms of addressing the diversity which defines women's employment patterns, the most important element of the recent pension reforms in the UK is the introduction of weekly credits towards both the BSP and the S2P, which can further facilitate pension entitlement among carers.

Women in modern pension systems: evidence of change?

Modern pension systems are currently being tested in their ability to adjust to population ageing and its financial implications, but their ability to cater for women's diverse employment patterns has been a continuous challenge since their establishment. Traditional pension systems were designed to provide old age pensions to workers, and women's more common pathway to pension entitlement was through their marital bond to their (working) husband. However, with the massive entry of women in the labour market, policy-makers have gradually faced the challenge of bringing care into the debate on social security and pension protection more broadly. The extent to which pension systems can shift away from the traditional model of employment over the life course, which implies continuity, professional promotion and rising wages, is the measure by which pension systems are seen to recognise diversity in employment patterns. A major part of this endeavour remains the recognition of periods of care provision towards pension entitlement, even if this practice in most European Member States is currently limited to the provision of childcare.

There is evidence that European Member States have certainly *tried* to address population ageing, rising pension expenditures and changing labour markets in ways which do not disadvantage women as a result of their more diverse life courses and employment patterns. In this respect, the British case is a good example. The reform of the minimum safety net, the strengthening of the BSP, the reform of pension entitlement rules (particularly for carers) which cover both the basic and the supplementary tiers of statutory pension provision, all reflect a commitment to supporting more people and in more diverse circumstances in accumulating pension rights. The additional element of 'soft compulsion' in the automatic enrolment to Personal Accounts or an employer scheme can also help expand coverage among low- and middle-income earners in the UK, who found it difficult to benefit from existing occupational and other private pension schemes. As the recent pension reforms are rolled out, one of the key challenges for the government will be to monitor the value of the BSP so that women with weak employment records are not threatened with a reliance on means-testing or with poverty in the latter part of their life course.

Bibliography

Arber, S. and Ginn, J. 1995. 'Gender differences in the relationship between paid employment and informal care', *Work, Employment and Society* 9(3): 445–71

Bardasi, E. and Jenkins, S. P. 2004. *The Gender Gap in Private Pensions*. Institute for Social and Economic Research Working Paper 29. Chelmsford: University of Essex

Barr, N. A. 2002. 'Reforming pensions: myths, truths and policy choices', *International Social Security Review* 55(2): 3–36

Bonoli, G. 2003. 'Two worlds of pension reform in Western Europe', *Comparative Politics* 35(4): 399–416

Bonoli, G. and Shinkawa, T. 2005. 'Population ageing and the logics of pension reform in Western Europe, East Asia and North America', in Bonoli and Shinkawa (eds.), *Ageing and Pension Reform around the World*. Cheltenham: Edward Elgar, 1–23.

Bubeck, D. E. 1995. *Care, Gender and Justice*. Oxford: Clarendon Press

Council of the European Union 2003. *Joint Report by the Commission and the Council on Adequate and Sustainable Pensions (7165/03) March 2003*. Brussels: Council of the European Union

Davis, P. E. 1998. 'Population aging and retirement income provision in the European Union', in B. Bosworth and G. Burtless (eds.), *Aging Societies: The Global Dimension*. Washington, DC: The Brookings Institution, 33–110

Department for Work and Pensions 2006. *Security in Retirement: Towards a New Pension System*. London: Department for Work and Pensions

    2007. *The Gender Impact of Pension Reform*. London: Department for Work and Pensions

    2010a. *Income-related Benefits: Estimates of Take-ups in 2008–9*. London: Department for Work and Pensions

    2010b. *The Coalition: Our Programme for Government – Pensions and Older People*. London: Department for Work and Pensions

Direct.Gov Online 2010. direct.gov.uk (accessed August 2010)

Disney, R. 1998. *Crises in Public Pension Programmes in OECD: What Are the Reform Options?* Nottingham: Department of Economics, University of Nottingham

Disney, R., Emmerson, C. and Wakefield, M. 2010. 'Tax reform and retirement savings incentives: take-up of stakeholder pensions in the UK', *Economica* 77: 213–33

Disney, R. and Johnson, P. 2001. 'An overview', in R. Disney and P. Johnson (eds.), *Pension Systems and Retirement Incomes across OECD Countries*. Cheltenham: Edward Elgar, 1–47

Economic Policy Committee 2001. *Budgetary Challenges Posed by Ageing Populations: The Impact on Public Spending on Pensions, Health and Long-term Care for the Elderly and Possible Indicators of the Long-term Sustainability of Public Finances. ECFIN/655/01-EN final*. Brussels: European Union

European Commission 2001. *Commission Decision on the Setting-up of a Committee in the Area of Supplementary Pensions*. Brussels: European Union

    2005. *Working Together, Working Better: A New Framework for the Open Coordination of Social Protection and Inclusion Policies in the European Union COM (2005) 706 final*. Brussels: European Union

2006. *Joint Report on Social Protection and Social Inclusion 2006 – Synthesis Report on Adequate and Sustainable Pensions.* SEC 2006 (304), 27/2/2006. Brussels: European Union

Eurostat Online 2010a. 'At-risk-of-poverty rate among elderly people', europa.eu (accessed August 2010)

2010b. 'Employment rate by gender', europa.eu (accessed August 2010)

2010c. 'Gender pay gap in unadjusted form', europa.eu (accessed August 2010)

Falkingham, J., Evandrou, M. and Vlachantoni, A. 2010. 'Gender, poverty and pensions in the UK', in S. Chant (ed.), *International Handbook on Gender and Poverty.* Cheltenham: Edward Elgar, 232–7

Falkingham, J. and Rake, K. 2001. 'Modelling the gender impact of the British pension reforms', in J. Ginn, D. Street and S. Arber (eds.), *Women, Work and Pensions: International Issues and Prospects.* Buckingham: Open University Press, 67–85

Fredman, S. 1996. 'The poverty of equality: pensions and the ECJ', *Industrial Law Journal* 25(2): 91–109

Gershuny, J. I., Godwin, M. and Jones, S. 1994. 'The domestic labour revolution: a process of lagged adaptation?', in M. Anderson, F. Bechofer and J. Gershuny (eds.), *The Social and Political Economy of the Household.* Oxford: Oxford University Press, 151–97

Ginn, J. 2001. *From Security to Risk: Pension Privatisation and Gender Inequality.* London: Catalyst

2002. 'Gender and social protection reforms', in G. Bonoli and H. Sarfati (eds.), *Labour Market and Social Protection Reforms in International Perspective: Parallel or Converging Tracks?* Aldershot: Ashgate, 133–9

2003. *Gender, Pensions and the Lifecourse.* Bristol: The Policy Press

Ginn, J. and Arber, S. 1995. 'Moving the goalposts: the impact on British women of raising their state pension age to 65', *Social Policy Review* 7: 186–212

1996. 'Patterns of employment, pensions and gender: the effect of work history on older women's non-state pensions', *Work, Employment and Society* 10(3): 469–90

1998. 'How does part-time work lead to low pension income?', in J. O'Reilly and C. Fagan (eds.), *Part-time Prospects: An International Comparison of Part-time Work in Europe, North America and the Pacific Rim.* London: Routledge, 156–73

Ginn, J., Daly, M. and Street, D. 2001. 'Engendering pensions: a comparative framework', in J. Ginn, D. Street and S. Arber (eds.), *Women, Work and Pensions: International Issues and Prospects.* Buckingham: Open University Press, 1–10

Ginn, J., Street, D. and Arber, S. 2001. 'Cross-national trends in women's work', in J. Ginn, D. Street and S. Arber (eds.), *Women, Work and Pensions: International Issues and Perspectives.* Buckingham: Open University Press, 11–30

Hinrichs, K. 2001. 'Elephants on the move. Patterns of public pension reforms in OECD countries', in S. Leibfried (ed.), *Welfare State Futures*. Cambridge University Press, 77–102

Holzmann, R., MacKellar, L. and Rutkowksi, M. 2003. 'Accelerating the European pension reform agenda: need, progress and conceptual underpinnings', in R. Holzmann, M. Orenstein and M. Rutkowski (eds.), *Pension Reform in Europe: Process and Progress*. Washington, DC: The World Bank, 1–46

Jenson, J. 1997. 'Who cares? Gender and welfare regimes', *Social Politics* 4(2): 182–7

Jenson, J. and Sineau, M. 2001. *Who Cares? Women's Work, Childcare, and Welfare State Redesign*. University of Toronto Press

Johnson, P., Conrad, C. and Thompson, D. 1989. *Workers versus Pensioners: Intergenerational Conflict in an Ageing World*. Manchester University Press

Kohli, M. and Novak, M. 2001. *Will Europe Work? Integration, Employment and the Social Order*. London: Routledge

Laczko, F. and Phillipson, C. 1991. *Changing Work and Retirement: Social Policy and the Older Worker*. Milton Keynes: Open University Press

Leitner, S. 2001. 'Sex discrimination within EU pension systems', *Journal of European Social Policy* 11(2): 99–115

Lewis, J. 1992. 'Gender and the development of welfare regimes', *Journal of European Social Policy* 2(3): 31–48

Luckhaus, L. 1997. 'Privatisation and pensions: some pitfalls for women?', *European Law Journal* 3(1): 83–100

Luckhaus, L. and Ward, S. 1997. 'Equal pension rights for men and women: a realistic perspective', *Journal of European Social Policy* 7(3): 237–53

Moerth, U. (ed.) 2004. *Soft Law in Governance and Regulation: An Interdisciplinary Analysis*. Cheltenham: Edward Elgar

Myles, J. 1984. *Old Age in the Welfare State: The Political Economy of Public Pensions*. Boston: Little Brown

Myles, J. and Pierson, P. 2001. 'The comparative political economy of pension reform', in P. Pierson (ed.), *The New Politics of the Welfare State*. Oxford University Press, 305–33

Myles, J. and Quadagno, J. 1997. 'Recent trends in public pension reform: a comparative view', in K. Banting and R. Broadway (eds.), *Reform in Retirement Income Policy: International and Canadian Perspectives*. Kingston, Ontario: Queen's University School of Policy Studies, 247–72

Nye, S. 2003. 'The rediscovery of politics: democracy and structural pension reform in continental Europe', in E. Holzmann (ed.), *Pension Reform in Europe: Process and Progress*. Washington, DC: The World Bank, 79–110

Office for National Statistics Online 2010. 'Ageing – fastest increase in the oldest old', statistics.gov.uk (accessed August 2010)

Organisation for Economic Co-operation and Development 2002. 'Women at work: who are they and how are they faring?', *Employment Outlook 2002*. Paris: Organisation for Economic Co-operation and Development

　　2004. *Reforming Public Pensions: Sharing the Experiences of Transition and OECD Countries*. Paris: Organisation for Economic Co-operation and Development

　　2009. *Society at a Glance 2009*. Paris: Organisation for Economic Co-operation and Development

Orloff, A. S. 2002. 'Women's employment and welfare regimes. Globalisation, export orientation and social policy in Europe and North America', United Nations Research Institute for Social Development Programme Paper 12

Palme, J. 1990. 'Models of old-age pensions', in A. Ware and R. E. Goodin (eds.), *Needs and Welfare*. London: Sage, 104–25

Pensions Policy Institute 2008. *Pension Facts*. London: Pensions Policy Institute

Pierson, P. 1994. *Dismantling the Welfare State? Reagan, Thatcher, and the Politics of Retrenchment*. Cambridge University Press

　　1997. 'The politics of pension reform', in K. Banting and R. Boadway (eds.), *Reform of Retirement Income Policy: International and Canadian Perspectives*. Kingston, Ontario: Queen's University School of Public Studies, 273–94

Pierson, P. and Weaver, K. 1993. 'Imposing losses in pension policy', in K. Weaver and B. Rockmann (eds.), *Do Institutions Matter? Government Capabilities in the United States and Abroad*. Washington, DC: The Brookings Institution, 110–50

Price, D. 2003 'Pension sharing in divorce: the future for women', *Social Policy Review* 15: 239–61

Rake, K. 1999. 'Accumulated disadvantage? Welfare state provision and the incomes of older women and men in Britain, France and Germany', in J. Clasen (ed.), *Comparative Social Policy Concepts, Theories and Methods*. Oxford: Blackwell, 220–46

Sainsbury, D. 1999. *Gender and Welfare State Regimes*. New York: Oxford University Press

Schokkaert, E. and Van Parijs, P. 2003. 'Debate on social justice and pension reform. Social justice and the reform of Europe's pension systems', *Journal of European Social Policy* 13(3): 245–79

Sefton, T., Evandrou, M. and Falkingham, J. 2010. 'Family ties: women's work and family histories and their association with incomes in later life in the UK', *Journal of Social Policy*, published online by Cambridge University Press, doi:10.1017/S0047279410000255

Social Protection Committee 2000. *Adequate and Sustainable Pensions: A Report by the Social Protection Committee on the Future Evolution of Social Protection. Brussels, European Union.* Brussels: European Commission

Steinhilber, S. 2005. 'The gender implications of pension reforms. General remarks and evidence from selected countries.' Draft Working Paper prepared for the UNRISD report 'Gender Equality: Striving for Justice in an Unequal World'

Street, D. and Ginn, J. 2001. 'The demographic debate: the gendered political economy of pensions', in J. Ginn, D. Street and S. Arber (eds.), *Women, Work and Pensions: International Issues and Perspectives.* Buckingham: Open University Press, 31–43

Thane, P. 1987. *Economic Burden or Benefit? A Positive View of Old Age.* London: Centre for Economic Policy Research

Vlachantoni, A. forthcoming. 'A good step forward but not far enough? The provision of care credits in European pensions systems', in E. Addis, F. Degavre, P. de Villota and J. Eriksen (eds.), *Institutions and Wellbeing: A Gender Approach.* Aldershot: Ashgate

Whiteford, P. 2004. 'Introduction: learning from pension reform experiences in OECD', in OECD, *Reforming Public Pensions: Sharing the Experiences of Transition and OECD Countries.* Paris: OECD

Zaidi, A., Grech, A. G. and Fuchs, M. 2006. 'Pension policy in EU25 and its possible impact on elderly poverty', CASE Discussion Paper 116. London School of Economics and Political Science

Zeitlin, J. 2005. 'What's left of the OMC: the future of Open Coordination', unpublished paper presented at the 4th ESRC Research Seminar, Implementing the Lisbon Strategy: Policy Co-ordination through Open Methods, London School of Economics and Political Science

5

Ageing and social class: towards a dynamic approach to class inequalities in old age

ALEXANDRA LOPES

Introduction

The inclusion of social class based inequalities in a book about diversity and discrimination in old age is certainly no surprise.[1] Social class understood as a system of social ranking and unbalanced distribution of opportunities, resources, prestige and power among social groups and among individuals is a building block of inequalities not only in old age but all along the life course. It is also a building block of sociological analysis and has been extensively explored in all corners of the world by a diversity of scholars interested in understanding the foundations of social organisation and social behaviour.

Although there is little or no theory specifically addressing social class differences in old age,[2] there is a growing body of empirical research about inequalities in later life that includes social class (often under the designation of 'socioeconomic status') as an independent variable that explains, if not entirely or dominantly, at least partially those inequalities. This empirical research is particularly rich in the field of health status and health care, a domain where scholars around the world have been accumulating data that sustain the association between class differences and differences in a series of health outcomes. The social gradient

---

[1] The statements and opinions contained in this paper are solely those of the author, who bears full responsibility for all its contents. The author would like to thank Professor Carlos Gonçalves for his comments on an earlier version of this paper.

[2] In this chapter I will consider old age as defined by the statutory age of retirement (65 in the majority of the European countries). Although it is acknowledged that different approaches to the definition of old age have been employed in the literature, in a study of social class differences, and given the widely used criterion of occupational status in many social class typologies, it was considered important to match the definition of old age with the most common cause for exiting the labour market: retirement.

in health outcomes has been signalled for both mortality and morbidity, disability rates and access to health care (Tabassum *et al.* 2009; Matthews, Jagger and Hancock 2006; Shoeni *et al.* 2005) and for health indicators that draw on the subjective measurement of health and quality of life, namely self-perception of health, satisfaction with life, perceived happiness and loneliness (Wenger *et al.* 1996; Breeze *et al.* 2005).

In all the studies mentioned above, statistical association between social class and a diversity of outcomes is frequently identified and most of the times in the direction one would reasonably expect to find it: those in lower social classes display disadvantaged positions in a series of dimensions of well-being. Yet, and despite the statistical significance of social class as a determining factor of inequalities in later life, little explanation is provided for why that is the case, and occasionally we are even confronted with some departures from the expected direction of the association.

My contribution to this book is primarily concerned with the discussion on why social class matters when analysing diversity and discrimination in old age and sets as the main goal to revise some theoretical contributions from social class and stratification analysis that researchers on ageing should consider taking on-board. It is my argument that studies on discrimination and inequality in old age would benefit from some investment in a conceptual framework that can illuminate some of the dynamics that have been empirically identified among that age group. This investment can also bring positive contributions to the mainstream approaches to social class analysis, which often fall short in accounting for class differences in old age. What is the scope of social class analysis when applied to older groups? How truthful are the impacts captured by the most well-established social class indicators when applied to older groups? How and why can social class differences become a factor of discrimination in old age? This chapter aims at bringing some contribution to answering these and other related questions that arise from an attempt critically to examine the importance of social class as a discriminating factor in old age.

Social class and modern analysis of social stratification

Although it is not my goal to develop a comprehensive revision of social class theories, it is important to include in this chapter a brief discussion of those theories, especially because in its roots social class analysis was associated with a set of substantive questions that had little, if anything, to do with ageing.

The concepts of social class and social stratification (often used inter-changeably)[3] are among the dearest concepts to a vast number of sociol-ogists. They are very much intertwined with the sociological understanding of human societies as structured systems of inequalities where individuals and groups display different levels of control over power and resources. Social class theory is at least as old as sociology itself and has been the arena for some vivid debates among sociologists coming from different traditions and schools of thought, ranging from those primarily concerned with social class formation and decomposition to those more focused on ana-lysing mechanisms of social class reproduction and resistance to change. Social class analysis has been rooted since its foundation in strong ideo-logical projects from which stem concepts about how societies should operate and about the nature of human beings.

In modern sociology researchers nurture a relationship with the con-cept of social class that varies, in the extremes, between those that remain truly fascinated with the importance social class still holds in moulding our lives and those who completely reject the relevance of the concept and see it as a relic of the past social order (the industrial order mean-while replaced by a new post-industrial society). The most bluntly put claim about the lack of interest in social class as a conceptual category with little empirical significance comes from post-modernists like Lyotard (1984) or Baudrillard (1983), two scholars who have become points of reference to all those who argue that the foundational principle of division and class struggle has lost its radicalism to the point of disappearing, something they see very much related to the rise of the media society and the consumer culture. Giddens, himself a former well-established authority on social class analysis, claims that class has a limited value to signal social differentiation when compared to lifestyle or consumption behaviour approaches (Giddens 1991).

The proclaimed end of social classes is partially associated to a wide debate that has been developing in recent decades about the emergence

---

[3] Although some sociologists insist on a clear conceptual distinction between social class system and social stratification, I will follow Crompton's approach and work with both, as complementary concepts that illuminate different parts of the whole (Crompton 2008: 6). Social stratification (and the derived measurements of social status) is considered as a more general framework that accounts for the hierarchically distinct positions individ-uals take in the social order. These positions, that bring different amounts of status, can be defined in a multiplicity of dimensions, from gender to ethnicity, from occupation to education, or others, depending on the society that is analysed. Social class offers a more specific framework to account for material inequalities and their origins.

of new forms of social inequality, new in the sense of falling outside the scope of social class differences. Among those we see included are, for example, gender differences or ethnic differences, categories that some scholars consider can hardly be seen as a novelty of our times. Instead, they argue these are categories that have been the source of inequalities for a long time, often operating as elements that reinforce (or dilute) the importance of the resilient sources of inequalities that derive from socio-professional differentiated positions and educational differences: income, opportunities to consume or lifestyles (Costa *et al.* 2000).

A strong reason, it appears, for many scholars to claim that social classes do not matter anymore is based on the fact that people do not acknowledge their existence and their own social class identity, as some surveys have been demonstrating (Birkelund 2002). It is as if there are no social classes because there is no subjective self-awareness of class, contrary to what those same scholars consider happens with other elements of identity formation: the body; sexual preferences and gender; relationship with the natural environment; relationship with food, among others (Beck, Giddens and Lash 1994).

In the two poles of social class theory, still with a great degree of influence on contemporary social class analysis, we have the Marxist school and the Liberal school. The first sees in social class struggles the process of social change. The second sees in the maturation of capitalism a process that will ultimately lead to the dissolution of social class struggles and inequalities. Alongside these two schools of thought, focused on understanding the rise (and fall) of social classes, we find a number of contributions that try to unravel the mechanisms of social class resilience. These range from those that see social class reproduction originating in non-material dimensions that operate without individuals consciously acknowledging them, namely in the form of distinctive social class norms and values,[4] to those that refuse the existence of such non-material dimensions and instead argue that the material dimension of social class, understood as opportunities and resources that derive from the situation of the individual in the labour market and the economic relations in which he or she is involved, constrains the universe of choices individuals consciously make in

---

[4] One example of such contributions would be Bourdieu and his theory about the *habitus*, defined as the pattern of unconscious preferences, classificatory schemes and taken-for-granted choices which differs between groups and classes and distinguishes them one from the other (Bourdieu 1984).

order to maximise the return they envisage as possible to achieve from where they stand.[5]

Despite its announced obsolescence, the concept of social class remains central in sociological theory and a structuring element to many analyses of how societies operate and of the status of each individual in the social space. In most of those analyses it is possible to identify a very strong link between social class and the analysis of inequality, in an effort to describe systems of social ranking and unbalanced distribution of opportunities, resources, prestige and power among social groups (Crompton 2008).

Although few would challenge the idea that human societies can be thought of as systems of social stratification, according to which individuals can be ranked, there is less consensus about how the ranking should be defined and about what measurement should be used to classify individuals. Social class analysis inspired in the Marxist tradition tends to emphasise class conflicts and social change and therefore pays great attention to ownership and class relations (Wright 1994). Scholars more inspired in the Weberian tradition, and more specifically in the British School of Class and Stratification, often prefer the concept of status to class and try to classify the relative positions of individuals in terms of people's social standing in a community, not defined exclusively by the place of the individual in the system of production.[6] The main emphasis of class typologies inspired by Max Weber is put on power resources and life chances which are undoubtedly dependent on work

---

[5] The analysis carried out by Goldthorpe on educational attainment and social class differences in educational attainment is an example of such an approach. Goldthorpe, a leading exponent of social class analysis within British sociology, insists that social classes are not mere classification dimensions but rather realities that acquire demographic and sociocultural identity, and as such reflect sets of resources and opportunities that constrain the choices individuals consciously make (Goldthorpe 1983). From a quasi-Weberian approach, Goldthorpe insists that the relevance of social class analysis does not come from any theory of class-based collective action, which he refuses to see as inherent to class analysis, but rather comes from the potential of social class analysis as a research programme that tries to understand the persistence and resistance to change of class-linked inequalities (Goldthorpe and Marshall 1992).

[6] The foundations of this approach can be traced back to Weber's analysis of social stratification in contemporary societies and to his theoretical model that intersected different hierarchies, corresponding to different types of capital: economic, relational and cultural. Weber acknowledged that although there is often a match between the positions individuals take in different fields, there are also cases of mismatch (Scott 2002). Put in other terms, if it can be said that status is statistically correlated with social class, it is not rare to find individuals that have inconsistent social class and status positions.

relations but are also related to market power. Crucial criteria in proposals rooted in this school include authority and hierarchical position (Dahrendorf 1959) or expert power and cultural capital (Parkin 1979).

In most empirical studies, though, sociologists tend to use the concepts of both social class and status to address social stratification and differentiation, especially because social class analysis nowadays is far more sophisticated and complex than it used to be. This is largely due to the statistical and methodological tools available, much more advanced than what was available in the early days of social class analysis, which has meant, among other things, that different approaches to class and stratification are being considered together, even if they sometimes appear to be diametrically opposed (Crompton 2008).

There are different dimensions in the contents of social class, and authors often tend to work with some dimensions and not with others. In this chapter I will consider two dimensions of social class (although one of them will be more in the spotlight than the other) and will deliberately exclude a third one. On one hand, classes will be addressed as prestige, status, culture and lifestyles and therefore as a broad system of social ranking. On the other hand, and focusing in particular on the material dimension of inequalities, classes will be addressed as structured social and economic inequalities that have their origins in the differentiated possession of economic and power resources. The dimension that will be excluded concerns social class as collective social and political actors. The exclusion of this dimension of social class does not imply any statement about its theoretical relevance. It results from a choice of not engaging in a discussion that I consider falls outside the scope of the aims of this chapter.

Social class analysis and old age

In the literature on social class it is only very rarely that one finds reference to older age groups. Most empirical studies that develop social class analysis tend to confine themselves to data for the working-age population, and the investment in social class theories has been drawing on the results of those studies. The analysis of social class in studies about old age usually translates into the use of some indicators of socio-economic status very much intertwined with the need to signal disadvantage and inequalities among the older groups of the population to inform policy design. Very rarely do we find any serious effort to mature the theoretical framework of social class analysis per se.

I believe there is a strong theoretical and analytical potential in the concept of social class to address diversity in old age and more specifically to address how the structured systems of inequalities and social distinctions captured by social class differences are reproduced (and eventually reinforced) in old age. That, however, can only be done if one critically disentangles the dimensions and the implications of current ways of performing social class analysis when applied to old age.

It is my belief that the neglect of social class theory production in the universe of ageing studies is not exclusively explained by the irrelevance old age represented for a long time as an object for social class theory in demographically young societies like those in the early twentieth century. That neglect is also the consequence of the difficulties in finding reliable indicators for socio-economic status and social class in that specific age group. For a range of reasons, the measurement of socio-economic status is extremely challenging in older age groups, and therefore one of the priorities for social class analysis in old age should be extending our knowledge about what indicators work better, namely taking into account the objectives of that classification when addressing the older age groups. Inspiration in well-established typologies of class is necessary, but a more promiscuous approach to a diversity of methods and tools may be required to refine the measurement of the concept, and improve its efficacy to address structured systems of inequality in old age. On the other hand, the analysis of the configurations of social class in old age must take on board a dynamic approach that considers life course events and not a static concept of social class. These ideas are developed in the next two sections.

Dynamic approaches to life chances in the measurement of social class in old age

My first claim is that there will be relevant benefits from adding a dynamic approach to social class differences in old age. Such an approach will yield implications both for social class theory and for intervention in inequalities in old age.

As a broad category, old age is frequently understood in a rather simplistic way as a condition that embeds a dimension of homogeneity in how it intersects social class and social status. Seen as a discriminating factor itself, old age is often associated with loss of social status. Entering old age is considered as triggering a sequence of events that together concur to a less favourable situation in the social space: exit from the labour market, loss of income, health problems and widowhood among others. This is very much the European tradition, that overall tends to consider old age as a mechanism of downward social mobility in itself, irrespective of the correlations it may hold with other discriminating variables. This is to a certain extent a by-product of the way social class analysis is performed in older age groups.

Measuring social class and establishing reliable indicators, taking as a reference that specific age group, is a difficult task. The two indicators that rank first in most typologies of social class are education and professional occupation, both posing some challenges when considering the older population.

As for education, and considering the known historical trends of schooling in a vast majority of European countries, the current older age group has predominantly left school at relatively younger ages. This means it is an indicator that tends to produce very little variation among individuals and has little discriminating power, a trend that is common to most European countries, as Grundy and Holt (2001) have demonstrated.

Occupational status, among older people usually measured as last occupation before exiting the labour market, is problematic in itself. On one hand, it does not capture the path of mobility in the labour market (that can be associated, in the extremes, with trajectories of upward or downward mobility), when it is this path that is likely to have more significant impacts in the quality of life of the older person. On the other hand, there are significant gender differences in employment histories, in terms of both labour market involvement and types of occupation (Adkins 1995). Finally, last occupation may have different implications depending on when the individual exited the labour market (e.g. early retirement in response to unemployment; early retirement for health reasons; early retirement due to restructuring of some occupational sectors and even the obsolescence of some job positions) (Walker 1981).

Confronted with these difficulties, it seems reasonable to consider the purpose of analysing socio-economic status and social class before deciding what method to adopt for measuring it. I contend that the analysis of social class in old age will have limited interest if limited to the classic classification of individuals along a scale of socio-economic status derived from educational attainment and occupational status (for most older people, translated into last job before retirement). The main reason for this is that it provides a static measurement of social positioning. Both educational attainment and last job are unlikely to change after a certain moment in time (typically after retirement) and therefore processes of social class mobility are not possible simply as the result of the measurement instrument in use. If one looks at the results of some research on inequalities among the elderly, the changing trends in the relationship between social class and inequalities as age progresses as well as the reversing trends in the relation between class and different dimensions of inequality suggest that the indicators themselves may be hindered. Taylor and Ford have done some analysis on Scottish samples of elderly people, and have demonstrated that the effects of class in the distribution of a set of personal resources (financial, social, health and psychological) are not constant along either the age line, the gender divide or the dimension of personal resources being addressed (Taylor and Ford 1983). Results like this suggest there might be a need to rethink how one captures social class among old people, more specifically among people who are passed their working-age years.

A classic example of the utility of a more dynamic approach to the classification of socio-economic status comes from studies on poverty. The persistence of the problem of poverty amongst the elderly and the growing gaps in poverty rates between the elderly and the rest of the society – a common trend in most European countries – has been a priority topic not only in the research agenda but also in the social policy agenda. Often we find the explanation for poverty in old age confined to the growing distributional inequalities in income that separate the elderly from the rest of the population, once more reinforcing the image of old age as a condition that triggers, just of itself, disadvantage. However, several authors have demonstrated, for the general population, that poverty is explained not only by distributional inequalities in income, but also by the position of families and individuals, relative to others, in the social class structure. It is that position that creates an unequal distribution of rewards and opportunities which are largely dependent on the command people have over other resources such as savings, interest, social services, etc., which together with income contribute to and protect their social status (Walker 1980).

Let me recall Titmuss who, in the mid-twentieth century, already warned about the impacts of the differential access to pension rights in what he termed the emergence of two nations in old age, with greater inequalities in living standards after work than during work (Titmuss 1955). Titmuss was discussing then what rests at the core of inequalities in old age in contemporary societies: inequalities that are forged in the labour market prior to retirement, and along the life course, are carried into old age. But they are carried not only in a static manner (which would not translate into the aggravation of inequalities among older people when compared to the rest of the population) but also in a dynamic manner. Inequalities resulting from low-paid employment, low status, disability, sex discrimination and other labour market disadvantages open different paths of access and accumulation of resources that will really determine if one is going to be poor or not in old age, and if one is going to be in a situation of aggravated disadvantage or not.

It is my argument that the measurement of social class in old age should not be limited to the traditional indicator 'last job', but should also include indicators that allow us to reconstruct the opportunities (or lack of opportunities) that have marked the participation of the individual in the labour market and that have (or have not) allowed for the acquisition of control over a set of resources that are what really can account for the situation of advantage or disadvantage that the person may experience in old age. Among the indicators to consider, we have unemployment spells, the existence of savings and interest income, ownership of house and amenities, but also access to occupational pensions and other social benefits (namely health benefits). When one browses through the main large-scope surveys that are used in most cross-national analyses on socio-economic status, these indicators are often available but have been used to a very limited extent in studies that focus on social class differentials in old age. I contend that there is a broader scope for analysing diversity, disadvantage and inequalities in old age if one starts from social class both as a dependent and as an independent variable. Taken as a dependent variable, social class has the potential to capture an entire life trajectory that defines the position of the older person as the result of a path of opportunities (or lack of them) that will in their turn constrain the opportunities available in old age. Only then does social class become an independent variable. Social class analysis allows placing the focus on the diversity of resources (or capital) that the older person controls and that creates opportunities (and therefore, automatically, impossibilities) to participate in a variety of dimensions of social existence. This potential will be reinforced if one starts from a dynamic life course perspective of the concept of social class and focuses on analysing processes of cumulative advantage/disadvantage along the social class divide.

Theoretical explanation and empirical efficiency in the measurement of social class in old age

Considerations on how the classification of social class is produced have impacts also on how one empirically captures the effect of social class. Arguing that social class should be taken as a dependent variable, the outcome of a series of life trajectories, strongly moulded by specific trajectories in the labour market and the opportunities and constraints they breed, also implies that social class effects need to be measured in a way that guarantees that social class differentials, as differentials in opportunities and in control over resources, are clearly captured at the arrival point.

One proposal that I believe can be particularly fruitful to measure social class differentials in old age, and that has been gathering less acceptance from social class scholars than what would be expected, is that of conciliating social class analysis with the social indicators approach (Payne, Payne and Hyde 1996).

Research on health status in old age, for example, has been establishing in a more or less consistent way that there is a strong correlation between material deprivation and poor standard of living and disadvantage in several health indicators. Inconsistencies have been signalled, however, in the association between social class, measured as occupational status, and those same indicators of disadvantage in health. This probably happens because, although it holds a positive correlation with income and wealth, occupational social class is largely a measure of social status and therefore a result of the social division of labour. Material standard of living on the other hand seems to operate more clearly as a measure of 'command over resources' (Weich and Lewis 1998).

We should call for some words of caution on how the social indicators approach is applied to older age groups, and some critical examination of the efficiency of the indicators in use is also in order. Like social class typologies, the most commonly used indicators of living conditions were also developed for the working-age population. For example, many older people do not have a car for reasons of infirmity and not poverty. Older people may own their houses, but these may be too costly to heat and maintain, leading to potentially unhealthy living standards. The combination of indicators is probably the best approach, and the only one that can shed some light on the multidimensionality of living conditions in old age.

The combination of both social class analysis and social indicators measurement serves to highlight the impact past social class trajectories have in the current situation of the elderly, namely by the accumulation of constraints or opportunities that may be particularly handy to deal with the limitations and the needs typical of old age. Payne argues that theories of social class offer the basis for the explanation of social deprivation and suggests there is no need to consider the two approaches as opposite, although some authors have been taking part as if that was the case (Payne *et al.* 1996). Social indicators are, simultaneously, a simpler and a more complex way of addressing inequalities. However, if it is true they offer enhanced quantification and multidimensionality, it is also true they have fewer theoretical arguments than the conventional class analysis approach. They are not, however, opposite. The way Townsend has defined relative deprivation is not very different from the approach of social class analysis that emphasises the distributional differences as outcomes of class. In Townsend's words, 'people can be said to be deprived if they lack the . . . conditions, activities and facilities which are customary, or at least widely encouraged and approved, in the society in which they belong' (Townsend 1987: 125–6).

In other words, if one starts from a social class perspective, one can use social indicators to look for evidence of continuing class differentials. This can be potentially very interesting to address old age, especially if combined with the dynamic approach to life course chances discussed in the previous section. Together, these two approaches have the potential not only to improve the empirical efficiency of the social class framework to signal inequalities, but also to clarify the link between social class differences and a series of outcomes in different dimensions of life, by explaining it as a process of cumulative advantage/disadvantage that defines the universe of possibilities of control over resources (material and immaterial) in old age.

Social class, diversity and discrimination in old age

Although in most cases the analysis of social class involves to some degree the analysis of inequalities, and therefore of the potential discriminating effect of belonging to different social groups, it does not have to be confined to that. In fact, diversity and discrimination do not have to walk hand in hand. If it is true that not acknowledging diversity may be a causing factor of discrimination, the sheer existence of diversity does not necessarily translate into inequalities and discrimination.

Following this idea, I consider that the analysis of social class, not only in old age but as a matter of fact when addressing any age group, may be applied in two different, although complementary, manners. First, social class can be considered, in Goldthorpe's approach, as an entity that materialises into objective socio-demographic realities that are derived from the economic relations that the individuals and households entail in the sphere of labour and production (Goldthorpe 1996). These objective realities constitute themselves into resources that individuals may activate in pursuit of their objectives and to maximise their well-being. One of the main goals of measuring social class is to identify the resources each individual controls and that may put him in a position of advantage or disadvantage when compared to other individuals. Typically, and considering older age groups, social class can reasonably be expected to translate into income and wealth, housing conditions, and health care and social care opportunities. These are objective conditions about which the individual is aware and that the individual will consider in any decision-making process related to his or her well-being. Some scholars doing research on social class in old age have been suggesting precisely that social class as traditionally measured should be considered as the arrival point of a life trajectory that acts as a context variable for a set of other indicators that reflect the accumulation of opportunities and constraints along that life trajectory (Dannefer 2003).

But there is another side to social class analysis that we could see as more aligned with Bourdieu's approach to social differentiation mechanisms. Social class also embeds the immaterial dimensions of social life where individuals are socialised and that will then be reflected in how each behaves in different situations and in how each perceives different situations. Life courses are not only paths of differentiated accumulation of resources and opportunities. They are also paths of socialisation in specific social milieux that can be captured as social classes. As socialised bodies in social class positions, individuals experience the process of ageing in different manners and are affected by public policies differently. Very often, this can translate into discrimination or be felt as discriminating.

Social class as material opportunity: accumulation of advantage/disadvantage and discrimination in old age

One way of approaching social class in old age is to consider it as the descriptor of a life trajectory that is characterised by different opportunities and constraints, and that ultimately materialises into certain objective realities that can be seen as manifest expressions of class.

Such would be the example of income (not only in absolute values, but also in terms of its source and its relative weight compared to income in working-life years); or the example of housing, including issues of ownership as well as issues of housing conditions.

Merton has described cumulative advantage as something that involves 'the ways in which initial comparative advantage of trained capacity, structural location, and available resources make for successive increments of advantage such as the gaps between the haves and have-nots widen' (Merton 1988: 606). There is abundant research that emphasises how material living conditions correlate strongly with a series of outcomes in different dimensions of life in old age. And there is also a good amount of empirical evidence that supports the thesis that living conditions in later life are the result of a pathway of opportunities that take place along life and that allow (or not) for the accumulation of resources that can come in very handy when certain problems emerge (Shoeni *et al.* 2005) There are studies that have tested and demonstrated that, in fact, the differences in standard of living across occupational strata are likely to increase with age (O'Reilly 2002; Dannefer 2003). Here rests one of the critical aspects of the discriminating potential of social class differences in old age.

I would like to consider three topics that are intimately related with the material accumulation of advantage/disadvantage throughout life and that are particularly sensitive to social class differentials. Moreover, they are sensitive topics in terms of their impacts on the quality of life of the older person – income, housing, and access to health and social care.

Income, understood not only as monthly disposable income, but also as access to savings or interest,[7] is an indicator that shows a high degree of correlation with occupational social class. In fact, some researchers have empirically demonstrated that different occupational strata display quite considerable differences not only in terms of amount of income generated but also in terms of the shape of the earnings-curve along the line of working life and in terms of access to complementary sources of income. Chan and Goldthorpe have recently highlighted, once again, the

---

[7] Considering income in this broader sense is particularly relevant for the analysis of income in old age. In some countries, in fact, anything different would be a gross methodological mistake given the different old age pension systems in place. In some states, pension systems tend to flatten income differences after retirement while in others they tend to have the opposite effect and increase income gaps.

importance of class to explain age–earning curves, a factor these authors consider a good indicator of economic life-chances and of security prospects. They recall, using data for British society, that it is known that the working-class age–earning curve tends to level out around the age of 30, while for the *salariat* groups it tends to rise up until the age of 50 (Chan and Goldthorpe 2007). On the other hand, there are known occupation-based differences in terms of access to complementary pension systems or health care benefits (Esping-Andersen 1996) as well as in savings behaviour and insurance taking rates (Snyder 1974). These differentiated income trajectories will then be reflected in the accumulation of a series of resources that will have serious consequences for the ability of each individual to manage the age-specific needs that may emerge in the later stages of life.

To a high degree correlated with the income curve, but having some unique effects as well, is housing. The material dimension of housing, usually measured using indicators of ownership and housing conditions and comfort, can be thought of largely as an outcome of income trajectories. In fact, as McMeekin and Tomlinson (1998) have demonstrated, occupational class is a powerful predictor of the rates of adoption and diffusion of certain consumer durables. This can certainly be explained, as the authors seem to suggest, by social class related behaviours (a theme that I will come back to in the next section), but surely also by the income trajectories of different occupational careers. This is particularly relevant in old age when, for example, house ownership, quite common in certain European countries in this age group (Castles and Ferrera 1996), may be accompanied by insufficient disposable income to heat the house during the cold winter, or to maintain it so as to prevent deterioration of living conditions. Once more, there pops up the methodological question of how to analyse social class in old age, and the need to combine more than one indicator even if they seem to be measuring the same. In any case, the point to be made is that housing differences are related to social class differences and have a significant discrimination potential in old age.

On one hand, poorer housing conditions are known to be correlated to physical disability and poorer health, and the material explanation, rather than the psychological one, seems to be gathering more support (Adamson, Ebrahim and Hunt 2006). On the other hand, there are known differences in the distribution of social groups in the urban space, with those in lower classes showing a higher likelihood of living in the most deprived areas of cities, with poorer infrastructure and worse social environment, particularly in terms of criminality and vandalism.

This is particularly harmful for the older population, as discussed in some literature that highlights how social class differentials are often projected in the urban space with impacts that are felt in a more severe way by those who are already in a frail situation, among which we find old people and children (Gottdiener 1985).

The third topic I would like to address, within this discussion about social class as material opportunity and how it impacts the life of the older as a discriminating force, is the topic of access to health and social care services. This is one domain where social class differentials are particularly visible, especially in some countries where social policies fail in providing a comprehensive response to old age related needs. Research on this has been showing that there is a social class gradient in the use of health care services (McNiece and Azeem 1999). National variations are quite relevant in this issue, given the differences in health care systems across Europe.

Social care services are equally relevant to consider, if we take into account that it is in the older population that we have the highest rates of loss of functional autonomy and therefore the highest rates of usage of social care services. One again there is considerable national variation, depending on the extent of the social care services coverage and on the eligibility criteria in place in each national system. However, social class differentials are likely to emerge, namely in those cases where private provision of services is required (Anneli 1996).

Social class in old age, understood as material opportunity, is very helpful to unravel how some individuals become trapped in a pathway of accumulation of disadvantage (if considering those in weaker positions in terms of the resources over which they have some control), and how little room they have to improve their situation and deal with the age-specific hazards that may occur. This is even more important because, as some researchers have been showing, the occurrence of hazards in old age, namely those related to problems of physical functioning and of mental health, are more likely to occur in individuals whose life trajectories are marked by a pathway of cumulative disadvantage (Breeze et al. 2005; Matthews et al. 2006). In other words, not only is the individual less equipped in terms of the resources he or she controls to deal with hampering problems that may occur in old age, but he or she is more likely to experience those hampering problems.

One of the crucial lessons to be drawn from social class analysis when addressing the welfare of the older population and when discussing social policy design to tackle disadvantage and discrimination in old age is this: it is necessary to understand that there are pathways of accumulation of disadvantage that need to be interrupted.

Social class as a mechanism of differentiation

Sociologists inspired by Bourdieu's work have been exploring the way social class translates into lifestyles and have been demonstrating how different lifestyles are rooted in the differentiated types and amounts of capital that individuals possess, depending on which social group they belong to (Bourdieu 1984). Although this approach has been criticised by some for diluting the role of the individual and for not considering how social differences associated to class have been reduced in modern societies (Beck *et al.* 1994), there is a good deal of evidence that suggests this is not the case and that social class still matters in understanding mechanisms of differentiation and the distribution of status. I will base my arguments about how this link operates in old age on some of those contributions.

First, it must be clarified that for the sake of this discussion the non-material or symbolic dimension of social class will be addressed as independent of the material opportunities that different social groups represent. It is not considered detrimental in this particular context to take a clear position about what it means to separate these two dimensions, and I am quite aware that it is a divisive topic for some theorists of social class analysis. The underlying rationale for my approach is to discuss the isolated discriminating potential of social class related behaviour, which allows us to analyse not only how individuals behave in terms of their social class but also how others behave in relation to them. It is an approach which allows thinking of the social space as a set of hierarchical relations, that express perceived and collectively accepted social superiority, equality and inferiority of a quite generalised kind and that translate into differentiated positions in terms of prestige and acceptance that can potentially discriminate.

I am particularly interested in highlighting one dimension of social class as a differentiation mechanism: how some behaviours are rooted in symbolic universes that may end up hindering the older person, even if they are felt as making sense.

Tomlinson mapped out a lifestyle space based on data from the Health and Lifestyles Survey, and showed how people from different social classes (obtained as occupational class) occupy in a distinctive manner separate parts of the lifestyle space, suggesting that social classes, according to Bourdieu's analysis, can in fact be thought of as socialisation

milieux where behaviours are forged, even if they hold negative consequences when approached from a rational choice perspective. In
Tomlinson's study, primarily addressing lifestyle health behaviour, it
was demonstrated that individuals in lower classes are more likely to
display unhealthy behaviour in terms of the types of food that are
consumed, and smoking habits, among others. Some changes were
signalled along the age line, but without ever questioning the fundamental divide that makes those in lower social classes more exposed to risky
and unhealthy behaviour (Tomlinson 2003). There are competing
explanations for these observed differences in behaviour associated to
social class, but ultimately the association is there, and it forces us to
consider the older population as a socially heterogeneous group.
Socialised in different social class milieux, individuals will form different
profiles of ageing as they grow older, and these highly symbolic ageing
profiles will largely determine the scope of possibilities that one can
reasonably expect to see implemented.

If it is true that this type of approach has been confined to the analysis of
health and quality of life associated to health outcomes, it can be expanded
to other themes. For example, if we consider leisure activities and social
networks of friends, there are social class differentials, as Blau had already
shown in the early sixties (Blau 1961). The research carried out by then
suggested the importance of past associational behaviour in terms of friendship networks across social strata to explain isolation and loneliness in old
age after loss of a spouse, with elderly working-class women showing the
worst situations. Other studies following Blau's conclusions point in the
same direction, suggesting a social class gradient in how older people live
their leisure time and in how they participate in social networks of neighbours and friends (Blum 1964; Lowenthal and Robinson 1976).

What seems to be definitely out of place is to think of aged groups of
the population as homogeneous in terms of their lifestyles or their
cultural *habitus* and dispositions, irrespective of the specific context
one is addressing.

Conclusion

Discussing social classes nowadays cannot be rejected as if it were some
reflection of a deterministic approach to social processes, or something
that involves one-dimensional and closed typologies. Social class, today
as before, remains a structuring element of the life of everybody: it
embeds asymmetric relations of power and it embeds differentiated

distributions of resources and opportunities. And these differences are reflected both as the basis of social processes, therefore operating as fundamental elements of how the social space is structured, and as the outcomes of those social processes, therefore operating as fundamental elements of how behaviour and values are structured.

Little research is done on how these arguments apply to the older population. Even those that claim that the older population cannot be treated as homogeneous fall short in including social class in the universe of factors of differentiation (and inequality). This is partially a result, I argue, of the way social class has been theoretically and empirically addressed in studies of older people.

The accumulation of evidence that links social class to disadvantage in old age is of limited interest, beyond signalling disadvantaged groups. The identification of the link, and its qualification as something that is a target for policies and that should be eliminated, does not produce any effects beyond the identification of the specific groups that may become the target of specific programs, and this is mostly because of the static nature of social class analysis as it has been performed in older age groups. A thorough understanding of why that link occurs should allow for preventive intervention, which will in the long run weaken the association between social class and disadvantage. It should also allow for a more in-depth understanding of how different profiles of ageing are built throughout life and of how those profiles appear associated to advantage or disadvantage in old age.

Plotting life trajectories to understand outcomes in old age seems to be a methodologically promising approach to social class differentials. Equally promising is adding multidimensionality to the indicators of social class by combining them with the analysis of social indicators of lifestyle. It is here that rests the explanation for the discrimination potential of social class in old age: the older person has his or her life chances defined by the path of accumulation of (dis)advantage that characterises his or her social trajectory in a social group, as well as by the process of identity building that is forged in each socialisation class milieu.

Bibliography

Adamson, J. A., Ebrahim, S. and Hunt, K. 2006. 'The psychosocial versus material hypothesis to explain observed inequality in disability among older adults: data from the West of Scotland Twenty-07 Study', *Journal of Epidemiology and Community Health* 60: 974–80

Adkins, L. 1995. *Gendered Work: Sexuality, Family and the Labour Market.* Bristol: Open University Press

Anneli, A. 1996. 'European social care services: is it possible to identify models?', *Journal of European Social Policy* 6(2): 87–100

Baudrillard, J. 1983. *In the Shadow of the Silent Majorities, or, The End of the Social Order and Other Essays* (trans. P. Foss, J. Johnston and P. Patton). New York: Semiotexte

Beck, U., Giddens, A. and Lash, S. 1994. *Reflexive Modernization: Politics, Tradition and Aesthetics in the Modern Social Order.* Stanford University Press

Birkelund, G. E. 2002. 'A class analysis for the future? Comment on Grusky and Weeden: "Decomposition without Death: A Research Agenda for a New Class Analysis"', *Acta Sociologia* 45(3): 217–21

Blau, Z. 1961. 'Structural constraints on friendship in old age', *American Sociological Review* 26: 429–39

Blum, A. 1964. 'Social structure, social class and participation in primary relationships', in, A. Shostak and W. Gomberg (eds.), *Blue Collar World.* Englewood Cliffs, NJ: Prentice Hall, 145–207

Bourdieu, P. 1984. *Distinction: A Social Critique of the Judgment of Taste.* London: Routledge

Breeze, E., Jones, D. A., Wilkinson, P., Bulpitt, C. J., Grundy, C., Latif, A. M. and Fletcher, A. E. 2005. 'Area deprivation, social class, and quality of life among people aged 75 years and over in Britain', *International Journal of Epidemiology* 34: 276–83

Castles, G. and Ferrera, M. 1996. 'Home ownership and the welfare state: is Southern Europe different?' *South European Society and Politics* 1(2): 163–85

Chan, T. W. and Goldthorpe, J. H. 2007. 'Class and status: the conceptual distinction and its empirical relevance', *American Sociological Review* 72: 512–32

Costa, A. F., Mautitti, R., Martins, S. C., Machado, F. L. and Almeida, J. F. 2000. 'Social classes in Europe', *Sociologia Problemas e Práticas* 34: 9–43

Crompton, R. 2008. *Class and Stratification.* Cambridge: Polity Press

Dahrendorf, R. 1959. *Class and Class Conflict in an Industrial Society.* London: Routledge and Kegan Paul

Dannefer, D. 2003. 'Cumulative advantage/disadvantage and life course: cross-fertilizing age and social science theory', *Journal of Gerontology* 58B(6): 327–37

Esping-Andersen, G. (ed.) 1996. *Welfare States in Transition: National Adaptation in Global Economies.* London: Sage Publications

Giddens, A. 1991. *Modernity and Self-Identity: Self and Society in the Late Modern Age.* Stanford University Press

Goldthorpe, J. H. 1983. 'Women and class analysis: in defense of the conventional view', *Sociology* 17: 465–88

1996. 'Class analysis and the reorientation of class theory: the case of persisting differentials in educational attainment', *British Journal of Sociology* 47(3): 481–505

Goldthorpe, J. H. and Marshall, G. 1992. 'The promising future of class analysis: a response to recent critiques', *Sociology* 26(3): 381–400

Gottdiener, M. 1985. *The Social Production of Urban Space*. Tucson: University of Texas Press

Grundy, E. and Holt, G. 2001. 'The socio-economic status of older adults: how should we measure it in studies of health inequalities?', *Journal of Epidemiology and Community Health* 55: 895–904

Lowenthal, M. and Robinson, B. 1976. 'Social networks and isolation', in R. Binstock and E. Shanas (eds.), *Handbook of Ageing and the Social Sciences*. New York: Van Nostrand Rheinhold, 432–56

Lyotard, J. F. 1984. *The Postmodern Condition: A Report on Knowledge* (trans. G. Bennington and B. Massumi). Minneapolis: University of Minnesota Press

Matthews, R. J., Jagger, C. and Hancock, R. M. 2006. 'Does socio-economic advantage lead to a longer, healthier old age?', *Social Science and Medicine* 62: 2489–99

McMeekin, A. and Tomlinson, M. 1998. 'Diffusion with distinction: the diffusion of household durables in the UK', *Futures* 30(9): 873–86

McNiece, R. and Azeem, M. 1999. 'Socioeconomic differences in general practice consultation rates in patients aged 65 and over: prospective cohort study', *British Medical Journal* 399: 26–8

Merton, R. K. 1988. 'The Matthew effect in science, II: cumulative advantage and the symbolism of intellectual property', *ISIS* 79: 606–23

O'Reilly, D. 2002. 'Standard indicators of deprivation: do they disadvantage older people?', *Age and Ageing* 31: 197–202

Parkin, F. 1979. *Marxism and Class Theory: A Bourgeois Critique*. New York: Columbia University Press

Payne, G., Payne, J. and Hyde, M. 1996. '"Refuse of all classes"? Social indicators and social deprivation', *Sociological Research Online* 1(1), www.socresonline.org.uk/1/1/3.html (last accessed 14 August 2010)

Scott, J. 2002. 'Social class and stratification in late modernity', *Acta Sociologica* 45(1): 23–35

Shoeni, R. F., Martin, L. G., Andreski, P. M. and Freedman, V. A. 2005. 'Persistent and growing socioeconomic disparities in disability among the elderly: 1982–2002', *American Journal of Public Health* 95(11): 2065–70

Snyder, D. W. 1974. 'Econometric studies of household saving behaviour in developing countries: a survey', *Journal of Development Studies* 10(2): 139–53

Tabassum, F., Verropoulou, G., Tsimbos, C., Gjonca, E. and Breeze, E. 2009. 'Socio-economic inequalities in physical functioning: a comparative study of English and Greek elderly men', *Ageing and Society* 29: 1123–40

Taylor, R. and Ford, G. 1983. 'Inequalities in old age. An examination of age, sex and class differences in a sample of community elderly', *Ageing and Society* 3: 183–208

Titmuss, R. 1955. 'The social division of welfare: some reflections on the search for equity', reprinted in P. Alcock, H. Glennester, A. Oakley and A. Sinfield (eds.), *Welfare and Wellbeing: Richard Titmuss's Contribution to Social Policy*. Bristol, Policy Press (2001), 59–70

Tomlinson, M. 2003. 'Lifestyle and social class', *European Sociological Review* 19: 97–111

Townsend, P. 1987. 'Deprivation', *Journal of Social Policy* 16: 125–46

Walker, A. 1980. 'The social creation of poverty and dependency in old age', *Journal of Social Policy* 9(1): 49–75

    1981. 'Towards a political economy of old age', *Ageing and Society* 1: 73–94

Weich, S. and Lewis, G. 1998. 'Material standard of living, social class, and the prevalence of the common mental disorders in Great Britain', *Journal of Epidemiology and Community Health* 52: 8–14

Wenger, G. C., Davies, R., Shahtahmasebi, S. and Scott, A. 1996. 'Social isolation and loneliness in old age: review and model refinement', *Ageing and Society* 16: 333–58

Wright, E. O. 1994. *Interrogating Inequality: Essays on Class Analysis, Socialism, and Marxism*. London: Verso

6

Age, sexual orientation and gender identity

MALCOLM SARGEANT

Introduction

To be an older bisexual, gay, lesbian or transgender person is potentially to suffer from multiple discrimination. Terry Kaelbar, Executive Director of SAGE (Senior Action in a Gay Environment) summed up the issues in the USA and elsewhere:

> Aging for GLBT seniors is informed by discrimination and anti gay bigotry, which impacts our ability and willingness to access needed programs and services as we age. It is informed by the fact that we, by and large, age as single people without the traditional familial supports of a spouse or children, supports available to the vast majority of heterosexual seniors, which makes us more reliant on the programs that we are not so willing to access. GLBT aging is informed by ... our invisibility; with care providers who assume that all old people are straight, one of many heterosexist assumptions.[1]

The subject of this chapter is older people who are lesbian, gay, bisexual or transgender and the disadvantage that they suffer because of the combination of their age and their sexual preferences/sexual identity. The acronyms LGB and LGBT are used to identify all these groups who are united in the sense that they are identified by their sexual orientation. This at least is the case with lesbians, gay men and bisexuals and may be the case with transgender people. Transgenders are usually included in the grouping but do have significantly different issues to deal with.

It is important, however, to consider all these groups separately where possible; for example, although lesbians and gay men have their attractions

---

[1] Presentation as part of 'Make room for all: diversity, cultural competency and discrimination in aging America', presentations, testimony, and organisational materials from the National Gay and Lesbian Task Force Summit and Hearing held in Washington, DC, 11 December 2005.

to those of the same sex in common, this does not mean that there are not issues that divide them. Lesbians may also suffer from gender discrimination by virtue of their sex, but also because, perhaps, of a failure to abide by stereotypical images of females and female characteristics. For gay men there are also issues of age discrimination within their community and to what extent they also conform to male stereotypes. For trans people the issue is not one of sexual orientation but one of gender identity, although they may also self-identify as gay, lesbian, straight or bisexual (Mitchell and Howarth 2009).

LGB

There are large numbers of people who are LGB. The statistics are estimates because of the perceived difficulty in asking people about their sexual orientation/gender identity. It is estimated that, in the UK, some 5–7% of the population is LGB.[2] This results in a figure of up to some 4 million people. Projections of growth in the older population also suggest that, by 2031, there will be up to 1.4 million people over the age of 60 who are lesbian, gay or bisexual (Musingarimi 2008). All the figures are, however, only estimates, with various surveys giving a range of from 0.3 to 7% of the population (Mitchell et al. 2009). In the USA it is estimated that there are some 3 million LGBT people over the age of 65, and that this will grow to 4 million by 2030 (Cahill, South and Spade 2000). Other estimates put the number of LGBT older people now at between 2 and 7 million (Grant 2010). It appears that lesbians will be 'disproportionately represented in these numbers reflecting both general population trends and the decimation wrought by HIV/AIDS, which disproportionately affected gay men' (Improving the lives of LGBT older adults 2010).

Bisexuals are people attracted to both sexes, and therefore cannot be defined in the same way as lesbians and gay men. 'Bisexuality means the capacity for emotional, romantic and/or physical attraction to more than one gender. The capacity for attraction may or may not manifest itself in sexual interaction' (Miller et al. 2007). The 2002 US National Survey of Family Growth found that nearly 13% of women and 6% of men were attracted to both men and women; 2% identified themselves as bisexual, compared to 1.8% who identified as homosexual (Miller et al. 2007).

[2] Figures from the website of Age Concern, which also states that Stonewall (the main LGB campaigning organisation in the UK) considers this a reasonable estimate: www.ageconcern.org.uk/AgeConcern/openingdoors_facts.asp.

Others (Yoshino 2000) have identified five studies which estimated the numbers of bisexuals as between 2 and 15% of the population. In each study, the incidence of bisexuality was greater than that of homosexuality. It is suggested that bisexuals are being 'erased' because both self-identified gays and self-identified heterosexuals have overlapping political interests in making them so. Bisexuals, it is suggested, threaten the sexual identification of homosexuals and heterosexuals.

Little is known, however, about the age profile of the LGB community in the UK and issues affecting young LGB people may not be the same as those that affect the older segment of the population. Indeed there is some evidence of ageism within the LGB population. Particular issues highlighted in research on older LGB people focus on alienation and isolation, and support and security, in old age (Mitchell *et al.* 2009).

Transgender

Transgender can be described as:

> A very broad term to include all sorts of trans people. It includes cross dressers, people who wear a mix of clothing, people with a dual or no gender identity, and transsexual people. It is also used to define a political and social community which is inclusive of transsexual people, transgender people, cross-dressers (transvestites) and other groups of 'gender-variant' people.
>
> (Whittle, Turner and Al-Alami 2007 cited in Mitchell and Howarth 2009).

Quite apart from the discrimination suffered as a result of their eventual sexual orientation, transgender people may go through a process of being exposed to bigotry and prejudice whilst undergoing serious physical and mental life-changing processes. It is the public nature of transgenderism that is an issue both for the individuals and for their SOFFAs (significant others, friends, families and allies). It is often their partners who are in the front line. Heterosexual partners can find themselves perceived as lesbian or gay. Often, it is suggested, LGB partners are also shunned by their own communities (Is Your T Written in Disappearing Ink? 2001).

It is estimated that there are also some 4,000 people in the UK who are receiving medical help for gender dysphoria,[3] indicating a total of some

---

[3] Gender dysphoria is a condition in which a person feels that they are trapped within a body of the wrong sex. It can also be known as gender identity disorder, gender incongruence or transgenderism. See www.nhs.uk/conditions/gender-dysphoria/Pages/Introduction.aspx?url=Pages/What-is-it.aspx.

15,000 in all. This cannot, of course, be an accurate measure of the number of transgender people, but it does suggest that it is a substantial number of people.[4]

> Studies carried out in the Netherlands suggest that the prevalence of transsexualism is between 1:11,900 and 1:17,000 in men over 15 years of age. The number of female-to-male transsexual people is far smaller, possibly in the region of one to every five male-to-female transsexual people. A further study carried out in primary care units in Scotland estimated the prevalence in men over 15 years at 1:12,400, with an approximate sex ratio of one to four in favour of male-to-female patients. These studies suggest that in the UK there are between 1,300 and 2,000 male-to-female and between 250 and 400 female-to-male transsexual people. 'Press for Change', however, estimate the figures at around 5,000 post-operative transsexual people.
>
> (Report of the Interdepartmental Working Group on Transsexual People 2000)

Institutionalised heterosexism

Whilst homophobia results in a dislike of LGBT people, heterosexism results from a belief that homosexuality is inferior to heterosexuality. Institutional heterosexism results from a social, economic and legal system which disparages homosexuality (Mitchell *et al.* 2009). Institutionalised heterosexism has been described as 'an ideological system that denies, denigrates and stigmatizes any non-heterosexual form of behaviour, identity, relationship or community ... heterosexism is manifested both in societal customs and institutions, such as religion and the legal system (cultural heterosexism), and in individual attitudes and behaviours' (Garrett 1994, in which she cites Herek 1990). The reaction of the state to non-heterosexual family structures and the interaction of LGBT elders with health and care providers can result, for example, from an apparent institutionalised heterosexism which is only now being tackled.

It is clear from the research that has been done that older people are not regarded by many as being sexually active. There is a prejudice that turns both heterosexual and homosexual people, as they age, into asexual beings. Interviewees in one project described encounters with health professionals where it was just assumed that the older patient was

---

[4] See www.nhs.uk/conditions/gender-dysphoria/Pages/Introduction.aspx?url=Pages/What-is-it.aspx. This National Health Service website also reveals that men are diagnosed with gender dysphoria five times more often than women.

sexually inactive. A difference between older heterosexual and older LGB people is that whilst the former came up against assumptions that they were sexually inactive, the latter came up against disbelief that they could be lesbian or gay (Bytheway *et al.* 2007). These and other issues are sometimes related to the apparent 'invisibility' of older people in general and older LGBT people in particular.

LGBs are defined by their sexuality in a way that heterosexual people are not. In old age this then becomes a particular issue in the clash between sexual identity and perceived asexuality. In one survey (Ward *et al.* 2008), lesbian and gay interviewees referred to sexuality in terms of identity shaped by a lifetime of discrimination. Heterosexuals, in contrast, spoke of sexuality in terms of feelings, desires and sexual practices. They did not mention what it was like to be a heterosexual. This issue is not one confined to LGBs, of course, as there is an issue of society generally 'de-sexing' old age. The issue may be compounded for those who do not conform to heterosexual norms, however. Certain behaviour and attributes are associated with age, e.g. the clothes and hair styles that are seen as appropriate. This attitude may hide an extra layer of problems for some LGB people, e.g. lesbians who may not wish to conform to an assumed feminine look with their hair styles (Ward *et al.* 2008).

Older LGBTs and discrimination

Homophobia is 'the irrational hatred, fear and intolerance of LGB(T) people' (Stonewall; www.stonewall.org.uk) and heterosexism is the institutionalisation of heterosexual assumptions in society. There are also other terms describing the same feelings towards particular groups, such as 'biphobia' with regard to bisexuals and transphobia with regard to transgender people. Discrimination on the grounds of sexual orientation and gender identity is, of course, not limited to older LGBTs. It is also suffered by younger members of the community. A survey by the UK Equality and Human Rights Commission (Bocherty and Creegan 2009) showed that, as a result of prejudice and discrimination, some 43% of lesbians and gay men and 24% of bisexual respondents had suffered stress; and around four in ten lesbians and gay men reported that they had been bullied (37%), or felt frightened (38%), and have suffered from low self-esteem (42%).

It is the bringing together of the stereotypes for older people and for LGBT people that helps create important issues for protection from discrimination and important issues for further research. As one study stated (Grossman, D'Augelli and O'Connell 2003):

> most people have opinions about aging, and many people have thoughts about homosexuality. But few individuals have considered them simultaneously; many scholars, advocates for older adults, and other individuals consider the terms gay and aging to be incompatible.

The LGBT population is, of course, as diverse as the general population and generalisations about discrimination need to take this into account. 'Anti-LGBT stigma and discrimination is a shared challenge that may or may not connect LGBT elders across the many different identities and communities in which they are situated' (Grant 2010).

Historical perspectives

To understand the discrimination suffered by LGBT elders it is important to consider how recent are many of the changes in society's attitudes and norms with regard to sexuality. A person who was 85 years old in 2010 was born in 1925. Such a person would have grown up in the 1930s, when homosexuality was regarded as a psychiatric disorder which required therapeutic intervention. Methods of treatment included drugs, aversion therapy, lobotomies and electric shock treatment (Knauer 2009). Someone who was 65 in 2010 would have been born in 1945 and would have lived as a young person through the 1950s and 60s, when homosexuality was still unlawful. It was not until 1967 that the Sexual Offences Act in the UK was adopted. This provided that homosexual acts in private did not constitute an offence, provided that it was consensual and that the participants were over 21 years of age (Section 1(1) Sexual Offences Act 1967). Not until 1973 did the American Psychiatric Association remove homosexuality from its list of mental disorders, and it was only in 1992 that the World Health Organization declassified homosexuality as a mental illness. Finally, it was in 2003 that the UK started to make discrimination against people on the grounds of their sexual orientation unlawful, with the adoption of the Employment Equality (Sexual Orientation) Regulations (SI 2003/1661), and it was not until 2007 that this also became unlawful in respect of facilities, goods and services (Equality Act (Sexual Orientation) Regulations; SI 2007/1263).[5]

---

[5] Both now superseded by the Equality Act 2010.

In contrast, in many parts of the USA there is still little protection, the situation probably being worse for transgender people than for lesbians and gay men. A San Francisco report (Towards Equality and Diversity 2003) summed up the situation:

> The older population of the Lesbian Gay Bisexual Transgender (LGBT) communities, particularly those over 60, have lived for decades in a society where LGBT people have been scorned, discriminated against, disowned by their families and religious institutions, fired from their jobs, arrested, beaten, and murdered. Though these conditions are vastly improved in today's San Francisco, all of these things still happen to some degree. Older LGBT people have learned to survive under these hostile conditions by staying in the closet or otherwise 'keeping a low profile'.

In 1969 people fought back against police harassment at the Stonewall Inn in Greenwich Village, New York. In June of that year:

> the New York City police department went on a routine assignment to harass patrons and to close a gay bar in Greenwich Village. They were unexpectedly faced with the anger and indignation of a handful of men and women who felt that they had had enough. That night began sub-sequent rioting and brought gays out of their 'closet' around the city. This capped a history of quietly suffered oppression.
>
> (Kochman 1997)

Three years earlier, at the Compton Street Café in the Tenderloin district of San Francisco, an event for transgender people also occurred when they resisted police harassment and fought back; other recorded incidents occurred at Cooper's Donuts in Main Street, Los Angeles in 1959, and Dewey's, a late-night coffee house in Philadelphia in 1965. These are both incidents where transgender people fought back against police harassment (Stryker 2008). It is worth noting that in 1969 our 65-year-old would have been 24 and our 85-year-old would have been 44.

The significance of all these events is that the current cohort of LGBT elders would have grown up in a time of harassment, illegality and discrimination against LGBT people. There are dangers, of course, in over-generalising and it is not argued here that all older people who share common experiences will react in the same way. If older LGBTs have grown up in a hostile environment and suffered from prejudice and bigotry, then the same can be said of those heterosexual elders of the same generation. One of the issues for older LGBTs entering care homes for the elderly is that the older residential population living there may exhibit the anti-LGBT prejudices of the society in which they grew up.

These older residents grew up and continue to operate within a society where heterosexism was the norm and homosexuality was an unacceptable deviation from that norm. In one US study of ninety-nine older people (Garrett 1994, cited in Cahill *et al.* 2000) it was concluded that some 52% of respondents aged 65–72 and 41% of respondents over this age were homophobic. US research gave examples of an older woman resident at a nursing home whom staff did not wish to touch because she was a lesbian; and a home care assistant who threatened to 'out' an older gay male client if he reported her negligent care. A UK study (River 2006) appears to substantiate this view when it states, in respect of care homes, that:

> The older lesbians we talked to said they would be worried how other residents would react. Older lesbians responded with comments such as 'it would be a nightmare' and 'I am hoping never to need one.' The perceptions behind these latter comments are, of course, shared by most heterosexual older people. However, older lesbians have particular concerns over and above the basic fears (amplified by television publicity about appallingly bad practice in some homes).

Evidence is further provided by a survey in the UK (Ellison and Gunstone 2009). When asked if they would be happy to vote for an openly LGB candidate for Prime Minister, those most likely to be happy to do so were the youngest age category with the highest levels of education (79%) and those least happy to do so were the oldest and least qualified (26%).

Coming out

One important consequence appears to have been that 'coming out' was much more difficult and challenging than it is perhaps today. One older respondent in a research project stated, for example, that

> I'm going back quite a long way . . . when I was young we didn't have any choices . . . we didn't have any choice about whether we would declare we were going to be gay or not, we didn't. You just accepted that fact, and you got on with it . . . You know, we were the twilight men then.
>
> (Heaphy and Yip 2006).

A survey of LGBs in the UK found that some 37% of men (particularly older ones) and 23% of women had hidden their sexuality throughout their lives (Heaphy, Yip and Thompson 2003). Heaphy *et al.*'s research suggests a number of reasons why LGBs were reluctant to come out and declare their true sexual orientation. These were, first, employer perceptions, second, the fear of 'queer bashing', third, geography as it was more difficult to come out in a small rural community compared to being in a big city. Importantly, many lived in heterosexual relationships which continued and, according to one participant, led to a 'very deep sense of isolation and loneliness'. Bisexuals also suffer from biphobia and are likely to remain invisible. Most bisexual elders do not come out at all (Towards Equality and Diversity 2003). A small US study of older lesbians in three West Coast states showed how carefully people thought about coming out and to whom (Jones and Nystrom 2002).[6] How much more difficult it may be for older LGBTs to come out is further shown in one study which commented, when analysing survey material, that 'older respondents (aged 50–64 and 65+) were under-represented in the gay or lesbian and bisexual categories and over-represented in the 'prefer not to say' category' (Aspinall 2009).

There are more issues for transgender individuals in transitioning and it appears that many do not transition until late middle age or beyond. These issues are concerned with the risks associated with surgery and age; the difficulties in changing speech patterns and physical mannerisms; and difficulties in making changes to long-term relationships. The public nature of the changes involved in transitioning make this an issue also for hetero-sexual partners who may now be perceived as gay or lesbian. There may also be substantial issues with other family members (Cook-Daniels 2002).

Peer discrimination

There is also some evidence that older LGB people suffer from discrim-ination within the LGB community. The 'gay scene' is said to be youth orientated. The view of older members of the LGB community who participated in research was that 'the pervasive story amongst older gay men is that visible signs of ageing can mark one as undesirable or unwelcome in gay culture' (Ward *et al.* 2008). There are also examples of internalised ageing, where gay men experience themselves as being old at an earlier age than their chronological age; this assumes importance for those 'who find much of their social acceptance and life meaning in physical attractiveness and desirability' (Cahill *et al.* 2000). Ageism manifests itself within the LGBT community by the use of 'beauty standards that privilege youth, the exclusion of old people from community

[6] Jones and Nystrom (2002) made a study of sixty-two lesbians and found that many participants reported that they were not out 'or were making very conscious and deliberate decisions about whom to tell about their sexual orientation'.

discussions, and the absence of senior issues from the mainstream GLBT political agenda'(Cahill *et al.* 2000). 'A culture which values youth and the body beautiful, and considers older gay men as predators looking for a young partner to boost their self esteem, can be very alienating' (Birch 2009).

According to Cahill *et al.* there are also structural problems associated with the separation of older LGBTs from the rest of the community, such as the age segregation of social organisations within the community, and the general lack of outreach to elders. There are few programmes that honour their contributions and very little material in the LGBT press featuring elders. One survey of older LGBTs in Chicago (Beauchamp, Skinner and Wiggins 2001) also confirmed the generational divide within the community, and its recommendations included promoting more awareness of seniors within the LGBT community, avoid opportunities for seniors to remain active and involved, and avoid opportunities for intergenerational activities.

Health provision

There are many problems, however, that are common to both LGBT and heterosexual communities in old age. These include concerns about loneliness, ill-health and financial issues (Turnbull 2001). It seems likely, however, that these issues are more prevalent amongst the older LGBT population. Grant (2010) describes the position thus: 'Recent studies show that lifelong experiences of social and economic marginalisation place lesbian, gay, bisexual and transgender elders at higher risk for isolation, poverty and homelessness than their heterosexual peers.' Grant also cites a study by the Williams Institute at the University of Los Angeles which compared couples which included members aged 65 or older in relation to poverty. The report found poverty rates of 4.6% for opposite-sex married couples, 4.9% for male same-sex couples and 9.1% for female same-sex couples (Albeida *et al.* 2009). Other research showed that, in California for example, transgender people are twice as likely to live below the poverty line as the population in general. Transgender people also suffered. A survey of 194 self-identified transgender people (Good Jobs Now 2006)[7] revealed that 40% said they had suffered discrimination when applying for work and 18% had been dismissed because of their gender identity.

---

[7] This, of course, did not relate to older transgenders alone.

There are, however, a number of issues that affect older people and are of particular importance to same-sex families. One issue is in health decision-making, especially when there are accidents and illnesses such as Alzheimer's (Gallanis 2002). The 'onset of dementia may mean that private matters become public, domestic arrangements and personal circumstances become more evident to outsiders and it is more difficult to keep the information given about oneself secure' (Out of the Shadows 2003). An Australian report (Birch 2009) also highlighted the issue with regard to dementia and older lesbians and gay men: 'While behaviour may have been modified outside the home, most lesbians and gay seniors would have felt that they could be themselves inside their homes. Dementia and age-related disabilities may mean that previously carefully guarded behaviour may be forgotten and an individual inadvertently reveals his or her sexuality to others.'

A related issue is the fear of negative responses from institutions such as hospitals and medical professionals (Musingarimi 2008). At times, when support is needed, a person's vulnerability to discrimination can be increased (Cummings and Galambos 2004). One example of this cited in research is the gay man caring for his dying partner who receives little support from neighbours and has a doctor who asks him if his wife has died (Ward et al. 2008). In a further US study, of some 205 older LGBTs, it was said that their greatest fear about growing older was being or dying alone. Some 19% also stated that they had little or no confidence that medical personnel would treat them with dignity and respect as LGBT people (Out and Aging 2006).

It is particularly important for older people, however, when it combines with heterosexual institutionalism. Older LGBTs are likely to come into contact with institutions that may not recognise their orientation/identity. In this regard, one survey showed that only one third of older non-heterosexuals believed that health professionals were positive towards LGB clients and only 16% believed that health professionals were generally knowledgeable about non-heterosexual lifestyles' (Heaphey and Yip 2006). This study of lesbians and gay men is illustrated in Table 6.1.

A UK Government report (Department of Health 2006) stated that 'Older LGBT people have told us about fearing responses on the grounds of their sexuality from institutions when life changing events occur, for example loss of independence through hospitalisation, going into a residential home, or having home-carers.' In a survey for the UK Commission for Social Care Inspection, some 45% of LGB respondents stated that they had suffered discrimination when using social care services. In addition, only 9% of service providers in the sample had

Table 6.1 *Number and percentage of participants who agreed or strongly agreed*

I am (open) about my sexuality to health professionals	142 (53%)
Health professionals are generally positive towards lesbian, gay and bisexual clients	92 (35%)
Health professionals are generally knowledgeable about lesbian, gay and bisexual lifestyles	43 (16%)

carried out any specific work to promote equality for LGB people, and only 2% had done this for transgender people (Commission for Social Care Inspection 2006). The LGBT community is itself diverse and there were further issues related to this shown in this survey, e.g. a disabled lesbian who stated that she had black lesbian friends who had stopped using services for fear of having a carer from the same community who will 'out' them; and the Asian gay man who was also a family carer and who found it unthinkable that he would tell staff about his sexuality.

Isolation and support

Older LGBT people do not, it has been suggested in US studies, 'access adequate health care, affordable housing, and other social services that they need because of institutionalised heterosexism ... studies have shown widespread homophobia amongst those entrusted with the care of seniors' (Cahill *et al.* 2000). The same report by Cahill *et al.* states:

> A number of the problems faced by LGBT elders also stem from the fact that they often do not have the same family support systems as heterosexual people. This is compounded by the failure of the state to recognize their same-sex families. Many gay men and lesbians already have experience providing care.

For older LGBTs this is a particular issue when faced with the need for care or medical intervention. For transgender people it can be significant as their medical histories will reveal, and their bodies may show the marks of, transition.

Older lesbians and gay men emphasise the lack of resources available to them and that they need to develop survival strategies which may further isolate them (Heaphey and Yip 2006). There is perhaps a greater reliance on non-traditional care-giving, and the differences when compared to heterosexual older adults include a lesser reliance on spouses, children, parents, siblings and in-laws and greater reliance on friends and other informal care givers (*Improving the Lives of LGBT Older Adults* 2010).

Maintenance of ties with the family of origin was important in making the decision on whether to come out or not. It is this potential isolation that is an issue. One study by the Brookdale Centre in New York (Musingarimi 2008) showed that up to 75% of the older LGBT population lived alone and 90% were childless. The subject of whom do older LGBT people rely upon as they age and need outside intervention is important. Relations with families of origin are important, but many rely upon networks and friendships developed from the sexual community in which they live (Heaphey and Yip 2006). A further important aspect of reliance upon networks is the disappearance of families as a result of HIV/Aids. It is estimated that over 17% of new HIV-positive cases occur in people aged 50 and above.[8] Such statistics may suggest that LGBT older adults in general are vulnerable to certain physical and mental health challenges for which older people who live alone are at greater risk; these include falls, malnutrition, depression and substance abuse. It has been suggested, however, that the life course experiences of LGBT older adults may have prepared them with greater resources to enable them to live alone successfully (Grant 2010).

Older LGBT people are more likely than the population at large to rely upon families of choice as they age, although there are further problems associated with this. As Nancy Knauer (2009) states:

> Beyond the issue of legal recognition, however, LGBT chosen families have a much more fundamental shortcoming: LGBT chosen families are almost always single-generational, due in part to the ageism within the LGBT community and internalized homophobia … The single-generational nature of these chosen families poses obvious problems in the case of eldercare and deprives LGBT elders of the benefits of multigenerational support groups. In the case of LGBT chosen families, the group's resources will be increasingly strained as the members of the group all age in unison. As the group members become progressively older and possibly more infirm, the level of care that they can provide to the other members of the group will naturally diminish.

---

[8] Presentation by Jim Campbell, President of National Association of HIV Over 50 (NAHOF) as part of 'Make room for all: diversity, cultural competency and discrimination in aging America', presentations, testimony, and organisational materials from the National Gay and Lesbian Task Force Summit and Hearing held in Washington, DC, 11 December 2005.

This is interesting because it appears to view families of choice in a heterosexual context, i.e. a multi-generational unit. LGB families are perhaps more complex. Many older gay men and lesbians had entered heterosexual relationships during their lifetime and there may be a resulting overlap with the friends who may make up the particular family (Weston 1991). A small but interesting study is reported in De Vries and Hoctel (2007) of a number of older gay men and lesbians who were asked questions about friendship and family. When asked whether they considered their friends to be their family, all but one considered this to be so in some manner. The dissenting person distinguished between the role of friends and family and is quoted as saying (p. 219) 'with a friend, there isn't an obligation to rescue, whereas with a family member there is'. The existence of that support network with 'the obligation to rescue' may be the issue for older gay and lesbian people, in contrast to heterosexual people; although it has to be said that some older people, regardless of their sexuality, live alone and do not have family support networks. The same study then asked how these 'family-friends' were defined. The answers were in terms of self-disclosure ('a true friend is someone you can confide in'); sociability ('you share good times and bad times with'); assistance ('a person you can count on for emotional support'); and shared activities ('someone willing to co-operate in doing things'). Finally they were asked whether they believed that friendships are more important to gays and lesbians than to heterosexuals. A small majority responded affirmatively and the authors (De Vries and Hoctel 2007) noted that:

> The vast majority of those responding affirmatively to this question raised issues about families of choice in their comments. The basic tenet in all of these remarks is that friendships are more important to gay men and lesbians because their friends, for various reasons, become their family. Inherent in this idea is that gays and lesbians need each other more than heterosexuals do, because the support that a family of origin might ordinarily supply is absent.

Legislative protection

The first same-sex couple to marry in California in February 2004 were an older lesbian couple. Del Martin was born as Dorothy Taliaferro in 1921 in San Francisco. She was married for four years and had one daughter before coming out. She studied journalism and human sexuality. Phyllis Lyon was born in 1924 in Oklahoma. She was a writer and reporter for several different newspapers in her career. They had lived together for more than fifty years.[9] Shortly afterwards, the State of California withdrew the possibility of same-sex marriage.

There is an important distinction in law to be made between lesbians, gays and bisexuals as a group and transgender people as a separate group (Cook-Daniels 2002). In the United Kingdom these different groups are recognised in protective legislation. The Equality Act 2010 defines sexual orientation as a sexual orientation towards persons of the same sex, persons of the opposite sex, or persons of the same sex and of the opposite sex.[10] Thus the legislation, which is designed to provide protection from discrimination, includes heterosexuals in the definition of sexual orientation. The Civil Partnership Act 2004 also provides for the legal recognition of same-sex partnerships.[11]

The USA does not have Federal legislation protecting LGBs from discrimination on sexual orientation grounds. There has been a long-running campaign for a national Employment Non-Discrimination Act (ENDA) to stop discrimination on the grounds of sexual orientation and gender identity. Although the draft legislation is making progress, there does seem to be a continuing reluctance to include gender identity as opposed to sexual orientation. Action has mostly been left to the states and municipalities in this regard. As a result, some twenty states and the District of Columbia prohibit discrimination based on sexual orientation.[12]

A major issue for older same-sex couples has been the need to have their partners given the same recognition as those in heterosexual relationships. In the UK this is achievable, since the adoption of the Civil Partnership Act. An example of such discrimination had occurred in *K.B. v. National Health Service*.[13] This case concerned a nurse who had worked for the National Health Service for some twenty years. She had a long-term emotional and domestic relationship with a person who was born a woman but, with surgery, transitioned to a man. He was unable to

---

[9] Information from the website of About.Com: http://lesbianlife.about.com/od/artistswriter-set1/p/DelandPhyllis.htm.

[10] Section 12(1).

[11] Background information can be found in the UK Government consultation document titled 'Civil Partnership: A Framework for the Legal Recognition of Same-Sex Couples', 2003.

[12] An example is California's Fair Employment and Housing Act; Government Code 12900–12996, which includes provisions concerning race, religious creed, color, national origin, ancestry, physical disability, mental disability, medical condition, marital status, sex, age or sexual orientation of any person; see further Lococo and Kleiner (2000).

[13] Case 117/01 *K.B. v. National Health Service* [2004] ECR I-541.

amend his birth certificate, and although they went through an exchange of vows at an 'adapted church ceremony' they were not regarded as married by the claimant's employer. The result of this was that there would be no entitlement to a survivor's pension in the event of the claimant's death. The European Court of Justice held that:

> It follows from the foregoing that Article 141 EC, in principle, precludes legislation, such as that at issue before the national court, which, in breach of the ECHR, prevents a couple such as K.B. and R. from fulfilling the marriage requirement which must be met for one of them to be able to benefit from part of the pay of the other.

Similarly, in *Christine Goodwin v. The United Kingdom*[14] the European Court of Human Rights had stated that a male to female transsexual who was refused a state pension at the same time as other women were entitled to it had suffered a disadvantage:

> The lack of legal recognition of her changed gender had been the cause of numerous discriminatory and humiliating experiences in her everyday life. In the past, in particular from 1990 to 1992, she was abused at work and did not receive proper protection from discrimination.[15]

Protection from discrimination on the grounds of sexual orientation is still an issue in many states in the USA, with some fifteen of them having actually passed anti gay partnership laws (Howenstine 2006). Campaigners have been able to use the prohibition against sex discrimination to fight discrimination based on gender, which is said to include sex stereotyping, i.e. on the basis of attributes which are stereotypically associated with different sexes. Thus in Price Waterhouse[16] a female senior manager was refused a partnership. She, according to the Court, was generally viewed as a highly competent individual, but she was also regarded by some as aggressive and difficult to work with. She was advised to walk, talk and dress more femininely as well as to wear makeup, have her hair styled and wear jewellery. Her aggressiveness and manner were not seen as feminine attributes. The Court concluded that 'an employer who acts on the belief that a woman cannot be aggressive, or that she must not be, has acted on the basis of gender'. This positive outcome has been relied upon elsewhere. In *Jimmie L. Smith v. City of Salem, Ohio*[17] a lieutenant in the City Fire Department had been diagnosed with gender identity disorder and began expressing a

---

[14] Application no. 28957/95 ECHR 11.7.2002.   [15] Para 60.
[16] *Price Waterhouse v. Hopkins* 490 U.S. 228, 109 S.Ct 1775; 104 L.Ed2nd 268 (1989).
[17] *Jimmie L. Smith v. City of Salem, Ohio* 2004 WL 1745840; 6th Cir (Ohio) 2004.

more feminine appearance. He was the subject of various comments from co-workers, so informed his immediate supervisor in confidence of his plans to transition. His supervisor nevertheless broke confidentiality and informed his superiors, who then took various actions against the complainant in order to encourage him to leave. He claimed that he had suffered sex discrimination contrary to Title VII. The Federal District Court held that Title VII protection was unavailable to transsexuals. Title VII of the Civil Rights Act 1964 provides that 'it shall be unlawful employment practice for an employer … to discriminate against any individual with respect to his compensation, terms, conditions, or privileges of employment because of such individual's race, color, religion, sex, or national origin'. On appeal, the Court concluded that a failure to conform to sex stereotypes amounted to sex discrimination:

> After *Price Waterhouse* an employer who discriminates against women because, for instance, they do not wear dresses or makeup, is engaging in sex discrimination because the discrimination would not occur but for the victim's sex. It follows that employers who discriminate against men because they *do* wear dresses and makeup, or otherwise act femininely, are also engaging in sex discrimination.[18]

For transgender people the issue is one of gender identity and it is treated, correctly, in the UK, as a sex discrimination matter. Transgender people in the United Kingdom are provided with protection by section 7 of the Equality Act 2010[19] which is concerned with discrimination on the grounds of gender reassignment. The legislation refers to discrimination on the ground that an individual intends to undergo, is undergoing or has undergone gender reassignment. In addition to this, the Gender Recognition Act 2004 provides that a person over the age of 18 years may make an application for a gender recognition certificate (Section 1(1)). The application will be reviewed by a Gender Recognition Panel who will grant a certificate if certain conditions are met. These are that the applicant has or has had gender dysphoria, has lived in the acquired gender throughout the period of two years ending with the date on which the application is made, and intends to continue to live in the acquired gender until death. The effect of obtaining such a certificate is to legally acquire the sought-for gender.

---

[18] At *7. [19] Previously contained in Section 2A of the Sex Discrimination Act 1975.

A UK Employment Tribunal decision shows the contrast now between the UK and the USA. In *X v. Brighton and Hove Council*[20] the Council was ordered to pay £34,765.18 for twice victimising and discriminating against a transgender ex-employee. In 2003 a teacher had registered with a teacher recruitment agency to try and find work. She lost the chance of work when her previous manager responded to a reference request with a secret fax providing information about her change of gender and the fact that she had previously alleged discrimination. This treatment was held to amount to discrimination and victimisation (retaliation).

The USA does not have Federal legislation protecting transgender people from discrimination on gender identity grounds. As noted above, the success in 2007 in the House of Representatives adopting ENDA was limited in that it did not include gender identity as an issue for discrimination. As with sexual orientation, action has been left to the state and local level, with the result that only some thirteen states have adopted some legislation aimed at stopping such discrimination (Ramos *et al.* 2008). One example of this is California, where a new law came into force at the beginning of 2007 specifically excluding discrimination on the grounds of sexual orientation and gender identity in state programmes and activities.

Bibliography

Albeida, R. 2009. *Poverty in the Lesbian, Gay and Bisexual Community.* Los Angeles: The Williams Institute, University of Los Angeles

Albelda, R., Badgett, Lee M. V., Schneebaum, A. and Gates, G. J. 2009. *Poverty in the Lesbian, Gay and Bisexual Community.* The Williams Institute, University of California, Los Angeles

Aspinall, P. J. 2009. *Estimating the Size and Composition of the Lesbian, Gay and Bisexual Population.* London: Equality and Human Rights Commission

Beauchamp, Dennis, Skinner, Jim and Wiggins, Perry 2001. 'LGBT persons in Chicago: a survey of needs and perceptions', Chicago Task Force on LGBT Aging

Birch, H. 2009. *Dementia, Lesbians and Gay Men.* Paper 15, Adelaide: Alzheimer's Australia

---

[20] Employment Tribunal decision: *X v. Brighton and Hove City Council* [2006/7] taken from the website of the Equality and Human Rights Commission www.equalityhuman-rights.com; there are other important decisions on the subject of discrimination against transgender people, in particular *P v. S and Cornwall County Council* [1996] IRLR 347 and *Chessington World of Adventure v. Reed* [1997] IRLR 556.

Bocherty, S. and Creegan, C. 2009. *Moving Forward: Putting Sexual Orientation in the Public Domain*. London: Equality and Human Rights Commission

Bytheway, Bill, Ward, Richard, Holland, Caroline and Peace, Sheila 2007. 'Sexuality and sexual orientation', in *Too Old: Older People's Accounts of Discrimination, Exclusion and Rejection*. London: Help the Aged

Cahill, S., South, K. and Spade, J. 2000. *Outing Age: Public Policy Issues Affecting Gay, Lesbian, Bisexual and Transgender Elders*. New York: The Policy Institute of the National Gay and Lesbian Task Force Foundation, www.thetaskforce.org/. Accessed 22 February 2011

Commission for Social Care Inspection 2006. *Putting People First: Equality and Diversity Matters; Providing Appropriate Services for Lesbian, Gay and Bisexual and Transgender people* (replaced by the Care Quality Commission in 2009)

Cook-Daniels, L. 2002. 'Transgender elders and SOFFAs: a primer'. Paper presented at the 110th Annual Convention of the American Psychological Association, Chicago, Illinois

Cummings, Sherry M. and Galambos, Colleen (eds.) 2004. *Diversity and Aging in the Social Environment*. Haworth Social Work Practice Press

Department of Health and Department for Work and Pensions. 2006. *A Sure Start to Later Life: Ending Inequalities for Older People*. A Social Exclusion Unit Final Report. London: Office of the Deputy Prime Minister

De Vries, B. and Hoctel, P. 2007. 'The family-friends of older gay men and lesbians', in Niels Teunis and Gilbert Herdt (eds.), *Sexual Inequalities and Social Justice*. Berkeley: University of California Press, 213–32

Ellison, G. and Gunstone, B. 2009. *Sexual Orientation Explored: A Study of Identity, Attraction, Behaviour and Attitudes in 2009*. London: Equality and Human Rights Commission

Gallanis, T. P. 2002. 'Aging and the non traditional family', *University of Memphis Law Review* 32: 607

Garrett, G. 1994. 'Homophobia among the elderly'. Masters dissertation, California State University, Los Angeles

'Good Jobs Now! 2006. A snapshot of the economic health of San Francisco's Transgender Communities'. Survey from the *San Francisco Guardian*

Grant, J. M. 2010. *Outing Age 2010*. National Gay and Lesbian Task Force Policy Institute, USA

Grossman, A. H., D'Augelli, A. R. and O'Connell, T. S. 2003. 'Being lesbian, gay, bisexual, and sixty or older in North America', in B. Heaphy, D. Thompson and A. K. T. Yip (eds.), *Uneven Possibilities: Understanding Non-heterosexual Ageing and the Implications of Social Change*. Sociological Research Online vol. 8 no. 4, www.socresonline.org.uk/8/4/heaphy.html para 5.1. Accessed 22 February 2011

Heaphy, B., and Yip, A. K. T. 2006. 'Policy implications of ageing sexualities', *Social Policy and Society* 5(4): 443–51

Heaphy, Brian, Yip, Andrew and Thompson, Debbie 2003. *Lesbian, Gay and Bisexual Lives over 50*. Nottingham: York House Publications

Herek, G. M. 1990. 'The context of anti gay violence', *Journal of Interpersonal Violence* 5: 316–33

Howenstine, David W. 2006. 'Beyond rational relations: the constitutional infirmities of anti-gay partnership laws under the equal protection clause', Washington Law Review 81: 417

Improving the Lives of LGBT Older Adults 2010. LGBT Movement Advancement Project (MAP) and Services and Advocacy for Gay, Lesbian. Bisexual and Transgender Adults (SAGE), http://sageusa.org/uploads/Advancing%20Equality%20for%20LGBT%20Elders%20%5BFINAL%20COMPRESSED%5D.pdf. Accessed 22 February 2011

Is Your T Written in Disappearing Ink? 2001. *A Checklist for Gender Inclusion*, FORGE and Transgender Aging Network, November, www.forge-forward.org/TAN. Accessed 22 February 2011

Jones, T. C. and Nystrom, N. M. 2002. 'Looking back . . . looking forward: addressing the lives of lesbians 55 and older', *Journal of Women and Aging* 14(3/4): 59–76

Knauer, N. 2009. 'LGBT elder law: toward equity in aging', *Harvard Journal of Law and Gender* 32(1)

Kochman, A. 1997. 'Gay and lesbian elderly: historical overview and implications for social work practice', *Journal of Gay and Lesbian Social Services* 6(1): 1–9

Lococo, Anna M. and Kleiner, Brian H. 2000. 'New developments concerning the fair employment and housing act', *Equal Opportunities International* 19 (6/7): 3–33

Miller, M., André, A., Ebin, J. and Bessonova, L. 2007. *Bisexual Health*. Binet: National Gay and Lesbian Taskforce

Mitchell, M. and Howarth, C. 2009. *Trans Research Review*. London: Equality and Human Rights Commission

Mitchell, M., Howarth, C., Kotecha, M. and Creegan, C. 2009. *Sexual Orientation Research Review 2008* London: Equality and Human Rights Commission

Musingarimi, P. 2008. *Older Gay, Lesbian and Bisexual People in the UK: A Policy Brief*. International Longevity Centre, www.ilcuk.org.uk/files/pdf_pdf_68.pdf. Accessed 22 February 2011

Out and Aging 2006. The MetLife Study of Lesbian and Gay Baby Boomers. MetLife Mature Market Institute

Out of the Shadows 2003. Accessed from the website of the Alzheimer's Society, UK; taken from Community Care, October 2003, www.communitycare.co.uk

Ramos, C., Badgett, Lee M. V. and Sears, B. 2008. *Evidence of Employment Discrimination on the Basis of Sexual Orientation and Gender Identity: Complaints Filed with State Enforcement Agencies 1999–2007*. Los Angeles: The Williams Institute, UCLA School of Law

Report of the Interdepartmental Working Group on Transsexual People 2000. Home Office www.pfc.org.uk/files/workgrp/wgtrans.pdf. Accessed 22 February 2011

River, L. 2006. *Report to Age Concern Camden: A Feasibility Study of the Needs of Older Lesbians in Camden and Surrounding Boroughs.* London: Polari

Towards Equality and Diversity: Report of Responses on Age 2003. DTI *Aging in the Lesbian Gay Bisexual Transgender Communities.* San Francisco: San Francisco Human Rights Commission and Aging and Adult Services Commission

Stryker, S. 2008. *Transgender History.* Berkeley, CA: Seal Press

Turnbull, Dr Annmarie 2001. *Opening Doors: The Needs of Lesbians and Gay Men: A Literature Review.* London: Age Concern England

Ward, R., Jones, R., Hughes, J., Humberstone, N. and Pearson, R. 2008. 'Intersections of ageing and sexuality', in R. Ward and B. Bytheway (eds.), *Researching Age and Multiple Discrimination.* London: Centre for Policy on Ageing London

Weston, K. 1991. *Families We Choose: Lesbians, Gays, Kinship.* New York: Columbia University Press

Whittle, S., Turner, L. and Al-Alami, M. 2007. *Engendered Penalties: Transgender and Transsexual People's Experiences of Inequality and Discrimination.* London: The Equalities Review

Yoshino, Kenyi 2000. 'The epistemic contract of bisexual erasure', *Stanford Law Review* 52(2): 353–460

7

Age and ethnicity

SHARON KOEHN AND KAREN KOBAYASHI

Introduction

Compared to many countries in Europe, Canada is a relatively 'young' nation, but its demographic profile is undergoing dramatic changes. Older adults are the most rapidly expanding population in Canada, expected to grow from 13.7% today to almost 24% by the year 2031 (BC Ministry of Health Services 2004). Equally striking is the increase of ethnocultural minority older adults (EMOA), who now comprise more than 25% of this age cohort (Statistics Canada 2006a). Diversification is especially apparent in Canada's three major immigrant-receiving metropolitan areas: Vancouver, Toronto and Montreal.

Somewhat belatedly, Canadian researchers, funding agencies and publishers are beginning to pay more attention to this diverse sub-population. Here we consider literature on both new immigrants and longer-term Canadians who, by virtue of their visible characteristics, may continue to experience discrimination. We recognise, nonetheless, that there are marked differences among them and that some EMOA are clearly more 'at risk' than others, with many such differences shaped by socially defined characteristics such as gender, race, class, sexuality, immigration status and so on (Iyer, Sen and Östlin 2008). Indeed, oppressions experienced throughout the life course influence a person's social capital,[1] which may be further diminished in the face of role reversal and loss of status, as well as discrimination experienced post-migration (Sadavoy, Meier and Ong 2004; Guruge, Kanthasamy and Santos 2008; Koehn 2009; Koehn, Spencer and Hwang 2010). Ultimately, then, 'statuses and their intersection influence a person's life

---

[1] Here defined, per Bourdieu, as the economic, social and symbolic power held by individuals and reproduced by institutions and practices (Siisiainen 2003).

chances, in terms of education, labour force participation, living arrangements, health status, and ultimately, the quality of life in old age' (McDonald, 2008: 139).

But these relationships are not well understood. A scoping review team (Kozak, Koehn and Khamisa, 2010), of which this chapter's authors are members, recently found that the literature on the health and health care access of EMOA was distributed across a broad span of diverse disciplines, as reflected by the publication of 791 eligible articles across 192 journals. The two journals publishing the most articles (twenty-five and seventeen) represented the distinct disciplines of social work and geriatric medicine; the dialectally opposed paradigmatic stances found in these two journals are characteristic of this field, which is rife with contradictory evidence.

Understanding the diverse experiences of ageing both across and within Canada's numerous ethnocultural groups thus requires complex theoretical and methodological approaches that move beyond a focus on ethnicity and age to explore the effects of other interlocking markers of social inequality in studying the lives of older adults. We suggest that it is time for a more decisive shift towards an intersectionality approach in ethnogerontology. To illustrate the value of this approach, we will limit our discussion to the context of health status and access to health care. For while many people lead healthy, productive lives as they age, older adults in general average more than two times the number of physician contacts per year than do persons under the age of 65 (Kelchner 2002) and this ratio doubles again amongst the old-old, aged 85+ (Nie *et al.* 2008).

Gerontological theories of difference

In the early years, efforts to construct theoretical models in the sociological and anthropological literature on ageing and culture or ethnicity were limited to an examination of conventional concepts such as disengagement (Vatuk 1980), activity (Palmore and Maeda, 1985), modernisation (Cowgill and Holmes 1972) and assimilation (Osako 1979). Overly simplistic and generalised to diverse populations of older adults, such theories did not stand up to the evidence and have been routinely critiqued (Driedger and Chappell 1987; Gelfand 2003).

By the late 1970s, however, new theories – such as the concepts of double and multiple jeopardy – recognised the negative impact that certain statuses, namely age and visible minority status[2] and later class and gender, conferred on individuals (Dowd and Bengtson 1978; Markides 1983). The concept of 'triple jeopardy' specifically identified the additive effect of age, sex and ethnicity as placing very old immigrant women at a relative disadvantage to other Canadians in terms of their mental functioning (Havens and Chappell 1983). This theory continues to be used as a framework for understanding the health status of older immigrant women (Public Health Agency of Canada et al. 2007). Other studies on mental health have nonetheless recognised that concepts such as ethnicity and SES are multidimensional, as reflected in their findings that factors such as living arrangements (e.g. co-residence with children), health status, experience of stressful life events, social connectedness, etc. (Wykle and Musil 1993; Mui 1998, 2002; Lai 2000; Kim 2007;) increase the probability of depression amongst EMOA. Yet others have explored the influence of social determinants of health[3] independently of gender and found similarly high rates of depression (Stokes et al. 2001) or have found that, while there are differences by gender, these are not statistically significant (Wu, Tran and Amjad 2004).

Cool's (1981) age-levelling hypothesis ran counter to multiple jeopardy theories by suggesting that age itself levelled out racial and ethnic inequalities experienced by older adults earlier in the life course. Theoretical developments like age stratification (Riley 1971; Foner and Kertzer 1978; A. Foner, 1979; N. Foner, 1984) and political economy (Estes 1979; Walker 1981), on the other hand, were grounded in the understanding that issues of structural inequality were central to understanding the experiences of EMOA. Age stratification theorists focused their discussion on inequities in access to various types of resources that were contingent on age. Feeling that age stratification theory failed to take into account the dynamics of inequality and power relationships, however, Marxist and neo-Marxist critics developed the political economy of ageing perspective to address this shortcoming.

---

[2] Statistics Canada (2006b) defines visible minorities as 'persons, other than Aboriginal peoples, who are non-Caucasian in race or non-white in colour'. More importantly, they are people subjected to *racialisation*, or 'the process through which groups and their practices are identified by reference to visible physical characteristics, thus grounding group distinctions in biology' (Johnson et al. 2004).

[3] The social determinants of health are the circumstances in which people are born, grow up, live, work and age, and the systems put in place to deal with illness. These circumstances are in turn shaped by a wider set of forces: economics, social policies and politics (Public Health Agency of Canada 2003).

Meanwhile, anthropologists were exploring, through ethnographic studies, the biological, psychological, social and cultural dimensions of age in order to comprehend its relationship to health (Fry 1981b). The discipline's 'concern for dimensions and complex interactions' sought to enrich gerontology 'both through comparative and holistic research' (Fry, 1981a: 2). While these studies provided valuable insights into the operation of various dimensions of difference, they nonetheless tended to be atheoretical and uncritical in their analysis, paying no heed to the manner in which power imbalances and discrimination shape the experience of age or its intersecting categories. Exploration of a variety of experiences of ageing nonetheless began to cast doubts on the validity and explanatory value of socially constructed categories such as ethnicity and the recognition of the importance of questioning such categories relative to social policy. Sokolovsky (1985, 1990a) has argued, for example, that an 'overemphasis on ethnicity as a resource has been overly optimistic, especially in the area of informal social supports and networks of exchange' (1990a: 203). While differences in networks between ethnic groups are evident in many studies, the nature of such support and their differential effect by gender, for example, are rarely interrogated. To illustrate, he cites Cohler's (1982) research demonstrating the benefit of ethnic embeddedness on adjustment to old age for Italian-American men, but the opposite for women. While the incipient deconstruction of categories and recognition of dynamic intersections between them were apparent here, it would take another twenty years for the notion of intersectionality to take hold in gerontology.

Other important contributions to the multidisciplinary hodgepodge of gerontological theory came from social work. The subdiscipline of ethnogerontology arose out of a concern with addressing the needs of a burgeoning heterogeneous ageing population (Crewe 2005). Jackson's (1967) early work with African-American older adults led her to define ethnogerontology as 'the study of the causes, processes, and consequences of race, national origin, and culture on individual and population aging in the three broad areas of biological, psychological, and social aging' (Jackson 1985: 266). Concerned initially with the confluence of old age and race (or rather its social construction), ethnogerontology brings a more critical gaze to the examination of age and ethnicity to which the lens of oppression is applied. Focused primarily on the 'inadequacies of access and availability of services and resources' (Crewe 2005: 50) to EMOA, ethnogerontological social workers advocate for cultural competence as a solution. Theoretical perspectives adopted by this group share a concern with access to resources. The 'multiple hierarchy stratification' theory draws on both the double jeopardy hypothesis and life course perspectives located at opposite ends of a continuum and 'focuses on the importance of the effects of history, social structure, and individual meaning to the aging process' (Hooyman and Kiyak 1996, as cited in Crewe 2005: 52).

The need for an intersectional approach to research was thus clearly established during the 1980s, yet few researchers in this area applied it in their work. With the growth of more critical perspectives since about 1999, research on ageing and ethnicity has started to recognise the diversity both across and within groups, and to address the complex interplay among statuses in ethnic older adult populations (e.g. Dossa 1999; Gee 1999; Kobayashi 2000; Calasanti and Slevin 2001; Estes, Mahakian and Weitz 2001; Koehn 2009). The remainder of this chapter will first describe intersectional approaches to research, and then furnish examples that illustrate the use of this approach in the analysis of our own work in the domain of health and ageing among EMOA. These in turn explicate how social inequities are generated through discrimination at multiple levels.

Adopting an intersectional approach

Intersectionality considers the *simultaneous* interactions between multiple dimensions of social identity (for example, sex, gender, age, visible minority and immigration status) that are contextualised within broader systems of power, domination and oppression (such as sexism, ageism and racism) (Hankivsky *et al.* 2009). Intersectionality differs from predecessors like multiple/triple jeopardy in that it is not an 'additive linear model': 'In the language of statistics, the analysis of intersectionality usually requires the use of "interaction effects" – or "multilevel," "hierarchical," "ecological," or "contextual" modelling – all of which introduce more complexity in estimation and interpretation" (McCall 2005: 1787–8). From this perspective, power imbalances and discrimination, as well as positive health care experiences, are thus understood as unique to each individual's constellation of intersecting identities, social roles and the broader social and political context in which they exist (Hankivsky *et al.* 2009). These intersections are at play at each of the micro, meso and macro levels – that is, relative to our identities, and to our interactions with others in different sociocultural contexts, and at the broader societal level wherein values are entrenched as policies (Colleen Reid, in Spence, Koehn and Kobayashi 2009).

For visible minority older adults, the process of racialisation greatly impacts health and quality of life. The social category of race and the corresponding social production of racial identities interact with other fundamental determinants of health such as ethnicity, age, gender and immigrant status to impact an individual's ability to access the key social resources necessary for health promotion and maintenance (Benoit and Shumka 2009). In practical terms, racism affects health through systemic and individual-level occurrences of discrimination, marginalisation and susceptibility to poverty, to name a few.

Intersectionality is essentially a theoretical and methodological counterbalance to the tendency for much research to reproduce the essentialising and 'othering' that occurs in society. 'Othering' practices, typically invisible to those who perpetrate them, take the form of ahistorical and abstracted over-generalisations that are applied to specific individuals to explain their behaviour (Johnson *et al.* 2004). Typically, these explanations invoke the socially constructed notions of 'race', culture or even gender as a means of creating distinctions between 'us' and 'them'. Othering thus fails to recognise the complex interactions between different 'categories' or sources of social inequity and how the construction of those categories is based on the experiences and hence the biases of the speaker. This form of inadvertent discrimination often originates or is supported by policies and institutional structures intended to be equitable but designed in accordance with Anglocentric, middle-class values (Brotman 2003).

An intersectional approach thus behooves us to ask how age, ethnicity, gender, visible minority and immigration status interact to create barriers to health and social care access for EMOA. The processes of discrimination are apparent in such an approach.

Methodological approaches to intersectionality

While much has been written about the theoretical premises of intersectionality, what is less clear is how one goes about *doing* it. McCall (2005) suggests that there are three stages or levels at which intersectionality is practised. The first of these – anticategorical complexity – finds its origins in anthropology, which has long since been successful in deconstructing categories that rarely hold water cross-culturally. In their critiques of modern Western philosophy, history and language, poststructuralists (Lechte 1994) in particular have been especially active in questioning the 'givenness' of categories of difference such as 'race' and even 'gender'. The importance of understanding such categories as complex social constructions within which specific manifestations may be infinite or at least range along broad continua entails a shift away from Cartesian dualisms or dichotomies such as male/female, black/white or ethnic/non-ethnic that underlie othering.

This leads us then to question the very premises upon which our enquiry is based. For example, *ethnicity* can be defined as 'a group's shared cultural heritage based on common ancestry, language, music, food and religion' (Hankivsky *et al.* 2009). Like 'race', it is often treated as a determinant of health. According to Illife and Manthorpe (2004: 283), however, 'Empirical research on dementia and ethnicity reveals that intra-ethnic group variation is greater than interethnic group variation; supporting the view that ethnicity as a category [when defined as particular shared cultural characteristics] may not have great explanatory power and may foster a category fallacy.' They add that a lack of clarity about the more salient determinants of health that are subsumed under the concept of ethnicity, such as migration, education, health beliefs and socio-economic status (SES), relegate broader health care access issues to an ethnic minority agenda.

Their observation also draws our attention to the uncritical treatment of the notion of *culture* as a determinant of health. Too often we see evidence of an inherent but unstated assumption that differences in health outcomes between ethnic groups are *de facto* attributable to cultural differences (e.g. Jones, Chow and Gatz 2006). This rests on a simplistic equation of culture with ethnicity, nationality and language that assumes that culture is static and homogeneous (Kleinman and Benson 2006). From a critical anthropological point of view, culture *does not* refer to essential identifiers of a group; rather it is a process of meaning-construction wherein people's practices – which are embedded in political, economic and social realities – operate in a dialectical relationship with systems of signification. Culture is defined in reference to these practices and vice versa (Wedeen 2002). Immigrants have thus been found to adapt cultural practices to their environments. For example, faced with the challenges of dementia care giving, the adult-child carers of Chinese-Canadian persons with dementia have shifted the meaning of filial piety that would traditionally mandate that they take care of ageing parents in the home, to the responsibility of ensuring that they seek out the most appropriate, high-quality long-term care facilities (Hicks and Lam 1999; Ho *et al.* 2003). This ability to renegotiate cultural meanings nonetheless depends on the individual's position in the matrix of social determinants, including age. Failure to acknowledge these determinants in explanations of behaviour that resort to culture are seen by critical theorists as essentialising and discriminatory – that is, they oversimplify the various influences on the person's thoughts and actions, and often do not take into account the conditions that give rise to them. In so doing, the burden of responsibility is shifted to the individual and his or her culture, and the underlying conditions are not addressed. For example, people may not adequately access the services they need due to barriers such as the unsuitability of the service (hours, language, etc.) or lack of appropriate outreach. Culture should nonetheless be understood as a determinant of health in so far as:

> Some persons or groups may face additional health risks due to a socio-economic environment, which is largely determined by dominant cultural values that contribute to the perpetuation of conditions such as marginalization, stigmatization, loss or devaluation of language and culture and lack of access to culturally appropriate health care and services.

> (Public Health Agency of Canada 2003)

These examples demonstrate that no category can be reduced to a single axis of difference. Yet the second type of intersectional analysis – intra-categorical complexity (McCall 2005) – zeroes in on a social location at the intersection of single dimensions of multiple categories. This typically entails analysis of a single social group at a neglected point of intersection of multiple master categories *or* a particular social setting or ideological construction, or both, and is characteristic of the ethnographic work already described (e.g., Fry 1981b; Sokolovsky 1990b). Thus while these studies question 'the homogenizing generalizations that go with the territory of classification and categorization', they do not reject them altogether. Most important is the 'process by which [categories] are produced, experienced, reproduced, and resisted in everyday life' (McCall 2005: 1783).

The third type of intersectional enquiry that McCall describes speaks to efforts to employ this approach in quantitative studies. Intercategorical complexity is thus concerned with 'the complexity of relationships among multiple social groups within and across analytical categories' (McCall 2005: 1786). Enquiries of this nature begin with the supposition that relationships of inequality exist between groups. Social determinants of health, such as age and ethnicity, are viewed as anchors in understanding inequities, but they are not fixed in their relationship to outcomes, because they interact with other determinants as well as biological factors in different contexts (McCall 2005). Categories are understood to be imperfect and ever changing, but the necessity of adopting them provisionally is accepted in order to proceed with analyses that explicate the relationships among them. Here, relationships of inequality are the *focus of* rather than the *background to* the analysis. Researchers are now beginning to develop methodologies that capture the multidimensionality of such categories. For example, Sen, Iyer and Mukherjee (2009: 401) probe the 'relative importance and magnitudes of class and gender inequities' as they relate to health outcomes.

Health inequities, ageing and ethnicity

A popular hypothesis concerning the health status of immigrants that is well supported in the Canadian literature is that of the 'healthy immigrant effect' (HIE), which posits that recent immigrants are healthier (and subsequently, that they use the health care system less) than their Canadian-born counterparts, but that, over time, this health status advantage decreases (Dunn and Dyck 2000; Newbold and Danforth 2003; Ali, McDermott and Gravel 2004; Gee, Kobayashi and Prus 2004; Newbold 2005a;). These studies also find that recent immigrants from Asia report better health status than those from Europe (Chen, Wilkins and Ng 1996; Laroche 2000; Ali *et al.*, 2004). This initial advantage is associated with self-selection for the lengthy and expensive process of migration and the medical screening required of all immigrants (Kennedy, McDonald and Biddle 2006). Health status declines, as indicated by higher morbidity of chronic disease (Newbold 2006), or increased body mass index (McDonald and Kennedy 2005) among longer-term immigrants, for example, are often associated with changes in behaviour following migration (Perez 2002; Newbold 2005b; Dean and Wilson 2010;).

Beiser (2005) denounces this emphasis on 'sick' and 'healthy' immigrants as 'wrong-headed' and asks instead what policy-makers in Canada are doing to ensure the ongoing health of its immigrants. Specifically, he argues, we need to adopt a model that examines 'salient resettlement stressors that act alone or interact with predisposition in order to create health risk, and the personal and social resources that reduce risk and promote well-being' (2005: S30). Support for this argument, which is consistent with an intersectionality approach, is found in the literature on older immigrants. For example, recent immigrants aged 65 and older have poorer health than both immigrants who have been in Canada longer and the Canadian-born population; this is especially true of Family Class (sponsored) immigrants and refugees (Gee *et al.* 2004; Statistics Canada 2005; Newbold 2005b). Gee *et al.* (2004) report that this disadvantage largely disappears when a number of sociodemographic, socio-economic and health behaviour factors are controlled. Still salient, however, is the fact that multiple markers of inequity recognised as social determinants of health – particularly age, SES, type of immigration, and possibly visible minority status – converge in the older Family Class immigrant or refugee. Controlling for such factors allows us to say that compared to a group of Canadian-born older adults who experience the same disadvantages, the immigrants studied are no worse off; this does not preclude the fact that the disadvantages or their intersecting influences may be found in higher proportions within a particular ethnocultural community.

Based on his study on the health care utilisation patterns of immigrants, Globerman (1998: 31) argues that age trumps immigration status as 'the strongest single determinant of health problems'. Kobayashi, Prus and Lin's (2008) comparison of self-rated health status and functional health differences between first-generation immigrant and Canadian-born persons of the same ethnocultural origin nonetheless establishes that being an immigrant does influence health status, but not always in the same direction: 'first-generation immigrants of Black and French ethnicity tend to have better health than their [Canadian-born] counterparts, while the opposite is true for those of South Asian and Chinese origins' (2008: 129). Menec, Shooshtari and Lambert's (2007) finding that Eastern European older adults in Canada are significantly more likely to rate their health as poor compared to older British Canadians, even when controlling for SES, language spoken and health status, similarly suggests that ethnicity and immigrant status do indeed matter in self-reported evaluations of health. But why is this so?

Predispositions to certain diseases exist among particular ethnic groups. For example, foreign-born populations from South Asia experience higher rates of diabetes mellitus and heart disease (Fikree and Pasha 2004; Gupta, Singh and Verma 2006; Raymond *et al.* 2009). The diversity in health status found among older adults is nonetheless better understood as the outcome of different life trajectories that are influenced only minimally by biology, genetic endowment or behaviour. Rather, it is sociocultural determinants that produce health inequities in vulnerable, at-risk populations and account for 75% of the influences on Canadians' health (Public Health Agency of Canada 2003; Canada: Standing Senate Committee on Social Affairs, Science and Technology 2009; Mikkonen and Raphael 2010). The differential impact of interactions of these factors across groups of older adults depends on their social location in Canadian society (Neysmith, O'Connell and Bezanson 2005).

Two examples of intersectional analyses

The following examples of the application of intersectional approaches to data on health inequities experienced by EMOA illustrate the relationships between markers of difference that help us to understand how the experience of immigration to Canada as older adults predisposes them to discrimination that contributes to inequities in health status and health care access. Kobayashi and Prus take an intercategorical approach to the analysis of quantitative data whereas Koehn's qualitative data is better suited to an intracategorical examination.

An intercategorical analysis of the 'healthy immigrant effect' (HIE)

In their examination of the HIE, Kobayashi and Prus (forthcoming) use an *intercategorical approach* to answer the questions, 'Do gender, age, and ethnicity matter in assessing the health of immigrants? And, if so, in what ways?' Such an approach is appropriate in that it recognises that 'pre-existing categories of difference' (Hankivsky *et al.*, 2009: 6) can be useful in exploring within- and between-group inequalities in health. Further, by including age as a salient marker of inequality, the study: (1) adds to an HIE literature that has, to date, been largely focused on examinations of the influence(s) of the typical research triumvirate of 'ethnicity–class–gender' on immigrant health; and (2) based on its findings, identifies and proposes policy responses to health inequalities among immigrant populations that can be translated cross-nationally to countries such as the USA, the UK and Australia, where similar results for the HIE have been found (Kennedy *et al.*, 2006).

By using an *intercategorical approach* to secondary data analysis to answer their research questions, Kobayashi and Prus acknowledge the potential of this type of analysis to transform the health and health care experiences of visible minority immigrant men and women at different stages of the adult life course. Further, it is their intention that findings from their study can then be explored qualitatively through in-depth interviews, focus groups and/or participant observation with mid-life and older visible minority immigrant men and women to provide insights into the self-reported and functional health statuses of individuals in these groups. Such a mixed-methods approach is a good 'fit' with an intersectionality perspective for studies on immigrant health.

The results of their study are based on data from the public-use microdata file of the 2005 (Cycle 3.1) Canadian Community Health Survey (CCHS). The sample consists of 132,221 Canadians aged 12 or older living in private occupied dwellings, with an overall response rate of approximately 85%. One of the key findings from the current study is that the *healthy immigrant effect* applies to mid-life males. Specifically, recent immigrant men – i.e., those who immigrated less than ten years ago – between the ages of 45 and 64 years have better functional and self-rated health compared to the Canadian-born. And, upon further examination, the results suggest that there is a convergence in health differences between foreign- and Canadian-born men in mid-life. Interestingly, the health advantage of recent immigrants is especially strong for visible minorities, suggesting that the observed HIE for middle-aged men is due, in part, to the exceptionally good health of recent visible minority immigrants. Finally, it should be noted that this advantage is not accounted for by differences in age, SES or health behaviours between the immigrant/visible minority groups, contradicting the argument that a healthier immigrant population can be attributed to advantages arising from such factors.

For mid-life women, the findings are less consistent with the HIE hypothesis, and the disparities are significantly influenced by visible minority status. Further, the study finds that unlike mid-life men, longer-term immigrant women in mid-life are actually disadvantaged in health (on both self-reported measures) compared to the Canadian-born, and that these differences are similar for visible and non-visible minorities even after controlling for sociodemographic, socio-economic and lifestyle factors.

A different picture emerges in later life for men, particularly for visible minority men, as recent immigrants 65 years of age and older are more likely to be disadvantaged vis-à-vis self-reported health, even after controlling for key factors. On the other hand, recent visible minority immigrant women in the latter stages of the life course fare much better on self-reported health measures. This advantage, however, disappears when the data are adjusted for other differences. The same holds true for longer-term visible minority immigrant women who are similarly disadvantaged when sociodemographic, SES and lifestyle factors are held constant.

Based on these findings, a key implication for health care policy and programme planning for immigrant men and women in mid to late adulthood – individuals that make up over one-half of the foreign-born adult population in Canada and increasingly larger proportions of the populations in the US, the UK and Australia – is noteworthy here. In particular, the findings underscore the necessity for policy-makers in these countries to address the differential health care needs of immigrant adults by gender and age group. Recent immigrant visible minority men in mid-life and, to a lesser extent, their later-life female counterparts may have fewer needs for services and programmes in the early years of their residency, while certain new immigrant subgroups, namely older men and mid-life women of colour, may actually have increased needs for services because of poor health status. This higher need is likely to persist for these women as they age.

In response to this reality, it is important that policies and programmes be developed at both the national and the provincial/state levels – particularly in urban centres in which the majority of immigrants choose to reside – that: (a) target mid-life immigrant and certain subgroups of older immigrant women as they age over time; and (b) respond to the needs of an older immigrant male population from the outset. The fact that 'evidence of strong positive selection effects for immigrants from all regions of origin in terms of education' (Kennedy et al., 2006: i) was found across all four countries in a study seeking to explain the HIE – despite differences in demographic composition and policy frameworks in the immigration and health care domains – supports the cross-national application of these findings and their policy implications.

An intracategorical analysis of sponsorship status, age and gender

A qualitative enquiry into the experiences of older Punjabi women in the Canadian province of British Columbia (BC) who were sponsored by their adult children (Koehn 1993) brought to light the importance of the *type* of immigration as a marker of difference that receives very little attention in the literature. Cultural values exert a powerful influence over family dynamics, gender roles, the construction of identity, and beliefs around health and illness, as detailed in previous work (Koehn 1993, 1999). We also know that the immigration experience itself is a strong determinant of health: 'resettlement stress, new pathogens, poverty, inter-racial and inter-generational conflict and family separation' that is common to many immigrants can exert a heavy toll on the physical and, most especially, the mental health of older immigrants (Health Canada and Kinnon 1999; Centre for Addiction and Mental Health (CAMH) 2009). Also salient, however, are the effects of discrimination and othering on the health of these sponsored older adults (Johnson et al. 2004; Koehn 2009).

In BC, almost one-third of sponsored or Family Class immigrants are aged 50+, and 60% are female (BC Stats 2006). Compared to immigrants overall, arrivals in this class have lower levels of education and English language ability. India has consistently accounted for the largest propor- tion of BC's Family Class immigrants (30% from 2000 to 2004). Unlike sponsored spouses, these older Family Class immigrants are dependent on their sponsors who must support them financially for a period of *ten* years, a significantly longer period than for any other Family Class group. During the initial dependency period, seniors may not be eligible for public pensions such as the Allowance, Old Age Security or the Guaranteed Income Supplement, social services, subsidised housing or housing subsidies, or other local benefits such as reduced fare bus passes (Koehn et al. 2010).

Family Class immigrants account for almost 80% of elders who arrive in Canada after the age of 60. Of these late-in-life immigrants, 25–40% report no source of income (Dempsey and Citizenship and Immigration Canada 2004). Approximately 60% of the income reported by this group is earned through participation in the labour market. Ageism and racialisation com- bine to limit job opportunities for these older immigrants, as do limited English skills. These inequities are perpetuated by the government's provi- sion of targeted funding to the settlement sector that prioritises return-to- work initiatives. English as a Second Language classes for seniors are thus extremely limited (Friesen and Hyndman 2004; Koehn 2009).

At least 50% of all elderly Punjabi Sikh women in Koehn's (1993) study participated in farm labour during the summer months. This can be extremely arduous work, typified by long hours, low wages and poor working conditions (Assanand, Koehn & Sethi 2007; Special Senate Committee on Aging 2009). They are nonetheless motivated to offset their sense of indebtedness to their sponsors and boost their self-esteem (Koehn 1993). Health hazards associated with farm work include der- matitis and respiratory problems associated with exposure to pesticides, and chronic musculoskeletal problems, heat stress and traumatic injury associated with stoop work over many hours under all weather condi- tions (Hansen and Donohoe 2004; Koehn 1993).

In addition, many older immigrants remain economically disadvantaged even after the ten-year period ends, because of the way the residency criterion for Old Age Security is calculated (Koehn *et al.* 2010). Reciprocal agreements on social security that Canada has with countries such as Australia, New Zealand and the United Kingdom translate into more residency credits which determine the eventual amount of Old Age Security the person will receive. Historical inequities in wealth between these Western superpowers and former colonies such as India, unable to offer reciprocal arrangements of this nature, are perpetuated by such policies, which are to the detriment of immigrants from these countries (Government of Canada 2006). Gender norms that have prevented women from participating full-time in the workforce also contribute to economic disadvantage among older women (Grewal *et al.* 2004). This is especially true of the immigrants in this age group who are among the poorest in Canada and other immigrant-receiving countries (Boyd 1989; Ahmad & Walker 1997; Choi 2002; National Advisory Council on Aging (Canada) 2005; Ordonez 2006; Joyce 2007; Zahno and Rhule 2008; Centre for Addiction and Mental Health 2009; Koehn *et al.* 2010).

As Family Class immigrants, older women can be especially vulnerable and dependent on their family sponsors. Oppressions experienced earlier in life by this cohort of older immigrant women often leave them with low levels of social capital (i.e., education, literacy, experience outside of the domestic sphere) (Raskin, Chiang-Piao Chien and Keh-Ming Lin 1992; Koehn 1993), that in turn influences determinants of health and their resettlement experience. Role reversals between younger and older Punjabi women from India often occur because younger women here typically enjoy more independence outside of the home, have a better understanding of Canadian society and its institutions, and speak more English than older women (Koehn 1993). The knowledge of older women is often deemed irrelevant here and they typically exert no economic control, resulting in a considerable drop in social status (Koehn 1993). This in turn can expose them to abuse and neglect (Choudhry 2001; Carefirst Seniors and Community Services Association 2002; Grewal, Bottorff and Hilton 2005; Tam and Neysmith 2006; Simmons 2007; Guruge *et al.* 2008; Hossem, 2009; Vancouver Cross-Cultural Seniors Network Society 2010). Elsewhere (Koehn *et al.* 2010) we have argued that this situation arises in large part due to the conditions of sponsorship itself.

Discrimination is especially apparent in Canada's immigration policy that determines that sponsored parents (i.e. older adults deemed to be an economic burden) should be dependent on their sponsors for ten years rather than the three years applied to sponsored spouses (Koehn *et al.* 2010). The reduction in the dependency period for spouses rested on evidence that the policy created power imbalances and dependency, and increased the risk of abuse or exploitation (Côté, Kérisit and Côté 2001). Yet the same concerns exist for older Family Class immigrants and for their families upon whom the responsibility for providing a social safety net falls (Koehn 1993; McLaren 2006). McLaren argues that this distinction arises from immigration policy and associated commentary (e.g. Collacott 2006) that increasingly focuses on immigrants' potential economic value as workers, and frames sponsored parents as an economic deficit and undesirable burdens on society. This position fails to recognise both the significant social and financial investment already made by working immigrants' parents in raising families to adulthood and their substantial contribution to the running of the immigrant household, particularly as childcare providers.

Among the older Punjabi participants in Koehn's (1993, 1999) research, the role of childcare provider is primarily assumed by women as per traditional gender roles. This unpaid position is accepted because it provides a role for sponsored women and offsets their sense of indebtedness to their sponsors. While it is satisfying for some, it is also tiring and precludes participation in activities that support mental and physical health such as exercise or social gatherings with peers, thus contributing to social isolation (Koehn 1993; Spence *et al.* 2009; Vancouver Cross-Cultural Seniors Network Society 2010). Frustration with the role can arise from a communication/culture gap between themselves and their children, grandchildren and the community at large. They may not share a language in common with older grandchildren, ideals around appropriate dress and activities often differ, and childrearing practices may be at odds with both the child's parents and the health and education systems in Canada. As a result, they say, the care giving affects their physical and mental health.

While a complete examination of the dynamics of inequitable access to health care experienced by EMOA in general is not feasible in this chapter (for which, see for example PRIAE (Policy Research Institute on Ageing and Ethnicity) 2003; Sadavoy *et al.* 2004; Koehn, Cameron and Kehoe, 2007; Public Health Agency of Canada *et al.* 2007; Koehn 2009), some features of the intersection of sponsorship with age and gender in particular should be noted. First, older Punjabi grandmothers responsible for care of their grandchildren and suffering from a loss of self-esteem often subjugate their own need for medical assistance to the needs of their grandchildren. Without income, English language skills or subsidised bus passes, they will also need to wait for a busy family member to provide transportation to the doctor's office – they rarely drive or even ride bicycles, as do some older Punjabi men – and to provide interpretation since interpreters are rarely available (Koehn 1993, 2009). As a result, care providers report that they often see these older sponsored immigrants, particularly women, in a crisis. Moreover, during their first ten years in Canada, they are not eligible for more than basic health services: rehabilitative services or long-term care, for example, are not publicly available to them. A decline in health status during this period can thus prove disastrous for family members and may result in a breakdown of the sponsorship relationship (Koehn *et al.* 2010). These factors in turn have deleterious consequences for their physical and mental health (Williams and Hunt 1997; Sadavoy *et al.* 2004; Public Health Agency of Canada *et al.* 2007; Centre for Addiction and Mental Health (CAMH) 2009; Vancouver Cross-Cultural Seniors Network Society 2010).

The above research examples provide two important illustrations of the different methodological approaches to interrogating intersectionality in ethnicity and ageing research. In particular, they underscore the need to appreciate and understand different epistemological standpoints in examining the complex nature – both social structural and cultural – of health inequities in multi-ethnic societies.

Conclusions

Significant changes in the demographic composition – i.e. the ethnicisation and ageing – of the populations in countries like Canada, the USA and the UK have been the impetus for much of the recent development in theory and research on ethnicity and ageing since the mid-1980s. Indeed, a large proportion of the research in this area comes from these increasingly multicultural countries, research that has focused for the most part on outcomes in the health and social support domains. This chapter has provided an overview of this emergent and diverse body of literature, and, in the process of reviewing the work, identified several key issues that warrant further research and/or policy attention.

First, in terms of theoretical directives, the application of an intersectionality perspective to the study of ethnicity and ageing has much promise, as it underscores the importance of understanding the differential impacts that markers of social inequality have on the social support and health outcomes of ethno-cultural older adults. In order adequately to address health and social inequities in such populations, a move beyond an analysis of one or two possible predictors like ethnicity and age to explore the intersecting influence of several markers of difference (gender, SES, marital status, geographic place of residence and sexual orientation, to name a few) is necessary. An acknowledgment of the complexity inherent in the production of health and social support in ethnic older adult populations calls for an understanding of the intersecting relations between these factors.

With regard to physical health status, Canadian research on the 'healthy immigrant effect' has shown that age does matter in evaluating the health of adult immigrants over time (Gee *et al.* 2004). Findings from this area suggest that older immigrants from South Asian or Asian source countries like India or China may experience changes in health status as lifestyle behaviours change at an accelerated rate after immigration, and that the rate at which such behaviours converge to the Canadian norm will, of course, vary according to a number of factors related to assimilation and acculturation processes including: age at immigration; country of birth; level of adherence to traditional (country of birth) value and belief systems; place of residence (urban versus rural); and degree of institutional completeness of the immigrant's ethnocultural group in the place of residence. And, as Koehn's work with South Asian older adults indicates, such processes are inherently marked by experiences of discrimination at the micro-, meso- and macro-level from pre- to post-immigration.

An examination of the intersections of gender and sponsored immigrant status reveals a plethora of implications for other determinants of health such as housing environment and SES as well as access to health care. Women who are sponsored by their adult children to provide care for grandchildren are economically dependent for ten years and isolated due to a combination of care giving responsibilities, lack of English language skills and experience with Canada or social institutions in general, and no access to subsidised transportation. They are unable to access health care without the assistance of busy adult children who must provide interpretation and transportation and, as a result, they have no means of communicating familial abuse to the outside world. Researchers thus need to pay more heed to the multidimensionality of immigrant status so as to acknowledge different types of immigration and their impact on access to resources, and their implications for social support and health care. In the end, these and other related factors should be considered in the development of any comprehensive Canadian health and social care policy and programme planning initiatives for ethnic adults in mid-life, given that adults currently in this group represent a rapidly growing age group in the country, and later life.

Finally, in the policy arena, a number of different recommendations emerge from an evaluation of the ethnicity and ageing research since the 1980s. First, as underscored earlier, health and social care policy-makers in Canada, the US and the UK must continue to address key issues related to the growing ethnic diversity in their populations; in particular, the differential health and social care needs of immigrant adults by gender and age group. For example, as Kobayashi and Prus (forthcoming) point out, recent immigrant visible minority men in mid-life, and to a lesser extent their later-life female counterparts, may have fewer needs for services and programmes in the early years of their residency in Canada, while certain new immigrant subgroups, namely older men and mid-life visible minority women, may have increased needs for services due to poor health status. This increased need is likely to continue for these women as they age in Canada. In response to this reality, it is important that policies and programmes be developed at both the federal and the provincial level, particularly in Ontario (Toronto), Quebec (Montreal) and British Columbia (Vancouver), provinces in which the majority of immigrants choose to reside, that: (a) target mid-life immigrant and certain subgroups of older immigrant women as they age over time; and (b) respond to the needs of an older immigrant male population from the outset.

Immigration and related policies and regulations ranging from pensions to housing bylaws also require scrutiny with respect to their implications for the health and health care access of older adults, as detailed by Koehn, Spencer and Hwang. Central is the recommendation, now adopted by the Special Senate Committee on Aging (2009), that the dependency period for sponsored parents be reduced from ten years to three in line with sponsored spouses. In critiquing the World Health Organization for paying insufficient attention to the power relations that shape social determinants of health, Navarro (2009: 440) states that 'It is not *inequalities* that kill people . . . it is *those who are responsible for these inequalities* that kill people.'

Over time, research on ethnicity and ageing has continued to reflect the increasing ethnic diversification of the older adult population globally. As social researchers increasingly facilitate the translation and exchange of this knowledge with various key stakeholders (including policy-makers, health care practitioners, front-line workers, family members, and the older adults themselves) we are likely to see continued growth and the uptake of important work in this area. Through the inclusion and exploration of the experiences of a broader group of older ethnic adults, individuals in their informal and formal support networks, and those who have the power to empower these individuals through the establishment of culturally appropriate policies and programmes in their home countries, we are setting a strong foundation for future research on ageing populations across the world.

Bibliography

Ahmad, W. I. U. and Walker, R. 1997. 'Asian older people: housing, health and access to services', *Ageing and Society* 17(2): 141–65

Ali, J. S., McDermott, S. and Gravel, R. G. 2004. 'Recent research on immigrant health from Statistics Canada's population surveys', *Canadian Journal of Public Health* 95(3): I-9–I-13.

Assanand, S., Koehn, S. and Sethi, B. 2007. 'Workshop 2: Immigrant status', in *Speaking to the Interface: A Symposium on Access to Care for Ethnic Minority Seniors*, Surrey, BC. Retrieved 30 August 2010, from www.hccrn.com

BC Ministry of Health Services 2004. *A Profile of Seniors in British Columbia.* Victoria, BC: Children's, Women's and Seniors' Health, Population Health and Wellness, Ministry of Health Services

BC Stats 2006. *Special Feature: Family Immigrants to British Columbia* (Immigration Highlights No. 05–4). Victoria, BC: Government of British Columbia. Retrieved from www.bcstats.gov.bc.ca/pubs/immig/imm054sf.pdf

Beiser, M. 2005. 'The health of immigrants and refugees in Canada', *Canadian Journal of Public Health* 96 Suppl 2: S30–44

Benoit, C. and Shumka, L. 2009. *Gendering the Health Determinants Framework: Why Girls' and Women's Health Matters.* Vancouver, BC: Women's Health Research Network

Boyd, M. 1989. 'Immigration and income security policies in Canada: implications for elderly immigrant women', *Population Research and Policy Review* 8(1): 5–24

Brotman, S. 2003. 'The limits of multiculturalism in elder care services', *Journal of Aging Studies* 17(2): 209–29

Calasanti, T. M. and Slevin, K. F. 2001. 'Gender, care work and family in old age', in T. M. Calasanti and K. F. Slevin (eds.), *Gender, Social Inequalities, And aging* Walnut Creek, CA: Altamira Press, 143–78.

Canada: Standing Senate Committee on Social Affairs, Science and Technology 2009. *A Healthy, Productive Canada: A Determinant of Health Approach*

(Final Report of the Senate Subcommittee on Population Health (co-chairs: W. J. Keon and L. Pepin). Ottawa: Parliament of Canada.

Carefirst Seniors and Community Services Association 2002. *In Disguise: Elder Abuse and Neglect in the Chinese Community*. Toronto: Carefirst Seniors and Community Services Association

Centre for Addiction and Mental Health (CAMH) 2009. *Improving Mental Health Services for Immigrant, Refugee, Ethno-cultural and Racialized Groups: Issues and Options for Service Improvement*. Ottawa: Mental Health Commission of Canada

Chen, J., Wilkins, R. and Ng, E. 1996. 'Health expectancy by immigrant status, 1986 and 1991', *Health Reports* 8(3): 29–38

Choi, N. G. 2002. 'Asian American elderly participants in congregate dining programs: an exploratory study', *Journal of Nutrition for the Elderly* 21(3): 1–13

Choudhry, U. K. 2001. 'Uprooting and resettlement experiences of South Asian immigrant women', *Western Journal of Nursing Research* 23(4): 376–93

Cohler, B. 1982 'Stress or support: relations between older women from three European ethnic groups and their relatives', in R. C. Manuel (ed.), *Minority Aging: Sociological and Social Psychological Issues*. Westport, CT: Greenwood

Collacott, M. 2006. 'Family class immigration: the need for a policy review', *Canadian Issues* 90. Retrieved 18 February 2011 from www.immigrationre-form.ca/doc/Family-Class%20Immigration.pdf.

Cool, L. E. 1981. 'Ethnic identity: a source of community esteem for the elderly', *Anthropological Quarterly* 54(4): 179–89

Côté, A., KéRisit M. & Côté, M. 2001. *Sponsorship . . . For Better or for Worse: The Impact of Sponsorship on the Equality Rights of Immigrant Women*. Ottawa: Status of Women Canada. Retrieved from www.swc-cfc.gc.ca/pubs/pubspr/ 0662296427/200103_0662296427_2_e.html

Cowgill, D. O. and Holmes, L. D. 1972. *Aging and Modernization*. New York: Appleton-Century-Crofts and Fleschner Publishing Company

Crewe, S. E. 2005. 'Ethnogerontology', *Journal of Gerontological Social Work* 43(4): 45–58

Dean, J. A. and Wilson, K. 2010. '"My health has improved because I always have everything I need here . . .": a qualitative exploration of health improvement and decline among immigrants', *Social Science and Medicine* 70(8): 1219–28

Dempsey, C. and Citizenship and Immigration Canada 2004. 'Elderly immigrants: income sources and compositions', *Horizons* 7(2): 58–65

Dossa, P. A. 1999. '(Re) imagining aging lives: ethnographic narratives of Muslim women in Diaspora', *Journal of Cross-Cultural Gerontology* 14(3): 245–72

Dowd, J. J. and Bengtson, V. L. 1978. 'Aging in minority populations: an examination of the double jeopardy hypothesis', *Journal of Gerontology* 33(3): 427–36

Driedger, L. and Chappell, N. L. 1987. *Aging and Ethnicity: Toward an Interface.* Toronto: Butterworth Legal

Dunn, J. R. and Dyck, I. 2000. 'Social determinants of health in Canada's immigrant population: results from the national population health survey', *Social Science and Medicine* 51(11): 1573–93

Estes, C. L. 1979. *The Aging Enterprise.* San Francisco: Jossey-Bass

Estes, C. L., Mahakian, J. L. and Weitz, T. A. 2001. A political economy critique of "Productive aging"', in C. L. Estes and Associates (eds.), *Social Policy and Aging: A Critical Perspective.* Thousand Oaks, CA: Sage Publications 187–199

Fikree, F. F. and Pasha, O. 2004. 'Role of gender in health disparity: the South Asian context', *British Medical Journal* 328(7443): 823–6

Foner, A. 1979. 'Ascribed and achieved bases of stratification', *Annual Review of Sociology* 5(1): 219–42

Foner, A. and Kertzer, D. I. 1978. 'Intrinsic and extrinsic sources of change in life-course transitions', in M. W. Riley (ed.), *Aging from Birth to Death: Interdisciplinary Perspectives*, Boulder, CO: Westview Press, vol. I, 121–36.

Foner, N. 1984. *Ages in Conflict: A Cross-cultural Perspective on Inequality between Old and Young.* New York: Columbia University Press

Friesen, C. and Hyndman, J. 2004. *A System in Crisis: 2004 Inter-provincial Report Card on Language and Settlement Services in Canada.* Burnaby, BC: Department of Geography, Simon Fraser University.

Fry, C. L. 1981a. 'Introduction: anthropology and dimensions of aging', in C. L. Fry (ed.), *Dimensions: Aging, Culture, and Health.* Westport, CT: Bergin & Garvey, 1–11

Fry, C. L. (ed.) 1981b. *Dimensions: Aging, Culture, and Health.* Westport, CT: Bergin & Garvey

Gee, E. M. 1999. 'Ethnic identity among foreign-born Chinese Canadian elders', *Canadian Journal on Aging* 18(4): 415–29

Gee, E. M., Kobayashi, K. M. and Prus, S. G. 2004. 'Examining the healthy immigrant effect in mid- to later life: findings from the Canadian Community Health Survey', *Canadian Journal on Aging*, Suppl., 23: S61–9

Gelfand, D. E. 2003. *Aging and Ethnicity: Knowledge and Services.* New York: Springer Publishing Company

Globerman, S. 1998. *Immigration and Health Care Utilization Patterns in Canada* (RIIM Working Paper Series No. 98–08). Vancouver, BC: Research on Immigration and Integration in the Metropolis

Government of Canada 2006. *Statements by Members: Penny Priddy (Surrey North, NDP). 39th parliament, 1st session: Edited Hansard* No. 036

Grewal, I., Nazroo, J., Bajekal, M., Blane, D. and Lewis, J. 2004. 'Influences on quality of life: a qualitative investigation of ethnic differences among older people in England', *Journal of Ethnic and Migration Studies* 30(4): 737–61

Grewal, S., Bottorff, J. L. and Hilton, B. A. 2005. 'The influence of family on immigrant South Asian women's health', *Journal of Family Nursing* 11(3): 242–63

Gupta, M., Singh, N. and Verma, S. 2006. 'South Asians and cardiovascular risk: what clinicians should know', *Circulation* 113(25): e924

Guruge, S., Kanthasamy, P. and Santos, J. E. 2008. 'Addressing older women's health', in S. Guruge and E. Collins (eds.), *Working with Immigrant Women*. Toronto: Centre for Addiction and Mental Health, 235–56.

Hankivsky, O., Cormier, R., DeMerich, D. and Chou, J. 2009. *Intersectionality: Moving Women's Health Research and Policy Forward*. Vancouver, BC: Women's Health Research Network

Hansen, E. and Donohoe, M. 2004. 'Health issues of migrant and seasonal farm-workers', *Journal of Health Care for the Poor and Underserved* 14(2): 153–64

Havens, B. and Chappell, N. L. 1983. 'Triple jeopardy: age, sex and ethnicity', *Canadian Ethnic Studies* 15(3): 119–32

Health Canada and Kinnon, D. 1999. *Canadian Research on Immigration and Health: An Overview*. Catalogue No. H21–149/1999E). Ottawa: Minister of Public Works and Government Services Canada

Hicks, M. H. and Lam, M. S. 1999. 'Decision-making within the social course of dementia: accounts by Chinese-American caregivers', *Culture, Medicine and Psychiatry* 23(4): 415–52

Ho, B., Friedland, J., Rappolt, S. and Noh, S. 2003. 'Caregiving for relatives with Alzheimer's disease: feelings of Chinese-Canadian women', *Journal of Aging Studies* 17(3): 301–21

Hooyman, N. R. and Kiyak, H. A. 1996. *Social Gerontology: A Multidisciplinary Perspective*. Boston, MA: Allyn and Bacon

Hossem, A. 2009. 'The South Asian older adult immigrant's barriers to accessing health services in Canada: what do we know? what can we do?', *Indian Journal of Gerontology* 23(3): 328–42

Iliffe, S. and Manthorpe, J. 2004. 'The debate on ethnicity and dementia: from category fallacy to person-centred care?', *Aging and Mental Health* 8(4): 283–92

Iyer, A., Sen, G. and Östlin, P. 2008. 'The intersections of gender and class in health status and health care', *Global Public Health* 3(1 suppl. 1): 13

Jackson, J. J. 1967. 'Social gerontology and the negro: a review', *Gerontologist* 7: 168
 1985. 'Race, national origin, ethnicity, and aging', in R. Binstock and E. Shanas (eds.), *Handbook of Aging and the Social Sciences*. New York: Van Nostrand Reinhold Company, 265–303

Johnson, J. L., Bottorff, J. L., Browne, A. J., Grewal, S., Hilton, B. A. and Clarke, H. 2004. 'Othering and being othered in the context of health care services', *Health Communication* 16(2): 255–71

Jones, R., Chow, T. and Gatz, M. 2006. 'Asian Americans and Alzheimer's disease: assimilation, culture and beliefs', *Journal of Aging Studies* 20: 11–25

Joyce, J. A. 2007. *Women, Marriage, and Wealth: The Impact of Marital Status on the Economic Well-being of Women through the Life Course*. New York: Gordian Knot Books

Kelchner, E. S. 2002. 'Physician/elder communication voices not heard', Unpublished PhD dissertation, University of Denver

Kennedy, S., McDonald, J. T. and Biddle, N. 2006. The healthy immigrant effect and immigrant selection: Evidence from four countries. *Social and Economic Dimensions of an Aging Population Research Papers* 164. Retrieved 18 February 2011 from http://socserv.mcmaster.ca/sedap/p/sedap164.pdf.

Kim, J. 2007. 'Relationship between acculturation level and depression among Korean older adults', UMI Dissertation Services, ProQuest Information and Learning, Ann Arbor, MI

Kleinman, A. and Benson, P. 2006. 'Anthropology in the clinic: the problem of cultural competency and how to fix it', *PLoS Med* 3(10): e294–e305

Kobayashi, K. M. 2000. 'The nature of support from adult *sansei* (third generation) children to older *nisei* (second generation) parents in Japanese Canadian families', *Journal of Cross-Cultural Gerontology* 15(3): 185–205

Kobayashi, K. M. and Prus, S. G. forthcoming. 'Adopting an intersectionality perspective to the study of the "Healthy immigrant effect"', in O. Hankivsky (ed.), *Intersectionality and Health Research*. Vancouver, BC: UBC Press

Kobayashi, K., Prus, S. and Lin, Z. 2008. 'Ethnic differences in self-rated and functional health: does immigrant status matter?', *Ethnicity and Health* 13(2): 129–47

Koehn, S. 1993. 'Negotiating new lives and new lands: elderly Punjabi women in British Columbia'. Master's thesis, University of Victoria, Victoria, BC

    1999. 'Fine balance: family, food, and faith in the health-worlds of elderly Punjabi Hindu women', PhD dissertation, University of Victoria, Victoria, BC. UMI Dissertation Services, ProQuest Information and Learning, Ann Arbor, MI

    2009. 'Negotiating candidacy: ethnic minority seniors' access to care', *Ageing and Society* 29(4): 585–608

Koehn, S., Cameron, L. and Kehoe, S. 2007. 'Speaking to the interface: a symposium on access to health care for ethnic minority seniors (proceedings). Surrey, B.C. 1–126', retrieved 30 August 2010, from www.hccrn.com

Koehn, S., Spencer, C. and Hwang, E. 2010. 'Promises, promises: cultural and legal dimensions of sponsorship for immigrant seniors', in D. Durst and M. MacLean (eds.), *Diversity and Aging among Immigrant Seniors in Canada: Changing Faces and Greying Temples*. Calgary, AB: Detselig Enterprises Ltd, 79–102

Kozak, J. F., Koehn, S. and Khamisa, H. 2010. *Final Report on a Population Health Approach to the Health and Healthcare of Ethnocultural Minority Older Adults: A Scoping Review*. CIHR knowledge synthesis grant (FRN 91772)

Lai, D. W. L. 2000. 'Prevalence of depression among the elderly Chinese in Canada', *Canadian Journal of Public Health* 91(1): 64–6

Laroche, M. 2000. 'Health status and health services utilization of Canada's immigrant and non-immigrant populations', *Canadian Public Policy* 26(1), 51–75

Lechte, J. (ed.) 1994. *Fifty Key Contemporary Thinkers: From Structuralism to Postmodernity*. London and New York: Routledge

Markides, K. S. 1983. 'Minority aging', in M. W. Riley, B. B. Hess and K. Bond (eds.), *Aging in Society: Selected Reviews of Recent Research*. Hillsdale, NJ: Lawrence Erlbaum, 15–37

McCall, L. 2005. 'The complexity of intersectionality', *Signs: Journal of Women in Culture and Society* 30(3): 1771–1800

McDonald, J. T. and Kennedy, S. 2005. 'Is migration to Canada associated with unhealthy weight gain? Overweight and obesity among Canada's immigrants', *Social Science and Medicine* 61(12): 2469–81

McDonald, L. 2008. 'Aging and ethnicity', in N. Chappell, L. McDonald and M. Stones (eds.), *Aging in Contemporary Canada* (2nd edn). Toronto: Pearson Prentice Hall, 136–66

McLaren, A. T. 2006. *Parental Sponsorship – Whose Problematic? A Consideration of South Asian Women's Immigration Experiences in Vancouver* (Research on Immigration and Integration in the Metropolis Working Paper Series No. 06–08). Vancouver, BC: Research on Immigration and Integration in the Metropolis

Menec, V. H., Shooshtari, S. and Lambert, P. 2007. 'Ethnic differences in self-rated health among older adults: a cross-sectional and longitudinal analysis', *Journal of Aging and Health* 19(1): 62

Mikkonen, J. and Raphael, D. 2010. *Social Determinants of Health: The Canadian Facts*. Toronto: York University School of Health Policy and Management

Mui, A. C. 1998. 'Living alone and depression among older Chinese immigrants', *Journal of Gerontological Social Work* 30(3–4): 147–66

  2002. 'Stress, coping, and depression among elderly Korean immigrants', *Journal of Human Behavior in the Social Environment* 3(3–4): 281–99

National Advisory Council on Aging (Canada) 2005. *Seniors on the Margins: Seniors from Ethnocultural Minorities*. Ottawa: Minister of Public Works and Government Services Canada

Navarro, V. 2009. 'What we mean by social determinants of health', *International Journal of Health Services* 39(3): 423–41

Newbold, K. B. 2005a. 'Health status and health care of immigrants in Canada: a longitudinal analysis', *Journal of Health Services Research and Policy* 10(2): 77–83

2005b. 'Self-rated health within the Canadian immigrant population: risk and the healthy immigrant effect', *Social Science and Medicine* 60(6): 1359–70

2006. 'Chronic conditions and the healthy immigrant effect: evidence from Canadian immigrants', *Journal of Ethnic and Migration Studies* 32(5): 765–84

Newbold, K. B. and Danforth, J. 2003. 'Health status and Canada's immigrant population', *Social Science and Medicine* 57(10): 1981–95

Neysmith, S., O'Connell, A. and Bezanson, K. 2005. *Telling Tales: Living the Effects of Public Policy*. Halifax: Fernwood

Nie, J. X., Wang, L., Tracy, C. S., Moineddin, R. and Upshur, R. E. 2008. 'Health care service utilization among the elderly: findings from the study to understand the chronic condition experience of the elderly and the disabled (SUCCEED project)', *Journal of Evaluation in Clinical Practice* 14(6): 1044–9

Ordonez, M. de los Angeles 2006. 'Lived experience of health among older Guatemalan women'. UMI Dissertation Services, ProQuest Information and Learning, Ann Arbor, MI

Osako, M. M. 1979. 'Aging and family among Japanese Americans: the role of ethnic tradition in the adjustment to old age', *The Gerontologist* 19(5 Part 1): 448–55

Palmore, E. B. and Maeda, D. 1985. *The Honorable Elders Revisited*. Durham, NC: Duke University Press

Perez, C. E. 2002. 'Health status and health behaviour among immigrants', *Health Reports-Statistics Canada* 13: 89–100

PRIAE (Policy Research Institute on Ageing and Ethnicity) 2003. *Minority Elderly Health and Social Care in Europe* (PRIAE Research Briefing). Leeds and London: Policy Research Institute on Ageing and Ethnicity

Public Health Agency of Canada 2003. *What Makes Canadians Healthy or Unhealthy? Underlying Premises and Evidence Table*. Retrieved 3 August 2010, from www.phac-aspc.gc.ca/ph-sp/determinants/determinants-eng.php#culture

Public Health Agency of Canada: Cornwell, L., Hendrickson, T., Lee, M., Lettner, M., Loli-Dano, L. *et al.* 2007. *Health Status and Health Needs of Older Immigrant Women: Individual, Community, Societal and Policy Links*. Ottawa: Public Health Agency of Canada

Raskin, A., Chiang-Piao Chien, A. and Keh-Ming Lin. 1992. 'Elderly Chinese- and Caucasian-Americans compared on measures of psychic distress, somatic complaints and social competence', *International Journal of Geriatric Psychiatry* 7(3): 191–8

Raymond, N. T., Varadhan, L., Reynold, D. R., Bush, K., Sankaranarayanan, S., Bellary, S. *et al.* 2009. 'Higher prevalence of retinopathy in diabetic patients of South Asian ethnicity compared with white Europeans in the community', *Diabetes Care* 32(3): 410

Riley, M. W. 1971. 'Social gerontology and the age stratification of society', *The Gerontologist* 11(1, Part 1): 79–87

Sadavoy, J., Meier, R. and Ong, A. Y. 2004. 'Barriers to access to mental health services for ethnic seniors: the Toronto study', *Canadian Journal of Psychiatry* 49(3): 192–99

Sen, G., Iyer, A. and Mukherjee, C. 2009. 'A methodology to analyse the intersections of social inequalities in health', *Journal of Human Development and Capabilities* 10(3): 397–415

Siisiainen, M. 2003. 'Two concepts of social capital: Bourdieu vs. Putnam', *International Journal of Contemporary Sociology* 40(2): 183–204

Simmons, N. 2007. 'Barriers, bridges and beyond: understanding perspectives in linguistically and culturally diverse clinical interactions'. PhD dissertation, University of British Columbia, BC

Sokolovsky, J. 1985. 'Ethnicity, culture and aging: do differences really make a difference?', *Journal of Applied Gerontology* 4(1): 6–17

  1990a. 'Bringing culture back home: aging, ethnicity and family support', in J. Sokolovsky (ed.), *The Cultural Context of Aging: Worldwide Perspectives* (1st edn). New York: Bergin and Garvey, 201–11

Sokolovsky, J. (ed.) 1990b. *The Cultural Context of Aging: Worldwide Perspectives*. New York: Bergin and Garvey

Special Senate Committee on Aging, Chairs: Carstairs, S. and Keon, W. J. 2009. *Canada's Aging Population: Seizing the Opportunity*. Ottawa, ON: The Senate

Spence, M., Koehn, S. and Kobayashi, K. 2009. *Summary Report: Knowledge.Power. Access Forum of the Immigrant Older Women: Care, Accessibility, Research, Empowerment (iCARE) Team, Held on June 25, 2009, Vancouver BC*. Vancouver, BC: ICARE team. Retrieved 30 August 2010, from www.hccrn.com

Statistics Canada 2005. *Longitudinal Survey of Immigrants to Canada: A Portrait of Early Settlement Experiences* (No. 89–614-XIE). Ottawa: Minister of Industry

  2006a. *2006 Census of Canada*. Statistics Canada (catalogue no. 97–562-XCB200601)

  2006b. *Concept: Visible Minority*. Ottawa, ON: Statistics Canada

Stokes, S. C., Thompson, L. W., Murphy, S. and Gallagher-Thompson, D. 2001. 'Screening for depression in immigrant Chinese-American elders: results of a pilot study', *Journal of Gerontological Social Work* 36(1): 27–44

Tam, S. and Neysmith, S. 2006. 'Disrespect and isolation: elder abuse in Chinese communities', *Canadian Journal on Aging* 25(2): 141–51

Vancouver Cross-Cultural Seniors Network Society 2010. Minutes, May 10th & June 14th meetings, including summary of member consultations following a report by Dr. Sharon Koehn, 'The health and health care of Canada's ethnocultural minority older adults: what we know and what we need to know.' Unpublished manuscript

Vatuk, S. 1980. 'Withdrawal and disengagement as a cultural response to aging in India', in C. Fry (ed.), *Aging in Culture and Society: Comparative Viewpoints and Strategies*. New York: J. F. Bergin Publishers, 126–48

Walker, A. 1981. 'Towards a political economy of old age', *Ageing and Society* 1(1): 73–94

Wedeen, L. 2002. 'Conceptualizing culture: possibilities for political science', *American Political Science Review* 96(4): 713–28

Williams, R. and Hunt, K. 1997. 'Psychological distress among British South Asians: the contribution of stressful situations and subcultural differences in the west of Scotland twenty-07 study', *Psychological Medicine* 27(5): 1173–81

Wu, B., Tran, T. V. and Amjad, Q. 2004. 'Chronic illnesses and depression among Chinese immigrant elders', *Journal of Gerontological Social Work* 43(2–3): 79–95

Wykle, M. L. and Musil, C. M. 1993. 'Mental health of older persons: social and cultural factors', *Generations* 17(1): 7–12

Zahno, K. and Rhule, C. 2008. *Information and Advice Needs of Black and Minority Ethnic Older People in England*. London: Zahno Rao Associates

8

Disability and age discrimination

GABRIELLE MASTIN AND MARK PRIESTLEY

Introduction

The connections between disability and ageing have been extensively discussed in the social gerontology literature but much less so within critical disability studies or in analyses of inequality. Partly as a consequence of this, there has been a tendency to focus discussion of disability in old age as a 'health' or 'quality of life' issue rather than an issue of intersectional discrimination. The main purpose of this chapter is to challenge this perspective and to elucidate some of the subtle, and not so subtle, ways in which disability discrimination and age discrimination combine and interact. This multiple discrimination has very real implications in the lives of older disabled people, including those who acquire impairments later in life and those who have aged with them. It has implications for the planning and provision of public services and for the redress of discrimination in law.

The discussion examines our understanding of the intersectionality between disability and age discrimination by outlining key conceptual models from critical disability studies to articulate the significance of both disability and old age as administrative policy categories with common characteristics (including cultural constructions of dependency and structural exclusions from labour market participation). This discussion highlights also some of the tensions and conflicts in identity construction for older disabled people themselves, and for the politics of social movements articulating claims to non-discrimination. After setting out the current basis for non-discrimination in the field of disability policy, the discussion then draws on data about local authority provision to illustrate the differential treatment of older disabled people in social protection, health and social care (thus, providing some links to the following chapter).

The association of older age and disability

There are many ways in which discussions of diversity and age discrimination can, and must, be connected with discussions of disability. There are strong associations between biological ageing and the onset of bodily impairments in later life. There are strong cultural associations in popular imagery of old age and disability, connections that impact also on ageing and disability identities. There are strong structural associations between the enforced dependency of older and disabled people in modern societies. There are strong similarities in the kinds of rights-based claims articulated by social movements representing older people and disabled people. In order to understand the interdependencies and complexities of the multiple discrimination experienced by older disabled people it is first useful to review some of these broader connections.

One of the major achievements in public health during the twentieth century was an increase in life expectancy. The average life expectancy of Europeans increased by twenty-eight years, from 45 to 73 years, and was predicted to increase a further 40% by 2015 (BURDIS 2004: 7). Western European countries are now amongst those with the highest life expectancy in the world (Muenz 2007). The potential to 'add life to years' (Hudson, Dearey and Glendinning 2005) has subsequently been much vaunted in efforts also to extend 'disability-free' years to life. In this context, the connections between old age, disability and quality of life have come increasingly into focus.

Demographic ageing has increased the number of older people now living with impairments, especially impairments acquired in advanced old age (Martin, Meltzer and Elliot 1988; Craig and Greenslade 1998; Disability Rights Commission 2000). At the same time, younger disabled adults have a much greater expectancy of living on into old age with impairments acquired earlier in life (Zarb and Oliver 1993; Salvatori *et al.* 1998). The consequence is that there is both an increasing number and an increasing proportion of older disabled people, and the majority of disabled people in Britain, as in some other developed economies, are older than the traditional age of retirement. The policy significance of these trends is striking but it has not attracted nearly so much attention as might be expected.

There has been a tendency to discuss disability in old age largely in medical terms, rather than in terms of inequality and discrimination (Priestley 2002a). For example, while 'disability' has been characterised as 'lacking an ability' to perform 'normal' adult tasks, ageing has been referred to as 'an inevitable loss of health' and a 'decline from optimum levels in youth' (Field and Blakemore 2007: 115). This prevalent way of thinking about disability and old age draws much from a discourse of 'biographical disruption' (Bury 1982), in which the onset of impairment is seen to interrupt positive life course expectations, requiring the negotiation of new, and more negative, ageing identities (Priestley 2005). Such constructions also tend to convey the social inequalities experienced by older disabled people as biologically determined and unavoidable. It is particularly important to challenge this view when considering intersections of age and disability discrimination.

The strong association between ageing and bodily impairment is very evident in discussion of identity transitions in old age. The onset of age-related impairment (perhaps as much as retirement) has been seen as one of the key factors that trigger personal identity transitions from adulthood into the *habitus* of old age. Indeed, research suggests that people often perceive the 'risks' of physical and mental decline as determinant factors in marking their own sense of ageing (Demakakos, Gjonca and Nazroo 2007: 284–5). Impairment may be seen as part of the 'mask of ageing' (Featherstone and Hepworth 1991), the presence of which makes it more difficult to 'choose' not to be old (Biggs 1997). However, as Williams (2000) points out, far from 'disrupting' biographies of ageing, the onset of impairment can also be seen as confirming or reinforcing that trajectory (see also Carricaburu and Pierret 1995). In this way, impaired bodies cease to be so 'out of place' or 'special' in old age as they may appear in childhood or younger adulthood (Zola 1989). In everyday terms then, impairment is often perceived as a very 'normal' part of ageing – and many older people with impairments do not identify themselves as 'disabled' people (Molloy, Knight and Woodfield 2003; Priestley 2004; NDA 2006).

This normalcy of impairment in old age may help to explain why older disabled people have been largely overlooked in discussions of inequality and disability discrimination. It may also explain how it is sometimes possible to simply dismiss 'disability' discrimination in old age as an inevitable consequence of 'getting older' (Barnes and Mercer 2003; Bytheway *et al.* 2007). As a consequence, older disabled people and their advocates may be less likely to articulate claims of discrimination and unequal treatment on grounds of disability. It is therefore important to consider whether disability discrimination in old age can, or should, be treated in any way differently from disability discrimination in younger adulthood or childhood (Breitenbach 2001; Priestley 2005).

Should experiences of disability discrimination, like experiences of bodily impairment, be viewed as an 'inevitable' consequence of ageing?

Assumptions about the inevitability of such disadvantage have been reinforced by the social dependency status attached to disability and old age, in which both have been viewed as 'deserving' and legitimate categories of exemption from full adult rights and responsibilities (notably the exemption from employment). This association between disability, old age and social exemption has been particularly evident in the fields of social policy and welfare. The social dependency of older disabled people has become a significant policy concern with the 'fear' that the country is in danger of being 'swamped by large numbers of frail and dependent old people' (McGlone 1992: 7). An alarming prospect for policy-makers, fearful of the strain this will have on scarce public resources, and threatening future economic prosperity (Dalley 1998; Field and Blakemore 2007).

Although sociological writings on ageing have revealed a great diversity of meanings and experiences (Fennell, Phillipson and Evers 1988; Bytheway 1989; Bytheway and Johnson 1990; Thompson 1992; Phillipson 1998), social policy constructs generational boundaries in a more reductionist way. We continue to be made 'older' through policies and practices that mark us out as different in later life (Phillipson and Walker 1986; Hughes 1995; Bernard and Phillips 1998; Vincent 1999). The same has been true of policies that create administrative or spatial segregation on the grounds of disability (Finkelstein 1991). Such distinctions are particularly evident in social policies that mark children, older people and disabled people as distinct and archetypal 'welfare classes' (Kaufmann and Leisering 1984; Rostgaard and Fridberg 1998).

The prospect of growing numbers of older disabled people stimulating greater demands on public services has focused political attention not only on the social policy implications, but on the implications for the national exchequer (Field and Blakemore 2007; Estes, Biggs and Phillipson 2003; Henwood 2001). For example, official statistics suggested that by 2003/4 spending on people over the age of 65 already accounted for 43% (£16 billion) of the total NHS budget (Healthcare Commission 2006: 4). As a consequence, the policy construction of disability in old age became increasingly preoccupied with managing and rationing social protection and social care on the basis of 'deficit and dependency' rather than 'wellbeing and independence' (Allen 2008). It is no surprise that public debates on ageing and disability have engaged with such concerns, and increasingly so as generational cohorts now reaching old age seek greater respect, rights and access to more sophisticated services (Roberts, Robinson and Seymour

2002; Field and Taylor 2007). However, within this debate there was scant recognition of the real inequalities and discrimination experienced by older disabled people in receipt of public services.

Despite the strong demographic, cultural and structural associations between ageing and disability, the development of disability equality and non-discrimination policies continued to focus much more on the needs of younger disabled people than older people (Walker and Naegele 1999; Priestley 2000, 2005). Conversely, policy and provision for an ageing society tended to 'conflate the needs of older disabled people with those of the wider (non-disabled) population of older people' (Drake 1999: 163). Thus, Kennedy and Minkler (1998) concluded that increasingly high expectations about disability rights during the 1990s were simply not being applied equally to older disabled people.

Disability discrimination and equal rights are relevant to people throughout the life course, and would seem to be particularly significant for the large numbers of those who experience impairment in advanced old age. Yet there has been a surprising lack of linkage between the demographic reality and debates about disability equality (Priestley 2002b), leaving the experiences of older disabled people almost 'completely overlooked' (Zarb 1992: 2). The result is that, while significant advances have been made in recognising disability rights, public expectations and responses still differ markedly for older and younger disabled people. An intersectional approach to equality and non-discrimination needs to consider both the impact of disability policies on older people and the impact of ageing policies on disabled people.

Connecting policies for disability and old age

Looking at the problem from a policy perspective, there are important similarities in the way that disability and old age have been produced and regulated within modern welfare states. Indeed, both old age and disability have been shaped by similar social claims and labour market forces, particularly in exemption, or exclusion, from adult employment (Irwin 1999, 2001). Consequently, disability and old age can be considered as rather similar kinds of 'non-adult' status, linked by their shared associations with structural 'dependency' on adult labour (Priestley 2005). In this context, it is helpful to consider the historical interdependency of old age and disability as administrative categories in British policy-making (Stone 1984; Priestley 1997).

Even prior to the 1601 Poor Law, the primary categories of welfare entitlement had been defined in relation to 'capacity' or 'ability' to work, and this laid the foundation for subsequent definitions of disability and old age in legislation. However, 'aged' and 'disabled' people remained largely undistinguished from one another in policy terms until at least the late nineteenth century. The subsequent introduction of retirement age and old age pensions then established a distinction between those who were exempt from employment on grounds of age and those exempt on grounds of disability. The (gendered) use of working age was no doubt an administratively simple way to draw a line on exemption from the adult labour market, but it masked the fact that most older people who had been dependent on public relief under the old Poor Law system were 'unable to work' not because of their chronological age but precisely because they were also disabled people (Priestley and Rabiee 2002). In this way, the significance of disability as a key factor in the social exclusion of older people became increasingly masked from critical attention. It is worth noting that the UK's recent commitment to abolish statutory retirement age in 2011 throws open again the need to consider more explicitly the relationship between disability and exit from the labour force amongst older workers.

The Second World War had created the social and political conditions for massive changes in the role of the state, and this manifested in the 1940s in a raft of new social legislation, much of it very relevant to the issues of disability. During this period National Assistance replaced the much-hated Poor Law, a new National Insurance scheme sought to protect against disruptions in employment, and health services were radically changed with the creation of a National Health Service. With massive investment in state education and employment-creation, citizens were now offered state protection 'from the cradle to the grave' (Dalley 1998). Although the policy emphasis was on rehabilitation there were also clear signs of social policies that sought greater social inclusion and recognition of rights to public participation (Topliss 1975; Barnes 1991; Borsay 2005). The transfer of welfare functions to local authorities provided greater choices in access to home nursing and domestic help for disabled people but also transferred the duty 'to provide residential accommodation for persons who by reason of age, infirmity or any other circumstance are in need of care and attention' (National Assistance Act, Section 21). Overall, during the 1950s and 1960s, although some of the legal issues around disability were clarified, there was growing concern at the preoccupation of state welfare services with residential provision rather than other more enlightened forms of community care. Townsend's report on residential homes for older people, *The Last Refuge*, suggested little had in fact changed from the Poor Law days, either in the housing of residents or in their treatment, whilst the Seebohm Committee (1968: para. 309) commented that 'the development of the domiciliary services (to enable as many older people as possible to stay in their own homes) . . . has been slow'.

The establishment of local social services departments, after Seebohm, the Health Services and Public Health Act 1968 and the Chronically Sick and Disabled Persons Act 1970, produced a wider range of options to support community living. In practice, however, there emerged a growing separation of provision for older and younger disabled people, administered through different arrangements and in different ways. Social services typically organised and funded their provision around generational constituencies 'intended to differentiate (i.e. discriminate) between different groups with different needs' (Roberts *et al.* 2002: 10). Moreover, provision by local authorities and the voluntary sector appeared to rely on more targeted and discretionary access to services than the equity-based framework that had been intended for the NHS (Healthcare Commission 2006; Field and Taylor 2007). The net effect was to establish a system of provision characterised by rather different life expectations and choices for younger and older disabled people – differences that were to be accentuated with subsequent advances in disability rights.

During the 1970s and 1980s, both 'disability' and 'ageing' policy remained largely focused on this problem of access to 'care' rather than on the problem of inequality and discrimination. However, this assumption was to be radically challenged by the mobilisation of new social movements representing the critical voice and claims of older and disabled people. In terms of disability, there were two key elements to these claims. On the one hand, disabled people's organisations lobbied increasingly for comprehensive non-discrimination legislation, and on the other hand, they sought to claim rights to dignity and self-determination in social care through the discourse of 'independent living' (Morris 1993; Priestley 1998; Barnes and Mercer 2006). Underpinning these claims was the development of a 'social model' of disability that characterised the inequalities experienced by disabled people as a consequence product of a disabling and discriminatory society rather than an inevitable consequence of individual impairment (Oliver 1983, 1990).

There has, however, been concern that older people – while being the largest group of disabled people – were somewhat marginalised from this revolution. Despite the obvious similarities in parallel social claims emanating from the disabled people's movement and the older people's movement, there remained little evidence of synergy or cross-fertilisation in their political strategies. Advocates of both groups articulated strong arguments about inequalities arising from poverty, access to public transport, inadequate housing options, inhumane and degrading treatment in institutions, dignity and choice. However, disability groups appeared to be primarily concerned with the interests of working-age adults while 'active ageing' lobbyists appeared reluctant to identify directly with 'disability' issues (Priestley 2002b). Indeed, Campbell (2008), writing in the *Guardian*, concluded that: 'Older people now and in the future will probably never identify with the disability movement, but they are equally impoverished, isolated and misrecognised as a consequence of our social care system's failure to support them to participate as full citizens.'

Community Care services in England were given legislative shape in the NHS and Community Care Act (1990), which sought to introduce a system of greater choice through a mixed economy of welfare. However, compared to the options that became available to disabled adults of working age during the 1990s (including the Independent Living Fund and the early introduction of direct payments), choice for older people lagged considerably behind. This was evident not only in the narrower range of community-based supports available to older people with significant impairments who wanted to live at home, but also in the lack of a clear underlying philosophy concerning their rights to independent living.

These concerns have since shifted towards an agenda based on personalisation and individual choice, as new principles established in the Green Paper *Independence, Wellbeing and Choice* (DoH 2005) have been developed and remain key drivers for 'inclusive' social services (Hudson *et al.* 2005). A major report from the Prime Minister's Strategy Unit (PMSU 2005) on *Improving the Life Chances of Disabled People* provided the focus for a new twenty-year strategy for the inclusion of disabled people by 2025. At the same time, policy co-ordination in Government was strengthened with the establishment of a cross-departmental Office for Disability Issues (ODI). ODI's transversal co-ordination of the 2025 strategy was consolidated, in 2009, with a 'Roadmap' based on fourteen themes (it is worth noting, however, that this initiative was developed under the previous government and that it is not yet clear what changes of priority can be expected). The 2008 Independent Living Strategy (ODI 2008) also established a five-year plan (2009–13), the main aim of which is to ensure that all disabled people who need support in daily life achieve 'greater choice and control over how support is provided'.

Although there is no explicit theme on older people in the Roadmap (as there is on outcomes for children) the Independent Living Strategy did address disabled people of all ages explicitly, throughout the life course – including the intention that 'older disabled people must have the same options and opportunities for independent living as anyone else' (2008: 5). A 'co-ordinated, strategic approach to investing in independent living for older disabled people' was promised (2008: 17) and there were specific proposals to develop exemplar practice through Action Learning Sites and toolkit resources. Indeed, there is reiteration throughout the document of the need to include and represent the voice of older disabled people in all aspects.

The aim of the five year Independent Living Strategy is thus that:

- disabled people (including older disabled people) who need support to go about their daily lives will have greater choice and control over how support is provided
- disabled people (including older disabled people) will have greater access to housing, transport, health, employment, and leisure opportunities and to participation in family and community life.

(2008: 31)

To summarise, the historical construction of disability and old age in social policy terms was somewhat dominated by a focus on 'dependency' and 'care', rather than debates about inequality and non-discrimination. In this historical context, disability and old age first emerged as rather similar and undifferentiated welfare categories (in which to be 'aged' was effectively to be 'disabled'). Over time, the two categories became more distinct, particularly as non-disabled older people acquired their right to exemption from employment in retirement. Later, systems of social support for older and younger people with impairments began to diverge somewhat, and to develop different expectations about older and younger people's rights to self-determination and community living. In the latter years of the twentieth century there were significant advances in the public recognition of disability rights but older disabled people remained somewhat marginalised from these developments. In the new century, the public policy debate has perhaps at last caught up with the recognition that most disabled people in Britain are older people too, and that they have equal claims to rights and non-discrimination.

Non-discrimination and disability rights

The disability studies literature has provided substantial evidence that people with impairments (of all ages) are consistently disadvantaged in important areas of social life, such as education, employment, income, family life, and political and cultural participation; or in access to public goods and services, like transport, housing, information and so on (e.g. Topliss 1975; Barnes 1991; PMSU 2005; Williams *et al.* 2008). We know, for example, from British Crime Survey data, that disabled people have a greater fear of crime and less confidence in the criminal justice system than non-disabled people. Housing surveys (such as the Survey for English Housing) show that fewer disabled people own their own house, and that more are unsatisfied with the suitability of their accommodation. Research commissioned by the Disability Rights Commission highlighted the 'transport gap' between disabled and non-disabled people (Jolly, Priestley and Matthews 2006). For example, disabled people attach greater importance to public transport but are less likely to go out or make long journeys (over half of disabled people would like to go out more often). Research on intersectional disadvantage suggests that 'Disabled people face one of the largest employment penalties of all social groups' and this has deteriorated over the past thirty years (Berthoud and Blekesaune 2007: 2). There is evidence that disabled people are less likely to access recreational and cultural activities, such as arts events, cinemas, museums, and so on.

The difficulty with much of this evidence is that the specific, or intersectional, situation of older and disabled people is not disaggregated (or, worse still, the data on which evidence is based only relates to disabled people of working age). This was addressed to some extent in a more comprehensive survey of the *Experiences and Expectations of Disabled People* in 2008 (sponsored by the government Office for Disability Issues). Almost half of the survey respondents were aged over 65. It is useful to look at some of the key findings from this survey for illustration (Williams *et al.* 2008). For example, older disabled people were more likely to live alone than for the general population of older people and less likely to take part in activities outside the home than younger disabled people, increasingly so for those aged over 75 (2008: 66). They were less likely to hold educational qualifications. Interestingly, in the context of earlier discussion on non-discrimination claims, 'younger disabled people were more likely than older disabled people to feel that they faced attitudinal and/or access barriers to participating in more social activities' (2008: 55). Indeed, 26% of disabled people aged 75 or above said that they 'do not encounter any barriers' to participation in social activity (which the authors also suggest may result from lowered expectations). To some extent this mirrors a more general trend for older people to express less dissatisfaction with public services, and with life in general (Bowling 2005) but of concern is the finding that older disabled people were the 'least likely to know that they had rights' under disability non-discrimination law. Many of those who were unaware of such rights also did not see themselves as disabled (2005: 97).

Alongside the burgeoning evidence of disability inequality, and the less well-known inequality experienced by older disabled people, there has been some optimism about changes in the treatment of disability as a public issue (including changes in public attitudes towards disability as well as a shift from welfare-based to rights-based social policies). The legal basis for protection of disabled people's rights has developed quite rapidly in recent years, albeit from a late start by comparison with other significant dimensions of discrimination (i.e. gender equality and racism). In a changing political climate, the 1970 Equal Pay Act, 1975 Sex Discrimination Act and 1976 Race Relations Act had begun to respond to equal rights claims from feminist and anti-racist movements. By contrast, parallel claims from disabled people were only beginning to be heard by the mid 1970s (non-discrimination legislation would take two more decades).

As Barnes (1991) catalogues in some detail, the 1980s witnessed growing political claims for a comprehensive legislative approach to disabled people's social exclusion. The first attempt to introduce anti-discrimination legislation was made by Jack Ashley, Minister for the Disabled, in 1982 (following establishment of a Parliamentary Committee on Restrictions against Disabled People in 1979). The little-referenced 1981 Disabled Persons Act also sought to address physical access in the built environment. However, it was to take a further thirteen years, and thirteen attempts, before a comprehensive legislation would gain Parliamentary approval. The passage of the 1995 Disability Discrimination Act (DDA) was certainly a landmark victory in establishing rights to non-discrimination across broad areas of policy affecting disabled people's lives. Its implementation was, however, phased over a ten-year period (beginning with a strong focus on discrimination in employment, extended to cover public goods and services in 1999).

The Disability Discrimination Act 1995 (as amended and extended in 2005) was intended to put an end to discrimination on grounds of disability. Section 1, for example, asserted that anyone could be considered as a disabled person if they could claim, at the relevant time, to have had a 'physical or mental impairment which has a substantial and long-term adverse effect on his ability to carry out normal day-to-day activities'. The framework of the Act thus differed somewhat from previous non-discrimination legislation on gender or 'race' by setting out a definition of those protected by its provisions (i.e. it set out to protect the rights of a specified minority group rather than to outlaw discrimination on a particular ground). The key principles of enforcement and interpretation in disability discrimination also differ somewhat from those in other areas. In particular, the DDA legislation has relied heavily on concepts of 'less favourable treatment' and 'reasonable adjustment' (Lawson 2008). In effect then, the legislation did not confer absolute rights to equal treatment and non-discrimination but only so far as they might be deemed 'reasonable' by the courts. It was, for example, permissible for employers and service providers to offer equivalent but different treatment to a disabled person, or to justify instances of exclusion and discrimination where the necessary adjustments could be proved too difficult (or costly).

To enforce the DDA, and promote its aims, an independent Disability Rights Commission (DRC) was established in 1999 to replace the pre-existing, but less significant, National Disability Council (mirroring more closely the work of the then Commission for Racial Equality and Equal Opportunities Commission). As well as dealing with individual cases of discrimination, the DRC sought to raise awareness and add to the evidence base on disability discrimination, pointing increasingly to its institutionalised character. Following the 2006 Equality Act, the DRC was closed in 2007 and merged into the new Equality and Human Rights Commission. On the one hand, this move should be welcomed for its potential to facilitate the consideration of intersectional claims to equal rights, and specifically for its inclusion of age discrimination alongside other grounds. However, the move also met with considerable concerns from the disability lobby about the likely loss of expertise and focus in the specificity of disability rights.

Implementation of the DDA brought some successes, but some population groups (including older people) remained much less aware of their rights than others. Part III of the Act (Provision of Goods, Facilities and Services) might be considered of greatest relevance to the older population, and it has resulted in a high success rate in legal judgments, yet many fewer cases have been brought under this section compared to Part II of the Act (Employment). The Act was extended in 2005 (along with the definition of those protected) and a new Disability Equality Duty was established from 2006, placing a positive duty on all public bodies actively to promote, as well ensure, the rights established in the Act (Gooding 2009). This means that, in theory, all public bodies have a positive duty to monitor, plan and evaluate their developing accessibility to disabled people. It is relevant to emphasise that this includes those that provide services specifically, or incidentally, to older people.

The first decade of the twenty-first century was thus marked by a continuing rise in the prominence of disability equality in public policy making. In this context, the UK's ratification of the United Nations Convention on the Rights of Persons with Disabilities, in June 2009, appeared to mark something of a watershed in public commitment. The far-reaching provisions of the UN Convention establish a comprehensive set of human rights, in all key areas of life, with obligations on states to ensure, protect and promote those rights through a variety of policy actions (Kanter 2007; Quinn 2009). The Convention establishes reporting mechanisms to monitor progress on rights and its Optional Protocol introduces the possibility of direct appeal by individuals or groups to the dedicated UN Committee. The Convention was adopted by the UN in 2006 and came into force in May 2008. However, the economic crisis and the election of a Conservative Liberal Democrat coalition Government, in 2010, have revived some uncertainty about the capacity of the state to fulfil its Treaty obligations in full.

The rights conveyed by the Convention can be taken to apply to disabled people of all ages, but older people are somewhat invisible as a group with claims to unique intersectional rights. There is one passing reference to the needs of older people in Article 25 (on health care and the prevention of impairment) and one point of recognition of the need to address the poverty of older disabled people in social protection programmes. The Convention does contain specific recognition of the intersectional rights of women and children (Articles 6 and 7) but there is no parallel recognition of the intersectional claims of older people. This is somewhat surprising but reflects the different legal status of women's and children's rights under existing UN Conventions protecting their rights. Recent advocacy by Global Action on Aging and others in 2010 has highlighted the case for establishment of parallel UN instruments and processes towards a future UN Convention on the Rights of Older People.

There have been further relevant developments with the 2010 Equality Act, which consolidates pre-existing legislation in a single Act. The new Act also broadens the definition of those protected from disability discrimination (e.g. by removing the requirement that a person's impairment must also affect certain functional 'capacities', and extending protection to those who are perceived to be disabled or associated with disability). More significantly for the present chapter, the Act introduces a new 'dual discrimination' clause, allowing consideration of direct discrimination based on a combination of two (but not more) grounds. In the case of disability and age discrimination it is worth emphasising that such provision would not include instances of indirect discrimination, for example where the provision of service indirectly disadvantaged older disabled people compared to younger disabled people (although the single ground of age discrimination may still be relevant here).

Age discrimination in disability services and entitlements

Discrimination against people based on their age is widespread, being 'part of the fabric of our everyday lives' (Bytheway *et al.* 2007: 5), and excludes older people, directly or indirectly, from full participation in a wide range of leisure activities, employment opportunities and care services (Allen 2008). In the context of public services this is supported by the finding that three-quarters of senior health and social services managers believed that age discrimination existed in some form within their system (Levenson 2003 in Field and Blakemore 2007: 131). In combating age discrimination, legislation has been introduced; for example, Standard One of the Older People's National Service Framework (DoH 2001) requires health and social care services to 'root-out age discrimination' in terms of both 'access', and the quality of services provided.

In the past, attention has been drawn to a number of inequities. For example, the publication of Social Services Performance Statistics at the end of 2000 drew attention to disparities in social care provision to older and younger disabled people. Local Authorities spent proportionately less on day and residential care for older people than for younger disabled people and many set lower cost thresholds when 'offering' residential care (Priestley 2002b). A report by Age Concern (1999) drew specific attention to ageism in the NHS. Older disabled people have been placed on different hospital wards and denied the sorts of treatments that younger people get (Pilling and Watson 1995; Iliffe, Patterson and Gould 1998). They have been subject to different arrangements for leaving hospital and denied the same kinds of continuing care as younger adults (Hughes 1995; Daley and Denniss 1997; Priestley 2002b).

A range of documents, including 'Opportunity age' (2005), have sought to bring together the various strands of policy in relation to ageing by offering 'for the first time, a complete strategy for an ageing society' (Help the Aged 2005: 1). The publication, a cross-departmental initiative, set out ambitious plans to extend the rights of older people to continue working, stressed the importance of active ageing and contributing to society, and highlighted the need for services that promoted well-being and independence rather than dependency. Although there was little extra money to underpin these ambitions, the publication did herald further plans, with the White Paper *Our Health, Our Care, Our Say* (DoH 2006), which reinforced earlier policy pronouncements about choice and control, and putting the client in the centre of the frame (Healthcare Commission 2006). However, many of the proposals remained unimplemented (Allen 2008). The increasing awareness of age discrimination within health and social care services has emphasised dignity, uniformity and fairness in service provision to meet identified care priorities (DoH 2001; McDonald and Taylor 2006), since reinforced in the report *High Quality Care for All* (DoH 2008).

Direct age discrimination occurs when a person is treated differently or denied services because of his or her chronological age. Although there are very few written policies specifying age criteria/barriers, some studies (e.g. Roberts *et al.* 2002), have found many senior managers describing examples of direct age discrimination (restricting access to particular services by setting age limits) within their services. Another example in the disability field is the use of chronological age in regulations governing Disability Living Allowance (DLA) and Attendance Allowance (AA). DLA is a non-contributory benefit, not dependent on an individual's National Insurance contributions record, nor is it means-tested. Rather it is paid to all disabled people who can demonstrate a need for help with care or mobility because of impairment. However, DLA is only available to disabled people aged 16–65, with those over this age entitled to apply for the substitute Attendance Allowance unless they were claiming previously. Thus, a clear distinction is introduced between disabled people who acquired impairments earlier and later in life. When compared, DLA proves a more generous allowance, including an additional 'mobility' component, while AA includes only the 'care' component. DLA is also paid at three rates (rather than two in the case of AA).

In addition there is a three-month qualifying period for DLA but a six-month qualifying period for AA (McKay and Rowlingson, 1999; McDonald and Taylor 2006). Indeed, Help the Aged (2007) argue that the use of arbitrary age in determining DLA 'flies in the face of the UK Government's own pledge to end age discrimination'.

In comparison to this, indirect age discrimination occurs when a service or practice has no explicit age bias, but is offered in such a way that older people are disproportionately affected. For example, 'geriatric care' has been seen as segregating older people from mainstream care provision, which consequently may result in reduced levels of funding and care (Bytheway *et al.* 2007). Likewise, unequal levels of intermediate or community-based care for older people in transition between hospital and home have been viewed in this way (McDonald and Taylor 2006; Field and Blakemore 2007). Although exploring evidence of direct age discrimination can be rather explicit in its differentiation of entitlements between older and younger disabled people, and between older disabled people who acquired impairments at different times in life. Finding evidence of indirect age discrimination in the field of disability entitlements requires a more sophisticated approach. The following examples draw on an investigation of data on access to resources for older people (carried out by the first author). Using the web-based modelling tool known as the *Care Calculator* (devised by the Personal Social Services Research Unit at the London School of Economics), it is possible to make some interesting comparisons between the level of social care provision available to younger and older disabled adults. In addition, the *Age Discrimination Benchmarking Tool* (developed by the Department of Health for Standard One of the Older People's NSF) can be used to illustrate differences in levels and patterns of services.

The *Care Calculator* provides hypothetical profiles of specific circumstances that produce a particular profile of 'needs' and entitlements. These can be modeled for different age groups. For example, one of the profiles describes a scenario in which: 'You were recently involved in a road accident; which has left you using a wheelchair. You cannot shower or dress independently or prepare your own meals.' Using this demonstrates clear differences between age groups who share the same disability-related needs, with a higher percentage of people aged 18–64 receiving 'services in the community', whilst the majority of people aged 80 and over receive 'residential care'. This suggests there is some truth in the proposition that older disabled people are likely to receive different social care services from younger disabled people.

Examining data from individual local authorities also shows that most are spending less on each 'package' of home care for older people than for working-age adults. For example, in Leeds (our own local authority) for every pound spent per week on home care for a working-age adult, only 66 pence was spent on an older adult. It has been argued frequently that high referral rates to residential care for older people may reflect cost ceilings that are lower than those for younger disabled people, and that discrimination is, therefore, occurring on grounds of age (Field and Blakemore 2007; Macfarlane 2003; King's Fund 2000). This appears to be confirmed by analyses using the *Benchmarking Tool*.

The example of direct payments was referred to briefly in the earlier discussion of policy development, highlighting the exclusion of disabled people over the age of 65 from entitlement (from 1996 until 2001). Less than 1% of total identified community care expenditure was spent on older people's direct payments in 2004/5, and as little as 0.2% in the Yorkshire and Humber region. Research on disparities in take-up of direct payments (Davey *et al.* 2007) indicated wide variations in the proportion of social care budgets spent on direct payments – between both different local areas and user groups. Within this context, it was clear that many more disabled people aged 18–65, with a physical or sensory impairment, were receiving direct payments than older people. According to the same research, the proportional expenditure on direct payments to older people was also much lower than for working-age disabled people. However, while the average weekly rates of payment for working-age disabled people were considerably lower than the average unit costs of residential care for this group, the comparable costs for older people were significantly higher.

Conclusions

Intersections between disability and age discrimination are of extreme importance to a society that is marked both by its demographic ageing profile and by its coming of age in terms of disability rights legislation. In the first decades of the twenty-first century we will continue to see increasing numbers of older people living with significant impairments. Increasing numbers of those who have aged with disability from childhood and younger adulthood will bring an awareness of their rights as disabled people into old age. It is essential that those rights are not denied by virtue of the ageing label. At the same time, it is clear that many who acquire impairments in old age may resist the adoption of disability identities and be unaware of their rights in that context.

Some commentators have observed that the age discrimination experienced by older disabled people may be caused by a lack of recognition of their needs, rather than a deliberate intention to treat them unfairly. Some have suggested that targets such as the NSF remain 'aspirational, rather than justiciable' (McDonald and Taylor 2006: 57) in the knowledge that UK legislation still lacks real legal protection from age discrimination in service provision relevant to disabled people. It could be argued that there is no need to define people with impairments over retirement age as 'disabled people' because their status as 'older people' over-rides the necessity to mark out other categories of rights and exemptions on grounds of disability. The disadvantages and barriers experienced in everyday life can simply be put down to the inevitabilities of the ageing process. A consistent finding in research is that older people's expectations of both disability rights and disability services remain low, and that such low expectations may be self-fulfilling.

The unequal treatment of older disabled people, and their marginalisation from the political claims of the disability movement, may stem, in part, from long-standing cultural prejudices and stereotypes that have linked old age with a particularly negative and individualistic view of 'disability', associated with passivity, failing physical and mental health, and dependency. It is a view that has been transformed by the social model of disability and by recent developments in disability law and policy. However, this reformulation has only recently been articulated to include older people explicitly, and older people have failed to attract strong advocacy for equal treatment within the disability rights lobby. The majority of disabled people in Britain are also older people and there can be no legitimate reason to overlook their entitlement to the same opportunities and choices as younger disabled adults.

Bibliography

Age Concern England 1999. *Turning Your Back on Us: Older People and the NHS*. London: Age Concern England

Allen, J. 2008. 'Older people and wellbeing', *IPPR*, available online at www.ippr.org/publicationsandreports/publication.asp?id=620, accessed September 2010

Barnes, C. 1991. *Disabled People in Britain and Discrimination: A Case for Anti-discrimination Legislation*. London: Hurst/BCODP

Barnes, C. and Mercer, G. 2003. *Disability*. Cambridge: Polity Press

2006. *Independent Futures: Creating User-led Services in a Disabling Society*, Bristol: BASW/Policy Press

Bernard, M. and Phillips, J. 1998. *The Social Policy of Old Age*. London: Centre for Policy on Ageing

Berthoud, R. and Blekesaune, M. 2007. *Persistent Employment Disadvantage*. London: Department for Work and Pensions

Biggs, S. 1997. 'Choosing not to be old? Masks, bodies and identity management in later life', *Ageing and Society* 17: 553–70

Borsay, A. 2005. *Disability and Social Policy in Britain since 1750: A History of Exclusion*. Basingstoke: Palgrave Macmillan

Bowling, A. 2005. *Quality of Life in Older Age*. Maidenhead: Open University Press

Breitenbach, N. 2001. 'Ageing with intellectual disabilities; discovering disability with old age: same or different?' in M. Priestley (ed.), *Disability and the Life Course: Global Perspectives*. Cambridge University Press, 231–39

BURDIS (Burden of Disease Network Project) 2004. *Disability in Old Age: Final Report Conclusions and Recommendations*. Jyvaskyla University Press

Bury, M. 1982. 'Chronic illness as biographical disruption', *Sociology of Health and Illness* 4(2): 167–82

Bytheway, B. and Johnson, J. 1990. 'On defining ageism', *Critical Social Policy* 27: 27–39

Bytheway, B., Ward, R., Holland, C. and Peace, S. 2007. 'Too old: older people's accounts of discrimination, exclusion and rejection', *Help the Aged*, available online at www.open.ac.uk/hsc/__assets/dh4bwtxdy7tqjqvhe2.pdf, accessed September 2010

Bytheway, W. 1989. *Becoming and Being Old: Sociological Approaches to Later Life*. London: Sage

Campbell, J. 2008. 'Joined-up thinking', *The Guardian*, 30 April 2008, available online at www.guardian.co.uk/society/2008/apr/30/disability, accessed September 2010

Carricaburu, D. and Pierret, J. 1995. 'From biographical disruption to biographical reinforcement – the case of HIV-positive men', *Sociology of Health and Illness* 17(1): 65–88

Craig, P. and Greenslade, M. 1998. *First Findings from the Disability Follow-up to the Family Resources Survey: Research Summary no. 5*. London: Analytical Services Division, Department of Social Security

Daley, G. and Denniss, M. 1997. *Patient Satisfaction: The Discharge of Older People from Hospital: A Survey*. London: Centre for Policy on Ageing

Dalley, G. 1998. 'Health and social welfare policy', in M. Bernard and J. Philips (eds.), *The Social Policy of Old Age*. London: Centre for Policy on Ageing, 20–39

Davey, V., Fernández, J. L., Knapp, M., Vick, N., Jolly, D., Swift, P., Tobin, R., Kendall, J., Ferrie, J., Pearson, C., Mercer, G. and Priestley, M. 2007. *Direct Payments Survey: A National Survey of Direct Payments Policy and Practice*. London: Personal Social Services Research Unit/London School of Economics

Demakakos, P., Gjonca, E. and Nazroo, J. 2007. 'Age identity, age perceptions, and health: evidence from the English Longitudinal Study of Ageing', *Annals of the New York Academy of Sciences* 1114: 279–87

Department for Work and Pensions 2005. *Opportunity Age: Meeting the Challenges of Ageing in the 21st Century*. London: DWP

Department of Health 2001. *National Service Framework for Older People*. London: DoH

  2005. *Independence, Well-being and Choice: Our Vision for the Future of Social Care for Adults in England*. London: DoH

  2006. *Our Health, Our Care, Our Say: A New Direction for Community Services*. London: DoH

  2008. *High Quality Care for All: NHS Next Stage Review Final Report*. London: DoH

Disability Rights Commission 2000. *DRC Disability Briefing*, available online at www.drc-gb.org/drc/InformationAndLegislation/Page353.asp, accessed June 2002

Drake, R. 1996. 'Charities, authority and disabled people: a qualitative study', *Disability and Society* 11(1): 5–23

  1999. *Understanding Disability Policies*. Basingstoke: Macmillan

Estes, C. L., Biggs, S. and Phillipson, C. 2003. *Social Theory, Social Policy and Ageing*. Milton Keynes: Open University Press

Featherstone, M. and Hepworth, M. 1991. 'The mask of aging and the post modern lifecourse', in M. Featherstone, M. Hepworth and B. S. Turner (eds.), *The Body: Social Process and Cultural Theory*. London: Sage, 371–89

Fennell, G., Phillipson, C. and Evers, H. 1988. *The Sociology of Old Age*. Milton Keynes: Open University Press

Field, D. and Blakemore, K. 2007. 'Health and disease in old age', in S. Taylor and D. Field (eds.), *Sociology of Health and Health Care*. Oxford: Blackwell, 113–33

Field, D. and Taylor, S. 2007. 'Health care in contemporary Britain', in S. Taylor and D. Field (eds.), *Sociology of Health and Health Care*. Oxford: Blackwell, 205–28

Finkelstein, V. 1991. 'Disability: an administrative challenge? (the health and welfare heritage)', in M. Oliver (ed.), *Social Work: Disabled People and Disabling Environments*. London: Jessica Kingsley, 63–77

Gooding, C. 2009. 'Promoting equality? Early lessons from the statutory disability duty in Great Britain', in G. Quinn and L. Waddington (eds.), *European Yearbook of Disability Law*. Antwerp: Intersentia, vol. I, 29–58

Healthcare Commission 2006. 'Living well in later life', 1–23, available online at www.audit-commission.gov.uk/SiteCollectionDocuments/AuditCommissionReports/NationalStudies/HCC_olderSummary.pdf, accessed September 2010

Help the Aged 2005. 'Opportunity age', available online at http://policy.helptheaged.org.uk/NR/rdonlyres/C27C1CA6–4995–4DAF-9971-D476F5AA912E/0/august_opportunityageresponse.pdf, accessed September 2010

2007. 'Disability benefits', available online at www.helptheaged.org.uk/en-gb/ Campaigns/Campaigns_old/PensionsAndBenefits/DisabilityBenefits/defa ult.htm, accessed May 2008

Henwood, M. 2001. 'Future imperfect? Report of the King's Fund Inquiry into Care and Support Workers', available online at www.kingsfund.org.uk/pu blications/kings_fund_publications/future.html, accessed May 2008

Hudson, B.; Dearey, M. and Glendinning, C. 2005. 'A new vision for adult social care: scoping service users' views', available online at www.york.ac.uk/inst/ spru/pubs/pdf/newvision.pdf, accessed September 2010

Hughes, B. 1995. *Older People and Community Care: Critical Theory and Practice.* Buckingham: Open University Press

Iliffe, S., Patterson, L. and Gould, M. 1998. *Health Care for Older People.* London: BMJ Publishing Group

Irwin, S. 1999. 'Later life, inequality and sociological theory', *Ageing and Society* 19(6): 691–715

2001. 'Repositioning disability and the life course: a social claiming perspective', in M. Priestley (ed.), *Disability and the Life Course: Global Perspectives.* Cambridge University Press, 15–25

Jolly, D., Priestley, M. and Matthews, B. 2006. *Secondary Analysis of Existing Data on Disabled People's Use and Experiences of Public Transport in Great Britain.* Leeds: Centre for Disability Studies

Kanter, A. 2007. 'The promise and challenge of the United Nations Convention on the rights of persons with disabilities. Symposium: The United Nations Convention on the rights of persons with disabilities', *Syracuse Journal of International Law and Commerce*, special issue 34(2): 287–321

Kaufmann, F. and Leisering, L. 1984. 'Demographic changes as a problem for social security systems', *International Social Security Review* 37: 388–409

Kennedy, J. and Minkler, M. 1998. 'Disability theory and public policy: implications for critical gerontology', *International Journal of Health Services* 28(4): 757–76

King's Fund 2000. 'Briefing note. Age discrimination in health and social care', available online at www.kingsfund.org.uk/publications/kings_ fund_publications/age.html, accessed May 2008

Lawson, A. 2008. *Disability and Equality Law in Britain: The Role of Reasonable Adjustment.* London: Hart Publishing

Macfarlane, A. 2003. 'Older people and direct payments', available online at www.independentliving.org/docs6/macfarlane200303.html#older, accessed September 2010

Martin, J., Meltzer, H. and Elliot, D. 1988. *The Prevalence of Disability Amongst Adults.* London: HMSO

McDonald, A. and Taylor, M. 2006. *Older People and the Law* (2nd edn). Bristol: The Policy Press

McGlone, F. 1992. *Disability and Dependency in Old Age: A Demographic and Social Audit*. London: Family Policy Studies Centre, Occasional Paper 14

McKay, S. and Rowlingson, K. 1999. *Social Security in Britain*. Basingstoke: Macmillan

Molloy, D., Knight, T. and Woodfield, K. 2003. *Diversity in Disability: Exploring the Interactions between Disability, Ethnicity, Age, Gender and Sexuality*. Leeds: Department for Work and Pensions

Morris, J. 1993. *Independent Lives? Community Care and Disabled People*. Basingstoke: Macmillan.

Muenz, R. 2007. *Aging and Demographic Change in European Societies: Aging and Demographic Change in European Societies: Main Trends and Alternative Policy Options*. Hamburg: Institute for International Economics

NDA 2006. 'Ageing and disability: a discussion paper', available online at www.nda.ie/cntmgmtnew.nsf/0/FBE570D7C6D435C28025710D004594B9/$F File/NDAAgeingandDisabilityDiscussionPaper.pdf, accessed September 2010

Office for Disability Issues 2008. *Independent Living: A Cross-government Strategy about Independent Living for Disabled People*. London: ODI

Oliver, M. 1983. *Social Work with Disabled People*. Basingstoke: Macmillan
  1990. *The Politics of Disablement*. Basingstoke: Macmillan

Phillipson, C. 1998. *Reconstructing Old Age: New Agendas in Social Theory and Social Practice*. London: Sage

Phillipson, C. and Walker, A. (eds.) 1986 *Ageing and Social Policy: A Critical Assessment*. Aldershot: Gower

Pilling, D. and Watson, G. (eds.) 1995. *Evaluating Quality in Services for Disabled and Older People*. London: Jessica Kingsley

Priestley, M. 1997. 'The origins of a legislative disability category in England: a speculative history', *Disability Studies Quarterly* 17(2): 87–94
  1998. *Disability Politics and Community Care*. London: Jessica Kingsley
  2000. 'Adults only: disability, social policy and the life course', *Journal of Social Policy* 29: 421–39
  2002a. '"It's like your hair going grey", or is it? Impairment, disability and the habitus of old age', in S. Riddell and N. Watson (eds.), *Disability, Culture and Identity*. Edinburgh: Pearson Education, 53–66
  2002b. 'Whose voices? Representing the claims of older disabled people under New Labour', *Policy and Politics* 30(3): 361–72
  2004. 'Generating debates: why we need a life course approach to disability issues', in J. Swain, S. French, C. Barnes and C. Thomas (eds.), *Disabling Barriers, Enabling Environments*. London: Sage, 94–9
  2005. 'Disability and old age: or why it isn't all in the mind', in D. Goodley and R. Lawton (eds.), *Disability and Psychology: Critical Introductions and Reflections*. London: Palgrave, 84–93

Priestley, M. and Rabiee, P. 2002. 'Same difference? Older people's organisations and disability issues', *Disability and Society* 17(6): 597–611

Prime Minister's Strategy Unit 2005. *Improving the Life Chances of Disabled People: Final Report*. London: PMSU

Quinn, G. 2009. 'A short guide to the United Nations Convention on the Rights of Persons with Disabilities', in G. Quinn and L. Waddington (eds.), *European Yearbook of Disability Law*. Antwerp: Intersentia, vol. I, 89–114

Roberts, E., Robinson, J. and Seymour, L. 2002. *Old Habits Die Hard: Tackling Age Discrimination in Health and Social Care*. London: King's Fund Publishing

Rostgaard, T. and Fridberg, T. 1998. *Caring for Children and Older People: A Comparison of European Policies and Practices*. Copenhagen: Danish National Institute of Social Research

Salvatori, P., Tremblay, M., Sandys, J. and Marcaccio, D. 1998. 'Aging with an intellectual disability: a review of Canadian literature', *Canadian Journal on Aging–Revue Canadienne du Vieillissement* 17(3): 249–71

Seebohm Report 1968. *Report of the Committee on Local Authority and Allied Personal Social Services (chair Frederic Seebohm)*. London: HMSO

Stone, D. 1984. *The Disabled State*. Philadelphia, PA: Temple University Press

Taylor, S. and Field, D. 2007. *Sociology of Health and Health Care* (4th edn). Oxford: Blackwell

Thompson, P. 1992. 'I don't feel old: subjective ageing and the search for meaning in later life', *Ageing and Society* 12: 23–47

Topliss, E. 1975. *Provision for the Disabled*. Oxford: Blackwell/Martin Robertson

Townsend, P. 1962. *The Last Refuge: A Survey of Residential Institutions and Homes for the Aged in England and Wales*. London: Routledge and Kegan Paul

Vincent, J. 1999. *Politics, Power and Old Age*. Buckingham: Open University Press

Walker, A. and Naegele, G. (eds.) 1999. *The Politics of Old Age in Europe*. Buckingham: Open University Press

Williams, B., Copestake, P., Eversley, J. and Stafford, B. 2008. *The Experiences and Expectations of Disabled People*. London: Office for Disability Issues/DWP

Williams, S. 2000. 'Chronic illness as biographical disruption or biographical disruption as chronic illness? Reflections on a core concept', *Sociology of Health and Illness* 22(1): 40–67

Zarb, G. 1992. 'Ageing with a disability: the experience of long-term male amputees', available online at www.leeds.ac.uk/disability-studies/archiveuk/Zarb/BLESMA.pdf, accessed September 2010

Zarb, G. and Oliver, M. 1993. *Ageing with a Disability: What Do They Expect after All These Years?* London: University of Greenwich

Zola, I. 1989. 'Towards a necessary universalizing of disability policy', *Millbank Memorial Quarterly* 67(2): 401–428.

9

New approaches for understanding inequalities in service use among older people

SARA ALLIN AND JOSE-LUIS FERNANDEZ

Inequalities in publicly funded services have received considerable attention in recent years. On the one hand, policy-makers have placed increased emphasis on ensuring a fair distribution of public services. On the other, researchers have responded by developing new methods to measure and understand inequalities. Inequalities can exist across a number of policy-relevant dimensions. These include, but are not limited to: socio-economic status, where there are concerns that individuals with less income or access to resources may be treated differently by public services such as health and social care; age, where the concern centres around age discrimination or differential access or treatment based on age; geography, where the availability of services or quality of services for a given need vary across regions; and racial/ethnic identity, language and culture. Policy attention has targeted all of these dimensions in recent years, and, in some cases, the policies have recognised the intersections of these factors. Overall, however, the bulk of the empirical research on inequalities in service use has focused on socio-economic inequalities. This chapter pays particular attention to the factors that explain socio-economic inequalities in health and social care service use among older people, and the methodological challenges that their study presents for this segment of the population.

Older people are the highest consumers of health and social services. Individuals aged 65 years and older are twice as likely as the younger population to be admitted to hospital in a year and they are heavy users of long-term care home services (Wanless *et al.* 2006; Fernandez and Forder 2008; Forder 2009). According to the British Household Panel Survey, from the period 1997 to 2006, almost a quarter of individuals aged 80 years or older had used some level of home help and almost half had seen a health visitor in the past year. Approximately 8% of those aged 65 years and older used home help and 13% saw a health visitor, while less than 1% of the under-65 population received home help, and about 6% had a health visitor. Investigating inequalities in service use within the older population is important, not only because they consume the majority of health and social services, but also because inequalities among older people are often linked to complex combinations of need factors relating to their socio-economic status, age and physical abilities, and the culture and organisation of health and social care. As discussed below, from a methodological perspective, understanding and measuring the impact on inequalities of such factors within the older people group also presents particular technical and conceptual challenges.

This chapter begins with an introduction of some of the methods used for measuring inequalities in the areas of health and social care services, paying special attention to the specific methodological issues that are raised in the older population. It then reviews the English evidence on the patterns of utilisation of the health and social services across socio-economic groups, and examines the role of different factors in explaining the observed distribution of state-funded support. It finishes with some directions for future research.

How do we measure inequalities?

Inequalities in services use can arise for a number of different reasons, each requiring different mitigation strategies and hence with different policy implications. Overall, differences in levels and quality of service use will depend on interactions between 'demand' related factors – such as variations between population groups in the need for services or in their degree of awareness of the availability of services – and 'supply' factors – such as variations in the 'offer' and accessibility of services to alternative groups (Fernandez *et al.* 2008). Building a full understanding of the policy implication of inequalities implies therefore first the measurement of the extent of inequalities across key groups, which is a descriptive exercise that combines information on services use with information on socio-economic status, and secondly an analysis of the factors at the source of such variations.

Numerous approaches can be used to describe and quantify the extent of inequalities. In the health economics literature, a major contribution to the measurement of inequalities has been made by the adaptation of the Lorenz curve and Gini coefficient, traditionally used in the estimation of income inequalities, to the health care context. As a result, concentration curve plots have been used to depict the cumulative distribution of service use amongst the population, ranked by income (Wagstaff and van Doorslaer 2000; O'Donnell *et al.* 2008). Using concentration curves, researchers are able to measure the extent to which service use is more (or less) concentrated among the lower (or upper) end of the income distribution. As an illustration of this approach, Figure 9.1 depicts a stylised concentration curve of inequality in service use. In situations in which all individuals use services equally, regardless of income, no concentration of service use by income exists, and the concentration curve falls on the line of equality. Graphically, the degree of inequality of service use is therefore illustrated by the area between the concentration curve and the line of equality. Figure 9.1 exemplifies a hypothetical inequality in service use, as can be seen by the fact that the poorest 20% of the population use much less than 20% (close to 5%) of the total services used in the population; the figure shows a visible concentration of services in the upper end of the income distribution. The concentration index is calculated as twice the area between the line of equality and the concentration curve.

The analysis of a bivariate relationship between income (or other indicators used to define population subgroups) on the one hand and

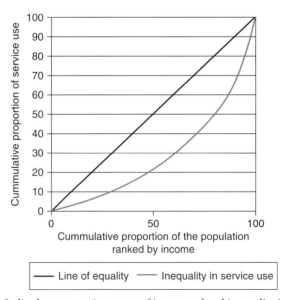

Figure 9.1 Stylised concentration curve of income-related inequality in service use.

service use on the other, such as is described by a concentration curve, is complicated by the unequal distribution of need for services between analysis groups. There is a great deal of evidence, for instance, of the unequal distribution of ill-health and disability by income, education, social class and other indicators of socio-economic status (Marmot and Shipley 1996; Marmot and Wilkinson 1999; Mackenbach *et al.* 2003). Individuals with socio-economic disadvantage have a greater prevalence of ill-health than those with socio-economic advantage; therefore, on average, there is greater need for health and social services among the lower socio-economic groups. This means that in many cases achieving equality of service use for given need implies a concentration of service use among the lower end of the income (or other indicator of socio-economic status) distribution.

From a policy perspective, we are in fact interested in the extent of inequalities in service use *controlling for need*. This means examining horizontal equity – the degree to which individuals of equal need enjoy equal levels of service – and vertical equity – the extent to which individuals with higher need receive more support (Musgrave 1959). In order to control for differences in need between subgroups, the concentration curve approach for measuring inequalities illustrated above has been adapted to the measurement of horizontal equity by adjusting the estimates of service utilisation used in the concentration curves for differences in needs, using multivariate regression methods.

Measuring individuals' need for services is therefore a key step in the methods for measuring inequalities in service use in terms of horizontal and vertical equity. In the economics literature, four definitions of need for health care have been proposed (Culyer and Wagstaff 1993): an individual's current health status; an individual's capacity to benefit from health care; the expenditure a person 'ought' to have (i.e. the amount of health care required to attain best possible health); or the minimum amount of resources required to exhaust capacity to benefit.

Which measures of need are used in the analysis will depend on the data sources that are available. When, as is often the case, studies of inequalities are based on survey data, the analyses have tended to use self-reported measures of health status, health conditions, disease symptoms, disability status and limitations with activities of daily living, to approximate need for health and/or social service use. Some surveys, such as the Health Survey for England, and the England Longitudinal Study of Ageing, include clinical measures of health that are collected by nurses about a subsample of survey respondents. These more objective need measures may help to remove some of the bias that is associated with self-reported health, and more importantly with the risk of differences in the systematic under- or over-reporting of health need across socio-economic groups (Sen 2002). There is, for instance, some evidence of differences in self-reported health bias by age and gender (Lindeboom and van Doorslaer 2004), and by income (Johnston, Propper and Shields 2009).

With administrative data, diagnostic information can also be used to measure need for services. For example, the Adjusted Clinical Group (ACG) system has been developed at Johns Hopkins University as a validated case-mix grouper for health services (Reid *et al.* 2001). This system classifies individuals into different categories on the basis of all diagnoses they have received in the past year in ambulatory or hospital settings with the aim to reflect expected health care utilisation. Therefore, individuals in the same ACG can be considered to have the same expected health care needs. However, one of the limitations of the use of administrative data is that the evidence will often include exclusively individuals who are known to the service collecting the data used, and therefore will exclude by definition individuals who are not in contact with services. With regards to social care, a number of assessment tools have been developed in order to measure need for services, such as the Residential Assessment Instrument (RAI) used to evaluate the needs of individuals in long-term care institutions (Ikegami 2004).

A literature review of inequalities in health services use in the UK found that empirical studies have tended to rely on one of the following assumptions about need (Goddard and Smith 2001):

- equal levels of need across the groups being studied (for example, in disease-specific studies);
- need is measured using self-assessed health (SAH), assuming there are no systematic variations between groups in reporting;
- need is measured with biomedical measures, assuming collection methods are standardised and that unmeasured factors are not related to need;
- levels of need are inferred through characteristics of the area people live in (e.g. through levels of deprivation);
- need is approximated with socio-economic measures;
- or need is inferred from the results of other studies.

In the epidemiological literature, need is commonly measured with biomedical measures, or disease-specific studies are undertaken and need is assumed to be equal across groups with the same conditions. In the health economics and health services literature, empirical studies most often measure need by level of ill-health (and risk of ill-health), with self-reported measures, clinical or diagnostic information, or area-level indicators.

Combining multivariate regression analyses with the concentration index approach for measuring inequalities allows us to account for differences in need for services along the income distribution. The same methods can be used to isolate and control for the impact of other policy relevant factors that independently affect the receipt of services. Such analyses allow us therefore to disentangle the impact of a wide range of mediating factors that lead to inequalities in service use, such as, for example, the impact of differences in the supply and thus availability of services, measured for instance in terms of bed numbers, distance to facilities, waiting times, density of providers and availability of informal care.

The effects of factors that are independently associated with service use can be estimated with regression models, and then the level of income-related inequality in service use can be statistically decomposed into the factors that contribute to inequality and those that do not (O'Donnell *et al.* 2008). Overall, the contribution of each determinant to total inequality in health care utilisation can be decomposed into three components: two deterministic components, equal to the combined effect of the concentration indices of need-related and non-need-related factors linked to variations in service use; and a residual component that reflects the inequality in health care use that cannot be explained by systematic variations in the indicators included in the analysis. Thus, the contributors to inequality can be divided into inequalities in each of the 'need' and 'non-need' variables (O'Donnell *et al.* 2008; Wagstaff, van Doorslaer and Watanabe 2003). Doing so is important, because although income-related inequity is often due directly to differences in income, it sometimes reflects the indirect effect of income through other factors such as education, place of residence, employment or immigration status. A positive link between income and educational attainment, for instance, together with a positive link between education and increased utilisation (for instance because of greater awareness among the better educated of the benefits of care) will result in a positive contribution of education to the income-based concentration of health care use. The intensity of this contribution will depend on the strength of the relationship between education and health care use and between education and income. In general, a factor's contribution can be either positive or negative, depending on the sign of the combination of the effects linking it to variations in service use. From a policy point of view, disentangling direct from indirect income effects on inequalities is very important because it will help inform the policy actions required to reduce inequalities.

Although very powerful, there are some general limitations with the concentration index approach to measuring inequalities. The approach above is for instance limited to consider factors that can be quantitatively measured at an individual level. Furthermore, the index does not impose any judgment about an appropriate level of utilisation in a population, and jurisdictions providing very different service levels may be associated with identical inequality indices. Also, a zero index can be obtained if the concentration curve crosses the diagonal, so visual depictions are useful to identify where along the income distribution there is inequality. Finally, the concentration curve by definition values all deviations in service use across the income distribution equally, in effect implying that inequalities among the richest people are equivalent in their contribution to overall estimates of inequalities as inequalities that predominantly affect the poorest people. Because policy-makers may choose to target inequalities at the lower end of the income distribution, or may view inequalities that affect the most deprived populations as more concerning, the 'extended concentration index' can be used to weigh inequalities among the poorest people more heavily (O'Donnell et al. 2008).

The methods described above are most often used to estimate income-related inequalities. However, income may not be the most appropriate indicator of socio-economic status among older people. Among older people, for instance, employment-related earnings are typically small and the variation (inequality) in income distribution more limited than for the general population. In England, for instance, only about 15% of individuals over age 65 reported any labour income in 2006. On average, this source of income was found to contribute approximately 5% of total household income, and the estimates of income inequality among older people were found to be lower than for the general population (Allin, Masseria and Mossialos 2010). It is not surprising therefore that the use of income indicators (and in particular of employment income) and activity status to capture variations in socio-economic status among older people has been called into question (Alessie, Lusardi and Aldershof 1997; van Ourti 2003). Some studies have pointed to home ownership as an alternative and more relevant proxy for socio-economic status among older people (Crystal and Shea 1990; Costa-Font 2008).

In terms of the analysis of inequalities, however, home ownership indicators offer little opportunity for differentiating between groups of individuals, and therefore limit the detail and scope of the analysis. Socio-economic status has also been defined by using area-level deprivation indices, such as the Townsend index of deprivation, which, although not defined at the individual level, can provide a more comprehensive measure of socio-economic status than solely income (Cookson, Dusheiko and Hardman 2007; Laudicella *et al.* 2009).

In general, the choice of indicator used for defining socio-economic status will impact directly the estimates of inequalities obtained. One recent study, for instance, concluded that the estimates of inequalities in service use among older adults in Europe tended to be higher when broader measures of wealth that considered assets in addition to income were used than when only income was considered (Allin *et al.* 2009).

What do we know about inequalities?

The majority of empirical studies of inequalities in service use have focused on health services, with most of the research investigating the extent of inequalities in separate sectors of the health care system, such as prevention, primary care and specialist care, or in separate services, such as hip replacements. Two early reviews of the literature on inequalities in health service use among the general population found evidence of some socio-economic inequalities in the use of some specific inpatient procedures, health promotion and prevention services in the period 1990–97 (Goddard and Smith 2001), and in the use of specialist care up to 2003 (Dixon *et al.* 2007). While these reviews did not focus on older people specifically, their findings are relevant to the older population because they make up the majority of service users.

An updated review that paid particular attention to older people found similar results (Fernandez *et al.* 2008): for services such as mammography, hip replacements, dental services, coronary revascularisation (among men) and ophthalmic services, the evidence demonstrates the existence of systematic differences in the utilisation of health care services across socio-economic groups of older people. Although based on a smaller body of research, the review also identified inequalities in the use of social care services. In England, the fact that the social care state system only provides support to individuals with very low resources and very high needs means that a significant proportion of older people with moderate means and/or moderate needs are faced with the full cost of their care, and as a result consume less care than wealthy older people, or than very poor individuals who qualify for state-funded support (Wanless *et al.* 2006). In general, means-tested social care systems are usually characterised by poor levels of horizontal and vertical equity (Fernandez *et al.* 2009).

Two recent studies employed the concentration index approach to measuring inequalities in health service use among older adults in England, drawing on different data sources – survey versus administrative data – and units of analysis – individuals versus small areas. Using the British Household Panel Survey for the period 1997–2006, Allin *et al.* (2010) estimated income-related inequalities in the likelihood of using primary care, specialist care, dental care and inpatient care among the older population. The study identified, in line with previous studies, evidence of income-related inequalities in needs-adjusted use in specialist care and to a greater extent in dental care. Cookson *et al.* (2007) used hospital episode statistics linked to area-level census deprivation data to examine socio-economic inequalities in the receipt of hip replacements among adults aged 44 years or older in 1991 and 2001. The study found a significant concentration of hip replacement rates in less deprived areas, thus suggesting inequalities in the use of the service between socio-economic groups. Both studies found some decrease in the extent of inequalities over time, which may be partly attributed to increased service capacity over the period.

In an earlier study, Morris, Sutton and Gravelle (2003) decomposed the concentration indices into the explanatory factors linked to inequalities in health care service use among the general population. The study showed the effect of education on inequality to depend on the service considered. Hence, higher educational attainment was associated with higher income and increased likelihood of specialist visits, but decreased likelihood of visiting a GP. The research also found that the contribution of supply variables on income-related inequality in probability of use of GP and outpatient visits, day cases and inpatient stays was near zero, even though there was a positive effect of these measures of supply on utilisation. In other words, the study concluded that better access to services, as measured by waiting times, distance to service and density of providers, was associated with increased use of services in all sectors, but that it was not correlated with income.

In addition to the studies aimed at assessing quantitatively patterns of variations in service utilisation, a significant body of research has explored which factors give rise to such inequalities (see Fernandez *et al.* 2008, for a fuller review of the evidence). First, the use of health care services has been found to vary across socio-economic groups because of differences in the nature of the doctor–patient relationship. In particular, studies have shown that better-educated patients and those from a higher social class enjoy increased access to specialist services, partly due to a privileged relationship with GPs, who in England are responsible for referring patients on to specialists. Second, there is evidence of lower awareness about the existence of (and/or the need for) services amongst disadvantaged groups. Hidden and late presentations of symptoms require further policy attention, as does the need for training of care staff in the recognition of under-presentation to services among low socio-economic groups. Third, studies have linked inequalities in service use among older people to differences across socio-economic groups in access to instrumental resources to the use of health care services, such as income, information sources (e.g. internet) and methods of transport. In addition to differences in actual utilisation, studies have found differences across socio-economic groups in other indicators of service provision. Hence, Siciliani and Verzulli (2009) identified longer waiting times across European countries for older people in low-income groups. There is some evidence, however, that over time the differences in waiting times across area of varying levels of deprivation for elective surgery have diminished in England (Cooper *et al.* 2009).

In terms of social care services, as indicated above, some of the patterns of inequalities in service utilisation in England are linked to the nature of funding arrangements for state support, and specifically to the targeting of public social care support on those with very high needs and very low means. Large numbers of older people with moderate levels of disabilities do not qualify for state support, and have either to rely on family and friends, to pay significant sums of money to fund their care, or to do without help. Thus, a number of studies have reported signifi-cant unmet social care needs among older people, and particularly among older people with moderate wealth (Forder and Fernandez 2009).

The needs of informal carers, who provide a majority of social care support and are often elderly themselves, should also receive greater policy attention. Many complain about lack of respite, and little information about the availability of services and the prognosis of the person being cared for. Whereas this does not point directly towards socio-economic inequalities, the lack of support for informal carers is particularly problematic among certain minority ethnic groups, owing to the expectation by services that among such groups informal support will always cover the social care needs of older people (Hanratty *et al.* 2007; Chui and Yu 2001).

There are also significant unmet social care needs linked to the lack of recognition by practitioners of mental health problems among older people, often because their symptoms are associated with the normal process of ageing. Again, whereas this problem is present across socio-economic groups, it is particularly acute among ethnic minority groups (Blakemore, 1999). Mold, Fitzpatrick and Roberts (2005) found a low take-up rate of nursing home services among Asians in Leicester because of cultural insensitivity of services to different dietary, religious and language needs, and a need to improve communication between ethnic minority users and formal carers. Cultural differences were also linked to the relatively low membership of self-help groups for carers in Munn-Giddings and McVicar's study (2006). A study of direct payments found that only a few black and minority communities accessed direct payments owing to a low level of awareness about the existence of the service (Spandler and Vick 2006).

Directions for future research

Whereas our understanding of inequalities in service use among older people has improved in recent times, important questions remain unanswered. Partly, these gaps in knowledge respond to limitations in the evidence base and analytical techniques currently available.

So far, most studies on inequalities have been based on cross-sectional evidence. Greater use of longitudinal data, however, would permit an investigation of the trends of inequalities over time, and would provide a number of important policy insights. For instance, it would allow the research to explore the dynamics leading to inequalities by linking outcomes and earlier life experiences and behaviours of individuals, such as for instance the longitudinal relationship between individual and family characteristics, factors leading to the take-up of insurance, accumulation of assets, health status and health care consumption. Longitudinal data would also enable the analysis to control for the possible endogeneity of need variables in the health care utilisation models (Sutton *et al.* 1999). For instance, the distinction between an initial state of health and the final state of health after receiving health care is often ignored because of limitations of cross-sectional survey data (Culyer 1993). If the relationship between morbidity and utilisation is bi-directional, then the endogenous and exogenous effects could be corrected, to some extent, by including past health status. The bias of reciprocal causality that stems from the causal impact of health care contacts on current health status, however, appears to be small (Windmeijer and Santos Silva 1997; Bago d'Uva, Jones and van Doorslaer 2007).

In addition to the use of longitudinal sources of evidence, it will be important for studies on inequalities to consider jointly the evidence for a wide range of services. By exploring patterns of variability for specific services independently, many studies in the area fail to recognise the substitutability and complementarity of alternative services (Fernandez and Forder 2008). Doing so is important because the apparent over/underutilisation of particular services by different socio-economic or ethnic groups could in fact be the result of differences in their preferences over alternative services or modalities of support (e.g. residential services versus community-based services). Patterns of inequalities, in other words, could compensate or exacerbate each other when measured across combinations of services.

Greater focus on final indicators of outcome (e.g. indicators of health status adjusted for quality of life) rather than on indicators of service receipt should also strengthen the usefulness of future research in the area. Focusing on variations in outcomes rather than in levels of service receipt should provide a more accurate picture of the true impact and possible shortfalls of the observed distribution of public resources on the well-being of individuals. By examining impact on well-being directly, focusing on outcomes would also contribute to tackling some of the current methodological problems, such as how to capture differences in the quality of services consumed by different socio-economic groups. Measuring outcomes, however, presents itself significant challenges in terms of the availability of appropriate outcome data, and of the ability of the analysis to attribute differences in final outcomes (such as mortality) to the effect of lack of services or to the impact of factors outside the control of policy-makers (Malley and Fernandez 2010).

In terms of tackling existing inequalities, more research is needed about how to use our understanding of human behaviour to develop appropriate incentives for increasing awareness among certain socio-economic groups about the benefits of healthy living, and about the existence of key health and social care services. It is often the case, for instance, that programmes aimed at reducing socio-economic inequalities in health by reducing risky behaviour (such as smoking) are most effective among the better-off and the more educated. From a front-line service point of view, an important focus of activity should be the development of processes and training for professionals in order to achieve a system which tailors flexibly for the specific needs of minority groups, and those most disadvantaged in society.

Bibliography

Alessie, R., Lusardi, A. and Aldershof, T. 1997. 'Income and wealth over the life cycle: evidence from panel data', *Review of Income and Wealth* 43: 1–32

Allin, S., Masseria, C. and Mossialos, E. 2009. 'Measuring socioeconomic differences in use of health care services by wealth versus by income', *American Journal of Public Health* 99: 1849–55

2010. 'Equity in health care use among older people in the United Kingdom: an analysis of panel data', *Applied Economics*. First published on 21 April 2010 (iFirst).

Bago d'Uva, T., Jones, A., and van Doorslaer, E. 2007. 'Measurement of horizontal inequity in health care utilization using European panel data'. Tinbergen Institute Discussion Paper TI 2007–059/3. Rotterdam: Erasmus University

Blakemore, K. 1999. 'Health and social care needs in minority communities: an over-problematized issue?', *Health and Social Care in the Community* 8: 22–30

Chui, S. and Yu, S. 2001. 'An excess of culture : the myth of shared care in the Chinese community in Britain', *Ageing and Society* 21: 681–99

Cookson, R., Dusheiko, M. and Hardman, G. 2007. 'Socioeconomic inequality in small area use of elective total hip replacement in the English National Health Service in 1991 and 2001', *Journal of Health Services Research and Policy* 12: 10–17

Cooper, Z. N., McGuire, A., Jones, S. and Le Grand, J. 2009. 'Equity, waiting times and the NHS reforms', *BMJ* 339: b3264

Costa-Font, J. 2008. 'Housing assets and the socio-economic determinants of health and disability in old age', *Health and Place* 14: 478–91

Crystal, S. and Shea, D. 1990. 'The economic well-being of the elderly', *Review of Income and Wealth* 36: 227–47

Culyer, A. J. 1993. 'Health, health expenditures, and equity', in E. van Doorslaer, A. Wagstaff and F. Rutten (eds.), *Equity in the Finance and Delivery of Health Care: An International Perspective*. Oxford University Press, 299–319

Culyer, A. J. and Wagstaff, A. 1993. 'Equity and equality in health and health care', *Journal of Health Economics* 12: 431–57

Dixon, A., Le Grand, J., Henderson, J., Murray, R. and Poteliakhoff, E. 2007. 'Is the British National Health Service equitable? The evidence on socio-economic differences in utilisation', *Journal of Health Services Research and Policy* 12: 104–9

Fernandez, J.-L., and Forder, J. 2008. 'Consequences of local variations in social care on the performance of the acute health care sector', *Applied Economics* 40: 1503–18

Fernandez, J.-L., Forder, J., Trukeschitz, B., Rokosová, M. and McDaid, D. 2009. *How Can European States Design Efficient, Equitable and Sustainable Funding Systems for Long-term Care for Older People?* Copenhagen: World Health Organization

Fernandez, J. L., McDaid, D., Kite, J., Schmidt, A., Park, A. and Knapp, M. 2008. 'Inequalities in the use of services among older people in England. A rapid review of the literature for Age Concern', PSSRU Discussion Paper DP2610. Canterbury: PSSRU

Forder, J. 2009. Long-term care and hospital utilisation by older people: an analysis of substitution rates', *Health Economics* 18: 1322–38

Forder, J. and Fernandez, J.-L. 2009. *Analysing Costs and Benefits of Social Care Funding Arrangements in England: Technical Report*. PSSRU Discussion Paper 2644. Canterbury: PSSRU.

Goddard, M. and Smith, P. 2001. 'Equity of access to health care services: theory and evidence from UK', *Social Science and Medicine* 53: 1149–62

Hanratty, B., Drever, F., Jacoby, A. and Whitehead, M. 2007. 'Retirement age caregivers and deprivation of area of residence in England and Wales', *European Journal of Ageing* 4: 35–43

Ikegami, N. 2004. 'Using residential assessment instrument minimum data set care planning instruments in community and institutional care: introduction by chair', *Geriatrics and Gerontology International* 4: S271–S273

Johnston, D. W., Propper, C. and Shields, M. A. 2009. 'Comparing subjective and objective measures of health: evidence from hypertension for the income/health gradient', *Journal of Health Economics* 28: 540–52

Laudicella, M., Cookson, R., Jones, A. M. and Rice, N. 2009. 'Health care deprivation profiles in the measurement of inequality and inequity: an application to GP fundholding in the English NHS', *Journal of Health Economics* 28: 1048–61

Lindeboom, M. and van Doorslaer, E. 2004. 'Cut-point shift and index shift in self-reported health', *Journal of Health Economics* 23: 1083–99

Mackenbach, J. P., Bos, V., Andersen, O., Cardano, M., Costa, G., Harding, S., Reid, A., Hemstrom, O., Valkonen, T. and Kunst, A. E. 2003. 'Widening socioeconomic inequalities in mortality in six western European countries', *International Journal of Epidemiology* 32: 830–7

Malley, J. and Fernandez, J. L. 2010. 'Measuring quality in social care services: theory and practice', *Annals of Public and Cooperative Economics* 81: 559–82

Marmot, M. G., and Shipley, M. J. 1996. 'Do socioeconomic differences in mortality persist after retirement? 25 year follow up of civil servants from the first Whitehall study', *BMJ* 313: 1177–80

Marmot, M. and Wilkinson, R. 1999. *The Social Determinants of Health*. Oxford University Press

Mold, F., Fitzpatrick, J. M. and Roberts, J. D. 2005. 'Minority ethnic elders in care homes: a review of the literature', *Age and Ageing* 34: 107–13

Morris, S., Sutton, M. and Gravelle, H. 2003. *Inequity and Inequality in the Use of Health Care in England: An Empirical Investigation*. York: Centre for Health Economics, University of York

Munn-Giddings, C. and McVicar, A. 2006. 'Self-help groups as mutual support: what do carers value?', *Health and Social Care in the Community* 15: 26–34

Musgrave, R. A. 1959. *The Theory of Public Finance: A Study in Public Economy* New York: McGraw-Hill

O'Donnell, O., Van Doorsslaer, E., Wagstaff, A. and Lindelöw, M. 2008. *Analyzing Health Equity Using Household Survey Data: A Guide to Techniques and Their Implementation.* Washington, DC: World Bank Publications

Reid, R. J., MacWilliam, L., Verhulst, L., Roos, N. and Atkinson, M. 2001. 'Performance of the ACG case-mix system in two Canadian provinces', *Medical Care* 39: 86–99

Sen, A. 2002. 'Health: perception versus observation', *BMJ* 324: 860–1

Siciliani, L. and Verzulli, R. 2009. 'Waiting times and socioeconomic status among elderly Europeans: evidence from SHARE', *Health Economics* 18: 1295–1306

Spandler, H. and Vick, N. 2006. 'Opportunities for independent living using direct payments in mental health', *Health and Social Care in the Community* 14: 107–15

Sutton, M., Carr-Hill, R., Gravelle, H. and Rice, N. 1999. 'Do measures of self-reported morbidity bias the estimation of the determinants of health care utilization?', *Social Science and Medicine* 49: 867–78

van Ourti, T. 2003. 'Socio-economic inequality in ill-health amongst the elderly: should one use current or permanent income?', *Journal of Health Economics* 22: 219–41

Wagstaff, A. and van Doorslaer, E. 2000. 'Equity in health care finance and delivery', in A. J. Culyer and J. P. Newhouse (eds.), *Handbook of Health Economics.* Amsterdam: North-Holland, 1803–62

Wagstaff, A., van Doorslaer, E. and Watanabe, N. 2003. 'On decomposing the causes of health sector inequalities with an application to malnutrition inequalities in Vietnam', *Journal of Econometrics* 112: 207–23

Wanless, D., Forder, J., Fernandez, J. -L., Poole, T., Beesley, L., Henwood, M. and Moscone, F. 2006. *Securing Good Care for Older People: Taking a Long Term View.* London: King's Fund

Windmeijer, F. A. G., and Santos Silva, J. M. C. 1997. 'Endogeneity in count data models: an application to demand for health care', *Journal of Applied Econometrics* 12: 281–94

INDEX

AA (Attendance Allowance) (UK), 174–5
Abrams, Kathryn, 30–2
accumulated disadvantage, pension security for women and, 67–8
ACG (Adjusted Clinical Group) system, 187
ADA (Americans With Disabilities Act 1990), age discrimination and, 24–6
additive discrimination, analysis of, 26, 29
ADEA (Age Discrimination in Employment Act 1967), 2, 4, 11–12, 25
Adjusted Clinical Group (ACG) system, 187
Age Concern, 173
age discrimination
    accumulation of advantage/disadvantage and, 101–5
    current trends in, 3–5
    disability services and entitlements, 173–6
    diversity as cause of, 100–1
    early in career, 51
    impact on older women of, 48–51
    intersectionality in, 24–9
    intracategorical analysis by sponsorship status, age and gender of participants in Canada, 144–8
    multiple discrimination policies and, 16–18
    of older homosexuals, 115–16
    of older women workers, 24–9, 37
    social class differences and, 89–107

Age Discrimination Act 2004 (Australia), 12
Age Discrimination Benchmarking (UK), 175–6
Age Discrimination in Employment Act 1967 (USA), 2, 4, 11–12, 25
age–earning curves, social class and, 102–3
age-levelling hypothesis, and ethnocultural minority older adults, 134
age limits, age discrimination using, 51–3
age stratification theory, ethnocultural minority older adults and, 134
Age UK report, 10
ageism
    age discrimination in disability services and, 173
    defined, 1–3
    framework for diversity and, 7–10
    gender differences in experience of, 43
    impact on older women of, 48–51
    institutionalised heterosexism and, 114–15
    in job advertisements, 51–3
    peer discrimination in GLBT community and, 119–20
    in workplace culture, 53–5
agency, identity theory and, 30–2
AIDS/HIV, social isolation of GLBT community in wake of, 122
Ain't I a Woman (hooks), 19–20
Alzheimer's, in GLBT community, 121
American Psychiatric Association, 116

198